the survivor's guide to
BUSINESS
travel

Herald INTERNATIONAL **Tribune**

the survivor's guide to
BUSINESS
travel

**how to get
the best
deals, travel
in style, mix
business
with
pleasure,
keep healthy
and much
more!**

roger collis

KOGAN
PAGE

First published 2000

Apart from any fair dealing for the purposes of research or private study, or criticism or review, as permitted under the Copyright, Designs and Patents Act 1988, this publication may only be reproduced, stored or transmitted, in any form or by any means, with the prior permission in writing of the publishers, or in the case of reprographic reproduction in accordance with the terms and licences issued by the CLA. Enquiries concerning reproduction outside these terms should be sent to the publishers at the undermentioned address:

Kogan Page Limited
120 Pentonville Road
London N1 9JN
UK

Kogan Page Limited
163 Central Avenue, Suite 4
Dover
NH 03820
USA

© Roger Collis, 2000

The right of Roger Collis to be identified as the author of this work has been asserted by him in accordance with the Copyright, Designs and Patents Act 1988.

British Library Cataloguing in Publication Data

A CIP record for this book is available from the British Library.

ISBN 0 7494 3074 5

Typeset by Kogan Page
Printed and bound by in Great Britain by Clays Ltd, St Ives plc

Contents

Part 2 Traveling

Part 3 Arriving

Acknowledgements

This book is a distillation of my column, The Frequent Traveler, in the *International Herald Tribune*. I owe the book to many people. But I owe the column to two people in particular. In July 1984, the late Philip M. Foisie, executive editor of the *International Herald Tribune*, invited me to write a weekly column for the paper. The idea originated from Katherine Knorr, now a deputy editor, for whom I had worked on management subjects for Special Reports and done a couple of humorous pieces. I had also written half-a-dozen satirical pieces for Sherry Buchanan on the op-ed pages of the *Wall Street Journal* – Europe, which Katherine had picked up and seemed to like. And my first book, *If My Boss Calls... Make Sure You Get His Name* – a collection of satire on corporate life – had just been published. I was a corporate executive with a promising future behind me who had decided that humour was the better part of valour.

Phil asked me what I'd like to write about. High on the fragile promise of my book, which Phil held in his hands, I ventured something like, 'Management, perhaps, an oblique, humorous look at the foibles of people in organizations...'.

'No, you can't do that: Sherry Buchanan has come over to write the International Manager column. What about business travel?'

I knew something about business. And I'd certainly traveled. But business travel? Business travel is now a genre, but few people were writing about it as a consumer issue at that time.

I came back with a list of ideas, then half-a-dozen sample pieces, and The Frequent Traveler (then called For Fun and Profit, which Katherine dreamed up over lunch) came into being on 18 January 1985. It was to run every Friday for a couple of years, then fortnightly. And take over my life. In the early days, it was like writing a term paper every week, on a steep learning curve. Wednesday was my day off!

At lunch that day in Paris with Phil, Katherine and Walter Wells, then news editor, Phil formally handed me over to Katherine ('You belong totally to Katherine') who has been my mentor ever since. I owe everything to her unfailing editorial judgement and support over the years.

I want to pay tribute to John Vinocur, who succeeded Phil when he retired as executive editor, Michael Getler, executive editor, and Walter Wells, managing editor, for their support and encouragement. And thanks to Jan Benzel, deputy travel editor at *The New York Times*, who has run several of my columns, for her kindness and encouragement.

I must not forget the hundreds of people in the travel community who have taken precious time out of their schedules to talk to me (not always in their best interest!) and answer my endless questions. Some of them are quoted in these chapters. I ask them to forgive me if their jobs, titles or circumstances have changed since we spoke.

Finally, I must thank all the people who have edited my copy with such skill and dexterity. All the material in this book has gone through their expert hands. Any inconsistencies, faults or factual errors are mine alone. I am especially grateful to David Stevens, Barney Kirchhoff, Brian Manning, Marti Stewart and Judy Burtt, the editors of Special Reports, for their patience and professionalism.

This book is dedicated to all my friends at the *Trib* and to road warriors everywhere.

Introduction

Road warriors of the millennium – state of the art travel

Know thyself is the lapidary advice on the temple of Apollo at Delphi. In present-day travel terms, that means deciding what kind of traveler you are for a particular trip. Travel decisions are made on a shifting equation of cost, convenience and comfort. We travel in different modes, different frames of mind, with different needs, motivations, priorities and prejudices, depending on why we're going and where we're headed.

Business travelers are not monolithic as the travel trade often assumes. Corporate travelers have expense accounts, but some have deeper pockets than others and are subject to travel policies reflecting status and company cultures. Individual and small-business travelers, for whom travel expenses are their bottom line, have different needs and priorities.

The hotel industry seems more aware than airlines of our diversity, our shifting needs, providing more choice and flexibility – recognizing that we may not only want to trade up or down between deluxe and budget hotels, but trade across as well, from serviced apartments to small, town-house hotels.

Major airlines are reporting lower yields, reflecting a downgrading from first and business class to economy, because they've got their branding out of sync with the emerging needs of business travelers; reading what they want to read from the self-fulfilling findings of consumer surveys.

Let the bad times roll! You don't have to be a professional cynic to believe that what's bad for the travel trade is good for the traveler. But this depends on the fine balance between supply and demand. Your crystal ball is as good as mine. The Asian financial collapse in 1998, followed by crises in Russia and Brazil, earned the economic pundits a reputation for perfect hindsight. In Europe and North America, we're still waiting for the other shoe to drop.

Whether the seller's market that airlines and hotels have enjoyed until now – with high load factors and occupancy rates – will shift to a buyer's market is an open question, depending on which newspaper you read. Analysts predict that passenger numbers will grow by about 6 per cent – slightly less than available seats. But airlines will be able to maintain high business fares as they consolidate their market dominance through alliances and code-sharing, in which one airline sells tickets on its partners' flights. Arguable benefits to travelers are better connections, a wider choice of destinations and 'seamless' transfers. But unless market forces increase competition, the only sign of better deals are lower costs for carriers.

The main generator of air traffic is not prices but economic activity. If GDP is growing at, say, 2.5 per cent, airline traffic will grow at about 5 per cent. This has been the main reason for the incredible growth in Asia – up till now. Asian economies were growing at 5 or 6 per cent with air traffic growing at 10 or 12 per cent. Load factors of 70 per cent or more mean that it's hard to get a seat at peak times, especially on the North Atlantic, which is 21 per cent of world international travel.

Road warriors of the millennium are often ambivalent about globe-trotting. Travel has become part of the job for many people. Some crave the challenge, the adventure of the road and the break from daily routines. Others miss their families and worry about work piling up on their desks.

Taking off on a business trip used to mean getting away from it all. But corporate downsizing and new information technology (which both allow and require you to be totally wired at all times) have forced travelers to be more accountable and productive when they're away. They are now expected to do two jobs – one on the road and one back in the office. For many, the most stressful part of business travel is the 're-entry syndrome' – catching up with family and work when they get home. Companies are increasingly aware of the cost of business travel – the third largest discretionary expense after salaries and data processing – and are subjecting travelers to rigorous travel policies that decree which airlines and hotels you can use and whether you go business class or economy.

For most business travelers what counts is choice, convenience and comfort at a competitive price. But 'state-of-the-art travel' is knowing how to cut corners in style. This might be taking off for a weekend in the middle of a business trip at a marginal cost; or knowing exactly how to pace yourself before vital meetings by allowing for stopovers and week-end breaks, often free or at marginal cost.

It never hurts to drive a bargain, especially as value for money in travel does not always depend on how much you pay. For example, it's possible to fly first class on some carriers for less than the cost of busi-ness class, or stay at the Ritz for about the same price as the Holiday Inn. On the other hand, there's no sense in going for the cheapest price if it's flexibility you need. A discount ticket can be costly if you suddenly have to change your itinerary. It sometimes pays to pay full fare. But only buy as much flexibility as you need.

State-of-the-art means checking out the options not only before you go, but also 'what if?' scenarios once you're on the road. You may be able to minimize hassles and expense by having alternative reserva-tions, avoiding back-to-back meetings on a multi-destination trip and allowing a day or two as a buffer for rest and rescheduling, especially before vital meetings in a new time zone. Don't forget to bone up on local lore (and law). The watchword is always to expect the unexpected (a corollary to Murphy's Law) and never take anything for granted (an optimist is simply a pessimist who is badly informed). It's thorough preparation, staying as flexible as you can and paying attention to detail that counts.

State-of-the-art travel is a state of mind; a belief that somewhere out there in the travel jungle is a buyer's market for you just waiting to be discovered.

PART 1

Preparing

Staying ahead of the game

Planning a business trip these days can be more complicated than doing business when you get there. With first class costing twice as much as business class, which in turn can be three times as much as full-fare economy class, you can easily pay more for a lot less. Faced with a blizzard of discount fares, upgrades, special promotions and the maze of frequent flier awards, it's sometimes hard to profit from a buyer's market. Or is it a seller's market? It depends which paper you read! I never know these days whether we're deep in a recession, just emerging from the last recession (with all the lessons learned and so on) or teetering on the edge of the next recession.

All may be fair in love and war but not with air fares. What incenses business travelers is that they are often unable to take advantage of low-cost excursion fares because they are so hedged with restrictions, such as a compulsory Saturday night stay, advance booking or limits on flights. Such fares are designed to frustrate their use by business people, who need to be able to change or cancel a flight at the last minute. It's pay top dollar for flexibility and a few frills.

The good news is that you can often cut the cost of full-fare travel in economy, business and first class by buying tickets through so-called flight consolidators and by the creative use of IATA published prices.

Consolidators are travel agents appointed by an airline to sell surplus seats for less than the published IATA fare – a kind of under-the-counter discounting. Consolidators buy seats at net prices and resell them either as a wholesaler to other agents or direct to the traveler at a mark-up, usually with fewer restrictions than in the case of APEX/PEX fares. A consolidation ticket is normally valid for a year and fully flexible, except that you can't change to another airline.

A trawl on the Internet or through the small ads will reveal a galaxy of cut-price fares, but you'll seldom see an airline mentioned. That is because airlines insist that the business be done ever so discreetly; you have to call to find out.

When buying a consolidator ticket, check whether you can upgrade with frequent flier miles. If it's a net-fare ticket (with no fare indicated in the fare box), you probably won't earn miles or be able to use them to make an upgrade. Tickets discounted to consolidators with an override commission will typically show a published fare in the fare box regardless of how much you pay. Many of these tickets can be upgraded; the only way to be sure is to ask your agent.

Value doesn't always depend on how much you spend; there are times when spending a little more can yield a great deal of extra comfort. It sometimes pays to book full fare. A consolidation fare may not be the best buy, especially if you are looking for maximum flexibility by being able to switch flights and carriers and make unlimited stopovers. A good travel agent can often save you more by exploiting IATA 'fare construction' rules allowing you to fly up to 25 per cent more miles between two points either free or for a small surcharge. Thus you can sometimes save as much as 40 per cent by combining separate round trips on the same ticket valid for a year. A full-fare ticket is usually a prerequisite for two-for-one promotions, upgrades and higher mileage credits.

Paying the full fare may also qualify for a free 24-hour stopover package that airlines sometimes offer to encourage people to fly via their main hub. Passengers arriving or departing on long-haul flights with full-fare tickets may get a free first-class hotel, lunch and dinner, sightseeing and airport transfers.

Not all stopover programmes are free, but they can be excellent value. Flying from Europe to the Far East it's always worth asking the airline if it can offer cheap hotel accommodation en route or at your destination – especially if you're passing or staying at its home city. Consider a fly-stay package from an airline or tour operator. Or ask your travel agent to customize one for you. You can save 50 per cent of the combined cost of the normal air fare and hotel.

Otherwise, a full economy fare is the worst buy in the sky – unless you plan to use it tactically to get an upgrade. (Airlines tend to upgrade people who've paid – or look as though they've paid – the most for their ticket or who belong to the frequent-flier programme.)

If you've got to sit in the back of the plane, it makes sense to shop for the deepest discount you can find – which can be as low as 30 per cent of full economy. Should your plans change, just throw away the return coupon – you'll be cash in hand. Avoid the Saturday night rule with 'back-to-back' ticketing. You buy two round-trip tickets – one at each end of the route – and travel out on the first coupon of the first ticket and back on the first coupon of the second ticket. And so on.

An 'open jaw' APEX ticket – whereby you fly to one gateway and return from another – is one way to combine economy with a degree of flexibility. Let's say you want to fly from New York to London, and back from Rome. First buy an APEX ticket that permits this. Then for the APEX leg London–Rome, buy an APEX round-trip ticket or a one-way fare on a no-frills carrier. This is cheaper than a one-way fare; either give the return ticket to a friend or throw it away.

A device that works well is to combine separate round trips on one ticket. You don't have to tie yourself down to dates and times: the combined ticket is valid for a year, with no cancellation or reissue charges other than rerouting. The technique works well for first class, business class, full economy or a mixture of classes.

Another device is to combine two types of fare on the same ticket; say a point-to-point on the way out and a fare allowing for unlimited stopovers on the way back. Or vice versa. Doing this can save you up to 40 per cent.

The converse is 'split ticketing', whereby you take advantage of a weaker currency by buying separate tickets for the outward and return journeys. If you travel often to a country with a currency weaker than your own, it makes sense to buy an initial one-way ticket and a series of round trips at the other end.

Don't assume that the best way to fly is with your national carrier from its major hub. Traveling between Europe, North America or Asia, you can save serious money on published round-trip fares by traveling via hub in another country – a strategy that I call 'cross-border hubbing'. Carriers offer the best deals in someone else's back yard. Thus, British Airways will sell you a much cheaper long-haul ticket if you're based in France or Germany. Likewise, airlines like Air France, Lufthansa and SAS for travelers in neighboring countries. Plan your trip wisely and well, and combine two trips for the price of one by stopping over to do business en route.

The right question at the right time

Before you pick up the phone to call the travel agent or reservations desk, ask yourself some questions. Are you concerned primarily with price or with the fastest routing? Are you prepared to change planes twice to earn frequent flier miles? Are there airlines or hubs you want to use or avoid? Ask about fly/stay or fly/drive packages.

Be clear about what you are being offered and ask for alternatives. Be aware that a 'direct' flight (even with one flight number) may not be non-stop. Do you have to change planes (if so, to which type?), airlines or terminals? Are connections guaranteed? Are there any special deals for hotels or car rental? Are there departures more convenient to the time you want to travel? If you were to travel at a different time, can you get a price break or a different routing? Are there other flights that get you there earlier? How can you get most frequent-flier miles or hotel points? Does this airline have a tendency to overbook? What about a free upgrade? Are there any penalties if you want to change your ticket? Would it be cheaper over the weekend? Will you be able to get a cheap ticket on that flight? Should you take the early flight so that you can get an empty seat next to you?

Always ask for consolidator tickets, which can provide discounts of up to 60 per cent off the published fares in first, business and economy. The only restriction is that you can't switch to another carrier. Airlines appoint certain agents as consolidators to sell surplus seats on some routes – a kind of under-the-counter discounting. The best deals are usually with foreign carriers, such as Air New Zealand, Singapore Airlines or Air India between the United Kingdom and North America.

A good agent can save you almost as much through 'fare construction', which allows you to fly up to 25 per cent more miles between two points either free or for a modest surcharge. If you plan to make more than one long-haul trip in a year, ask the agent to combine the trips on one ticket. You can save up to 40 per cent. For example, such a ticket might read London–Singapore–London with London–New York–London at a later date. You don't have to tie yourself down to flights or dates, and the combined ticket is valid for a year, with no cancellation or reissue charges except for rerouting.

You may be able to save 10 to 40 per cent on air fares by 'split ticket-ing', a device whereby you buy a one-way ticket out and a one-way ticket back based on local currency. If you travel frequently to a destina-tion with a softer currency – especially in Asia – consider buying a one-way ticket out and a series of round-trip tickets at the other end.

Always test the agent with your own information. The best way to do this is by subscribing to a neutral database, such as an electronic edi-tion of OAG flight guide or hotel disk. Failing this, consult a hard-copy edition. I find the OAG *Pocket Flight Guide* handy at home and on the road. Be warned, however, that even OAG does not always show the best connections between some cities (connections are paid for by car-riers) so you may have to search for them.

Priorities

 Do decide your priorities and how much flexibility you need before calling the travel agent or reservations desk. Don't be caught by the bait-and-switch scam. If an airline can't find a seat at the low advertised fare, shop around until you find one that can.

 Don't be deterred by the ignorance of reservations staff. They may not know or care about other possibilities. Test them with your own knowledge. Hit them with 'what if?' scenarios.

 Do call hotels direct to ask about promotions. These do not always make it into central reservations.

 Do be clear about what you are offered and ask for alternatives. If you travel at a different time, can you get a better routing or a price break? Will you get a better rate by extending your stay?

 Do compare advertised discount fares and special promotions, consolidator fares, and using frequent flier miles to upgrade.

Do check fares at each end of a route. It can make sense to buy an initial one-way ticket to a country with a weaker currency, and a series of round-trips at the other end.

Tips for stopovers

 Do make sure that your ticket allows for the stopovers you want. Discount fares may be restricted to a point-to-point routing. Weigh the extra cost of an unrestricted ticket.

 Don't be deterred by the ignorance or protests of airline sales staff. 'I've had trouble getting this stopover information together,' says an airline PR manager.

 Do exploit the maximum mileage rules when traveling full fare, which allows extra stopovers at no additional cost.

 Do choose a carrier that doesn't have an onward connecting flight on the day you travel. Failing that, make sure you arrive too late to catch it.

 Do make sure you understand the rules and conditions for stopovers. If the airline doesn't promote a stopover package, try to get hold of a sales service manual. The local sales manager or station manager has discretion to bend the rules.

 Don't ask questions like, 'What rules apply to stopovers in London?' Better to say, 'I'm thinking of flying business class with you to Tokyo. What kind of deal will you offer me in London?'

Dos and don'ts when buying airline tickets through a 'bucket shop'

 Do check out travel restrictions.

 Can you change flights and dates?

 Can you switch to another carrier?

 Do you have to change planes en route?

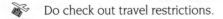

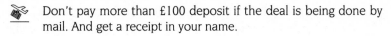 Don't pay more than £100 deposit if the deal is being done by mail. And get a receipt in your name.

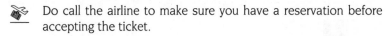 Do call the airline to make sure you have a reservation before accepting the ticket.

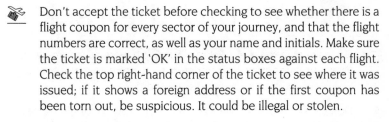 Don't accept the ticket before checking to see whether there is a flight coupon for every sector of your journey, and that the flight numbers are correct, as well as your name and initials. Make sure the ticket is marked 'OK' in the status boxes against each flight. Check the top right-hand corner of the ticket to see where it was issued; if it shows a foreign address or if the first coupon has been torn out, be suspicious. It could be illegal or stolen.

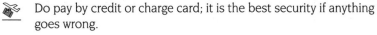 Do pay by credit or charge card; it is the best security if anything goes wrong.

Never pay the rack rate at hotels

Hotel rooms are discounted just like airline seats, and in many cases savings can be greater. A recent trade survey of 27 European cities found that the average corporate discount on published hotel rates was 32 per cent. Hotel costs can account for as much as 60 per cent of the cost of a business trip. But many travelers are much less efficient at booking hotel rooms than buying airline tickets.

The worldwide boom in business travel has made getting a discount more difficult and more important. There has been a dramatic rise in occupancy levels, and therefore room rates.

It has become a seller's market in many parts of the world, so it's tougher to negotiate deals. Hotels are smarter these days at 'yield management'; that is, adjusting the room rate in line with occupancy to get the maximum 'yield'. Some hotels renege on negotiated corporate rates when it comes to 'last room availability'. In other words, turn up at the last minute and you may be charged a high rate. (On the other hand, you may get a cheap last-minute 'walk-in' rate if you turn up late and there are rooms to spare. Like airline seats, nothing is more perishable than an empty hotel room. You can't save it for another day; it's gone forever.)

Big companies can make big savings by negotiating directly with hotel groups and committing, long-term and worldwide, to the one that offers the best price. If you are traveling to just a few key destinations, it's often best to negotiate with individual hotels. A good travel agent can pull a company's total hotel spend together and negotiate with a few hotels. It's often the case that three of four travelers from the same company pay different rates at the same hotel.

A similar approach can work for small companies and independent business travelers. If you travel a lot to a particular city, you may have more purchasing power than you think. Even for 15 or 20 room-nights a year – and don't forget to mention meals and entertaining – a smaller hotel may be prepared to make you a special customer.

Failing that, a good travel agency should be able to get you a 'corporate rate' (a 10 to 20 per cent discount at a good four-star hotel; less in cheaper hotels). Some travel agents also offer 'consortium' or 'preferred rates' at hotels with which they have a volume discount. But not all agents have the best deals everywhere. So it pays to shop around.

But the best value comes from negotiated rates. And even where a hotel seems reluctant to cut its price, don't stop negotiating: you may still be able to get an 'added-value' deal – a discount in kind – which could be an upgrade to an executive room or executive floor, either free of charge or at a preferred rate. Take either option and you won't pay the full whack at a hotel. But there are times – especially when hotel rooms in a city are hard to find – that the highest discount is not always the best buy. Consider negotiating a slightly higher rate to ensure 'last room availability'. Hotels sometimes renege on discounted rates and will let your room go if they can sell it at a higher price.

Whatever discount you're offered, it always pays to call the hotel direct and ask the right questions. This is how the ideal conversation should go:

'Hi, what can you offer me for next Thursday?'
'I have a deluxe king for $400.'
'Is there a corporate rate?'
'Yes, $270.'
'And other rooms?'
'Executive twins are $230, regular twins are $180.'
'What does that include?'
'Service and tax. English breakfast is extra.'
'That's more than I'm ready to pay. What about weekend deals or promotions?'
'I can give you 50 per cent off a regular twin for Friday, Saturday or Sunday night.'
'What does that make the room rate?'
'That's $90.'
'Can you give me that rate if I stay Thursday and Friday?'
'Yes, I'd be pleased to do that.'
'Any chance of an upgrade?'

'I can probably give you an executive twin for the same.'
'If you can do it with breakfast as well, I'll take it.'
'Fine. Your name please?'

An ounce of chutzpah can go a long way.

Choose a hotel for location as well as price. It's worth paying a bit more to be close to where you need to be. Nothing beats being able to walk to the office, restaurants and shops. Check whether breakfast is included in the room rate. If not, ask if it is a mandatory extra. Breakfast in a big hotel, especially continental breakfast, can be exorbitant. A big breakfast can be much better value. Unless you're hosting a power breakfast, you may find a nearby café much cheaper and more congenial.

When it pays to pay more

'Never pay the rack rate at hotels' has become a kind of mantra with business travelers, and rightly so. Everyone should be able to save 10 per cent and sometimes as much as 40 per cent off the published rate at most four- and five-star hotels. You can usually get some kind of 'corporate' rate just by calling or asking at the desk: a good test of your management style and chutzpah. Serious discounts can come through travel agency 'consortium' rates, typically available to all comers, or corporate deals negotiated with hotel chains or individual properties.

Fewer than 10 per cent of hotel rooms are sold at rack rate; and, according to a trade report, the average corporate discount on published hotel rates in 27 European countries in 1998 was 32.5 per cent.

During the last recession, some hotels sold rooms at pretty well any price they could get – some income being better than none – striving for higher occupancy at the expense of profit. Others reacted more creatively by tempting business and leisure travelers with a raft of inducements – anything from room upgrades and 'welcome' fruit baskets and champagne to buffet breakfasts, late check-outs and airport limos – to justify higher prices and improve yields.

Whether an 'added-value' package adds up to good value for you depends, of course, on your needs and priorities. Do you need fruit and champagne and a guided tour of the Kriegsmuseum? Or just a room for the night at a decent price and breakfast in the café next door? But there are occasions when a larger room with your own fax, coffee-making facilities, early check-in or late check-out, and a limo to fetch and carry you to the airport would make the right statement.

There are times when it pays to pay a bit more for better value. Hotels are looking for loyalty, repeat business; business travelers want recognition, the personal touch, which they are more likely to get as members of a smaller club.

'You're dealing with sophisticated customers. Most people who buy added-value business packages are seasoned travelers; the occupancy of our Regency Club rooms is better than the rest of the hotel,' says John Wallace, vice president marketing at Hyatt Hotels Corporation in Chicago. 'People can work these things out for themselves; they do their sums; they know what the room rate is, how much the cab ride is going to cost from the airport. These programmes only work if they are to the benefit of the customer.'

Peter Yesawich, president and CEO of Yesawich, Pepperdine & Brown in Orlando, Florida, co-publishers with Yankelovich Partners of the *Business Travel Monitor*, says: 'Hotels are moving to an inclusive pricing strategy. Six out of 10 business travelers tell us that having breakfast included in the room rate is a very desirable attribute in hotel selection. The wave of the future is something called self-service. Four out of 10 travelers tell us they want services and technology delivered in the room. They don't want to go to the front desk to send a fax. They don't want to wait for half an hour for room service to get a cup of coffee; they'll make it themselves. Or if they wake up hungry in the night, they want to be able to put a dish in the microwave and serve themselves. The guest-room has become what we call a command centre from which you can manage your business and communicate with clients and the office. Three out of 10 travelers say they'd like voice-mail, multiple phones, and computer data ports and a monitor in the room, along with coffee-makers and refrigerators.'

'There's been a seller's market; hotels have been able to increase rates at all levels so companies have a tougher job to negotiate deals', says Carolyn Moore, hotels specialist at Hogg Robinson Travel in London. 'Hotels have also become much smarter at yield management – adjusting room rates in line with occupancy and anticipated demand. This means that your locally negotiated volume rate may only be available when more than 50 per cent of the rooms are vacant. You may be told the hotel is full, but it may only be full at your rate. Try to negotiate a rate as near to "last room availability" as possible.'

Paradoxically, this can make added-value business packages more attractive. This is because you typically pay a surcharge – from $15 to $30 – on top of your discounted rate.

The most uncompromising added-value package is Shangri La's Valued Guest Program, available at all its hotels and resorts in the Asia-Pacific region, which requires you to pay the full rack rate. But the benefits – airport limo transfers, guaranteed room upgrade, unlimited laundry and dry cleaning, breakfast, tea and coffee, fax and phone calls at cost with free local calls and a 6 pm check-out – add up to good value.

Radisson Hotels worldwide Business Class programme, averaging an extra $20 a night, gives you a 'deluxe' room (your partner stays free), breakfast, in-room movies and coffee-maker, no phone or fax access charges for calling cards, and computer hookup.

Hyatt's Business Plan programme costs an extra $15 and provides 24-hour access to printers, photocopiers and office supplies, complimentary breakfast and newspapers, coffee-making facilities, and a large desk, fax machine and computer hookup. Another $25 buys you access to the Regency Club floor, which has its own concierge and lounge and offers free evening snacks and cocktails.

Hilton International's Hilton Club is worth joining for a raft of benefits including an upgrade (when available) to an 'executive' room (your partner stays free), run of the club lounge with free drinks, snacks, newspapers, a 20 per cent discount on business services, early check-in from 9 am and late check-out at 6 pm or later. Annual membership costs $150 a year. But this is waived if you have stayed five times at a Hilton hotel in the past year, regardless of the rate you paid.

Tips for choosing your travel agent

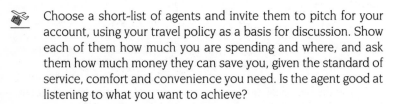

- Choose a short-list of agents and invite them to pitch for your account, using your travel policy as a basis for discussion. Show each of them how much you are spending and where, and ask them how much money they can save you, given the standard of service, comfort and convenience you need. Is the agent good at listening to what you want to achieve?

- Choose an agent where YOU will be important. For an independent business traveler, this is likely to be a small independent agent rather than a large multiple, though some large agents have divisions specializing in small-business clients.

- Meet the person/people who will be booking your travel. What is their experience? How long have they worked with the agent? Experience and continuity are important in an industry with transient, often low-paid, personnel.

- Ask what CRS/GDS (computer reservations/global distribution system) the agent is using; be especially vigilant if it is hosted by a national airline. Such systems are supposed to be unbiased these days, but you may become a victim of CRS bias – by which airlines manipulate the displays in favour of their own flights. It may be worth sitting down with the travel booker to understand the system, so that he knows that you know that he knows. (High-tech systems have the capability of finding you the cheapest, most convenient flight and the cheapest hotel room; what counts is being able to play your criteria against the system.) Reservations people often try. But they're inclined just to read off the screen.

Expediency is a pernicious form of bias when 80 per cent of airline reservations are made on the first screen.

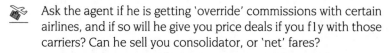

Ask the agent if he is getting 'override' commissions with certain airlines, and if so will he give you price deals if you fly with those carriers? Can he sell you consolidator, or 'net' fares?

Can the agent help you get a 'route deal' with an airline on frequently traveled itineraries? This depends on how much business your provide. Companies can get a discount of up to 50 per cent on the cost of business-class fares on some routes. Most airlines that offer preferred deals to companies pay retrospective cash rebates when, for example, you book an agreed number of city-pair sectors. Sometimes, you may get a discounted price up-front, which may come in the form of upgrades, say from economy to business class.

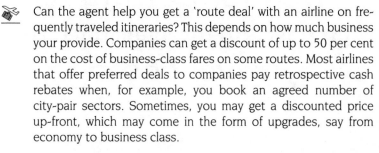

An agent needs the skill and motivation to hunt through the jungle of fares and come up with the best option – in terms of price, convenience and routing. Few agents – who work on commission from travel suppliers – are willing to save you money in this way unless you are a big customer. The harder they work at finding you the best deal, the less money they make. Independent travelers should consider joining a 'travel club' such as WEXAS International in London. For annual dues of around $75 you get expert travel advice and efficient booking on the phone.

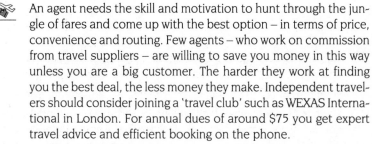

Consider a fee-based arrangement to make sure the agent is working for you, whereby he passes all commissions over to you (or splits the commissions) and you pay an agreed sum of money to the agent for managing your travel, based on open-book accounting. But always establish a performance target – having benchmarked what you're paying already through your travel patterns. If the agent can take your spending down from, say, $1 million to $900,000, you can decide the split on the incremental savings. So the agent has an incentive to save you money, and it takes the ambiguity (who is the agent working for, the suppliers or me?) out of the relationship.

Expect an agent to provide a round-the-clock service (he may even give you a direct line or terminal in your office), a courier service and other travel documents, help with visas and passports, health, climate and weather advice, traveler's cheques without charge, and discounts on travel insurance.

Tips for getting to grips with company travel costs

 Appoint somebody in the company to co-ordinate and centralize global spending. In large companies this person may be the travel manager, or the head of finance or central purchasing. This can be a major task: pulling together travel expenditure from several departments and subsidiaries. But make sure you seek advice from someone in the company who understands travel management.

 The first task of a co-ordinator is to look at where and how money is spent on travel. To what destinations do people travel most often? How do they obtain tickets and settle hotel bills? What class of travel and accommodation are executives entitled to? What controls are there?

 The next step is to write a travel policy, setting out guidelines on class of travel (say, according to pecking order and journey time), grades of hotels and rental cars, daily spending allowances, and latitude to be allowed in choosing flights, hotels and other suppliers and frequent flier programmes. (It's worthwhile consulting local companies or companies in the same industry on what they do.) Review the policy regularly. Make sure all executives read and understand if. Give your travel agent a copy. The agent needs to know what you're seeking: economy above all else or the best service.

Focus your spending to maximize your purchasing clout. You might want to put all your business with an agent, or just your air tickets and buy hotels and car rental direct. My advice is to select the best flight specialist, then shop around for hotel discounts.

 Large companies can usually cut the best deals by negotiating directly with a hotel group. This may also work for the small business or independent traveler. You may have more purchasing clout than you think. If you travel frequently to a particular city, consider patronizing just one hotel. Even 30 nights a year might make you a special customer.

 Minimize cash advances through the use of a corporate charge card, or tell travelers to use their own plastic for hotels and restaurants (reimburse them before their bills become due). Other benefits are insurance coverage, itemized statements and emergency cash.

 Get your agent to prepare a management report each month, showing how much he has saved you (or could have) by comparing the published air fare with the fare he offered. Typically, this will be broken down by traveler, department, destination and type of travel service.

Airline alliances: are they passenger friendly?

You can never be sure these days whether the airline you were booked on is the one you will actually fly, whatever your boarding card says. Or whether you will set out on one type of plane and arrive on another, perhaps on a connecting flight with a second or third carrier.

Buy a ticket from Air France from Nice to London and you will find yourself on a British Midland flight. Continental Airlines passengers from Gatwick to Orlando, Florida, may be surprised (though not dismayed) to board a Virgin Atlantic plane. Nobody told you that Delta was operating what you thought was your Swissair flight from Zurich to Cincinnati; or that your Sabena flight from Brussels to Heathrow (for which you paid the business-class fare) turns out to be operated by Virgin Express. And what you thought was an Air Canada flight from Toronto to Copenhagen was really SAS.

Whether you're pleased, perplexed, angry or indifferent may depend on whether you find yourself on your most- or least-favourite carrier. This is what happens with 'code-sharing' – a system by which two or more airlines agree to use the same 'designator' or flight number for a flight or series of connecting flights in order to attract new business by extending their networks through partner carriers. They can disguise an 'online' change of plane or change of 'gauge' to a feeder line. There's also a 'double designator', whereby one airline or another operates the flight.

There is growing criticism that code-sharing is misleading because the traveler is buying one product and getting another. An analysis by the US Department of Transportation found that 30 per cent of passengers on code-share flights are not told which carrier they will be flying.

'If you buy a ticket on British Airways and wind up flying on a US carrier that's almost broke, you may not want to fly on that,' says Dr Hans Krakauer, international senior vice president government and industry affairs at IAPA in Lisbon. 'As a passenger, you are entitled to be told when the flight you booked is operated by another carrier. You must have the right of refusal to travel on that flight and have your ticket refunded.'

Krakauer is concerned that code-sharing may replace the passenger's right to 'interline' from one carrier to another under IATA rules – whereby baggage is checked through, a through fare rather than a 'sector' fare is applied, and the tariff attribution between the carriers is done automatically by the IATA clearing system.

'You must maintain the passenger's right to switch carriers to go to a specific destination,' Krakauer says. 'I was traveling from Lisbon to San Antonio: I flew to Newark and then had to get a separate ticket on Delta because there was no interline. Why? Because you've now got airlines going all the way through code-sharing. Interlining represents a real chance of competition for smaller and medium-sized carriers. To prevent it would be to reduce the competitive capacity of these smaller airlines – which has already begun to happen in the USA.'

Code-sharing is the most visible consequence of the alliances that airlines are now forging in their quest for global dominance. These accords include loose marketing agreements, reciprocal sales and marketing pacts; co-ordination of schedules and fares; cross-equity holdings and aircraft-buying consortia; and franchising deals where one airline pays another for the right to carry its name.

Imagine arriving at the airport to find that instead of the familiar airline check-in desks, there is just one long row of desks displaying the logo Star Alliance. At other airports, you might have a choice of Oneworld or Atlantic Excellence. But this is Hamburg, a Star Alliance hub. Your ticket reads: Hamburg–Copenhagen–New York–Toronto–Frankfurt–Hamburg. You have no idea on which airline you will be flying in these sectors – perhaps Lufthansa, SAS, United or Air Canada. You can expect the same standards of service and comfort, similar seating, food and in-flight entertainment. You will earn double miles because the entire journey is with Star Alliance partners, and diamond membership of the Star Alliance frequent-flier programme will give you the run of VIP lounges along the way. But don't expect any price breaks because there is no competition on the route you are traveling.

This scenario may be only slightly futuristic as airlines carve up the skies into four major alliances, accounting for more than 60 per cent of world airline traffic: Star Alliance; Oneworld; Atlantic Excellence; and KLM-Northwest-Continental Airlines.

Airline alliances are the most seminal issue in air travel since deregulation went into effect in the United States in 1978 and in Europe in April 1997, allowing carriers to fly anywhere at any time charging any fare they want. 'Open-skies' agreements between many European countries and the United States – Austria, Belgium, Denmark, Finland, Germany, Luxembourg, Sweden, the United Kingdom (except for London airports) and Italy – have stimulated business in a market that represents nearly 12 per cent of world airline traffic. Trans-Atlantic travelers have the choice of more than 40 new non-stop services between Europe and North America this summer compared with last year, according to Airports Council International in Brussels. Open skies is supposed to mean more choice, more competition, more players in the marketplace, breaking the hegemony of major carriers on trunk routes and providing more options for travelers, and lower fares. But many insiders fear that alliances herald a return to the bad old days before the deregulation of monopoly and duopoly routes, with 'pooled' schedules and revenue, and the threat of higher fares.

Alliances are in the business of reducing operational and distribution costs through shared facilities and economies of scale. This is packaged to the public as 'seamless' travel through one global network. Indeed, there are benefits – especially to the corporate traveler – such as great scope to earn and redeem FFP miles and reciprocal use of lounges between partner airlines. But not always when it comes to getting the lowest fare.

Even benefits of FFPs are ambiguous. Business travelers can accumulate miles more rapidly on alliance partners, But the promise of rewards serves to lock up their loyalty and discourage them from seeking cheaper fares outside the alliance.

Ironically, upgrades – one of the most sought-after benefits of FFPs – could be one of the first casualties of airline alliances. The problem for 'elite' frequent-flier members is sharing scarce upgrade seats with travelers belonging to partner programmes. Some alliances prohibit 'cross-upgrades'.

Murray Greenfield in Tel Aviv complains that Swissair refused to redeem an award for miles earned on Delta, its alliance partner. When he remonstrated with Delta, Greenfield was told that his 'free' ticket would cost nearly twice as many miles as the same ticket issued by Swissair anyway. So much for reciprocity.

Regulatory authorities in Washington and Brussels are concerned about the antitrust implications of the growth of alliances. Alliances claim that they are not inimical to free-market forces because they compete with one another. But the US Department of Justice is concerned about 'fortress hubs' dominated by one alliance. There is also a worry that non-alliance airlines will be forced out of business.

'We're faced with virtual monopoly pricing as a result of airline alliances,' says Danamichele O'Brien, vice president and chief travel scientist at Rosenbluth Travel International in Philadelphia. 'As you create these monopolies, prices go up. Air fares have been projected to increase from 5 to 7 per cent year over year through 2001.'

'Travelers are about to be cheated again: we're going back to the old IATA days of price-fixing: airline alliances are nothing more than monopolies,' says Moritz Suter, president of Crossair, Swissair's regional subsidiary, in Basel. 'We are in the Qualiflyer/Atlantic Excellence group because of Swissair. But I'm not allowed to compete any more against a guy in the same alliance. I don't know what's going to happen; but I don't think alliances will last too long.'

'You can be sure that airlines didn't form alliances to offer the traveler cheaper fares,' says Mike Platt, director commercial affairs at Hogg Robinson Travel in London. 'They formed alliances to reduce their costs and increase their ability to sell on broader markets.'

Jackie Gallagher, deputy editor of *Airline Business* magazine in London, says: 'Whether we end up with four or five global alliances depends on the regulators. All the alliances except Oneworld have US antitrust immunity, which allows them to co-ordinate fares and split revenues and profits, ruling out competition. This is because countries like The Netherlands, Switzerland and Germany have open skies agreements with the United States. But they haven't yet been given European antitrust immunity, which normally they would require to do the things they are doing.'

Mathew Davis, manager of the purchasing management group at American Express in London, says: 'Alliances are targeting traveler satisfaction, like FFPs and airport lounges, but this doesn't help the corporation in managing its travel policy. We're not yet seeing benefits in terms of hard dollar savings.'

He adds: 'Travelers are getting confused because the airline they fly is not the one they thought they had paid for and services are very different, especially between US and European carriers. The traveler is being sold short. The question for corporate travel managers is: "Do you – can you – make deals with the alliance or the partner airlines?" We have clients in Germany who had excellent deals with United until the alliance started. Lufthansa then took over corporate sales and the discounts offered have gone down to the lowest denominator.'

Lucas Dendieval, director of European travel services at Johnson & Johnson in Brussels, says: 'We haven't seen the benefit from any alliance. I don't mean smoother connections and being able to use a Qantas lounge on a BA flight: nice to know, but it doesn't really add any value to the customer.

'We're seeing monopoly markets like Sabena and Delta between Brussels and the States where you can no longer negotiate with individual carriers; you have to deal with the Atlantic Alliance. The same goes for Lufthansa, United and SAS in the Star Alliance. You call the SAS rep; they automatically refer you back to the Lufthansa rep. I mean, you see the Lufthansa guy walking around in the United Airlines office. It gets scary. KLM walks in the door and they know what our deals are with Alitalia.

'Our concern is control. Alliances will be able to control markets – city pairs – and control prices. Alliances may split if companies insist on doing business with a particular airline. We're testing this right now with Atlantic Excellence. We're going to try and break it up: we don't want to talk to the alliance any more.

'You never see an alliance with two US partners – like American-Continental or Continental-Delta. If that were to happen, I think the United States regulators would step in. I don't think they care if BA wants to do something with American. But Congress is getting interested. We're getting calls from Congress asking what we feel as a corporation and what our travelers feel about alliances.'

Craig Jenks, an aviation consultant in New York, says: 'The hub-to-spoke emphasis in new non-stop services on the Atlantic undermines the more monopolistic hub-to-hub concept engendered by recession and alliances in the early and mid-1990s. Competition is again increasing. For how long remains to be seen as alliances evolve.

'Alliance hub-to-hub services are monopolistic by nature. Hub-to-spoke is much more creative – it means that airlines are throwing out new non-stops from their hubs into competing airline territory. When Continental starts flying from Newark to Brussels and Newark to Zurich as they're doing this summer, then they are flying from their hub in New York into what for them is a spoke, but for someone else is their turf. In that case it happens to be the Swissair group. And when Lufthansa sends a flight from Frankfurt to Philadelphia – which is USAir territory, or Frankfurt to Detroit – which is Northwest territory – it's saying, we're not going to stay away from your fortress hub.'

Good news for the traveler. 'Yes, the options on the North Atlantic keep increasing,' Jenks says. 'And even when what's growing is hubs, the reality is that every time you grow a hub, you are growing it by adding non-stops. If every alliance wants to compete in every market, and we end up with four or five alliances, then we're going to see a bunch of competitive non-stops on the North Atlantic. On the other hand, if there were to be a consolidation of alliances so we ended up with only three, that would be very negative.'

Rupert Duschesne, senior vice president international at Air Canada in Montreal, says: 'The Star Alliance has allowed us to develop services that would not otherwise have been possible, such as our Toronto–Copenhagen service in a code-share with SAS, whereas previously you had to fly Toronto–Newark–Copenhagen or Toronto–London–Copenhagen. Our principle is to do point-to-point as much as we can rather than one-stops. As we convert to smaller planes – such as the 200-seat 767 – we're going to fly more, thinner routes. Going from a two-stop to a one-stop or even non-stop makes a huge difference.

'Our view is not that prices will rise. The whole game for us is taking passengers away from other airlines, because we've got a better network than they have, through the alliance. You're going to see more competition for the individual traveler's loyalty.'

Cracking the airline codes

Cracking the airline codes comes down to asking the right questions. Which airline will be operating this flight? How many times does it stop and where? Is there a change of aircraft or airline? Will my seating and meal requirements be respected throughout the journey, especially if I am decanted to a smaller plane? Is my connection 'guaranteed'? How long will I be on the ground? Can I use an executive lounge? Will I earn frequent-flier miles on both code-sharing carriers? Is there an alternative (more convenient) routing with a cheaper fare?

It's not supposed to happen these days, but airlines 'hosting' a CRS/GDS tend to manipulate display screens – or give incentives to travel agents – in favour of their own flights. Code-sharing allows airlines to offer on-line connections that may involve a change of plane or carrier as direct flights. So ask the agent to check all screens for a through flight before putting you on a connecting code-sharing flight. Be aware that a direct flight does not mean non-stop. It means you are stopping somewhere, but staying on the same plane.

Airline timetables should reveal code-sharing flights. But the only way to be sure is to subscribe to a database such as the IAPA traveler manager or the OAG electronic flight guide. OAG is 'neutral' but does accept paid advertising from airlines to list connecting flights – which may not be the best option. If in doubt, call the airline.

Carving up the skies:

*STAR ALLIANCE: 720 destinations in 110 countries
Air Canada
Lufthansa
SAS
Thai International
United Airlines
Varig Brazilian Airlines
Air New Zealand
Ansett Australia
All Nippon Airlines
Mexicana Airlines (2000)
Austrian Airlines/Lauda Air

(Singapore Airlines co-operates with some Star Alliance partners.)

*ONEWORLD: 648 destinations in 139 countries
American Airlines
British Airways
Canadian Airlines
Cathay Pacific
Qantas
Iberia
Finnair
LanChile (in 2000)

(Japan Airlines co-operates with American and British Airways on code-sharing and frequent-flier programmes. LOT Polish Airlines, Avianca and Aerolineas Argentinas co-operate with certain Oneworld carriers. BA owns 25 per cent of Qantas and 9 per cent of Iberia.)

*ATLANTIC EXCELLENCE/QUALIFLYER:
Swissair/Crossair   655 destinations in 139 countries
Sabena

Turkish Airlines
TAP Air Portugal
Austrian Airlines/Lauda Air
AOM French Airlines/AirLittoral

(Swissair has acquired a 20 per cent stake is South African Airways (SAA). SAA, Swissair and the Qualiflyer group account for more than 40 per cent of air traffic between South Africa and Europe.)

*ALITALIA/KLM/NORTHWEST/CONTINENTAL:
500 destinations in 100 countries

*AIR FRANCE/DELTA/AERO MEXICO

*VIRGIN ATLANTIC code-shares with NORTHWEST and CONTINENTAL AIRLINES.

*VIRGIN ATLANTIC/SINGAPORE AIRLINES

High-tech help for the corporate traveler

'The lowest air fare isn't always the best fare when you take into account the travel policy of the corporation, deals with certain airlines, and the needs of the traveler. Our system really flips the whole travel purchasing process upside down. The only yield management systems that exist today are owned by the airlines; they're designed to maximize the profit per seat. What we have is a yield management system for our clients.'

This is how Hal Rosenbluth, president and chief executive of Rosenbluth International in Philadelphia, describes DACODA, a travel management programme that he claims enables corporations to 'model' factors such as travel patterns, policies and priorities (how important are convenience and comfort?), meeting negotiated targets for rebates with various airlines and coming up with the optimum deal. Rosenbluth claims that DACODA can quantify such intangibles as the value of an executive's time when it comes to deciding between a more costly direct flight and a cheaper flight with stopovers. This is an example of how high tech is helping to establish business travel agencies to streamline their service and save their customers money.

'Travel agents as order takers will very quickly find themselves out of business. A really fine travel agency is one that use technology and blends that with competent people,' Rosenbluth says. "Questions may come in which lead to a simple answer. But more important is to provide options to the traveler that they would not have known about.'

Rosenbluth, third largest travel agency in the United States, introduced DACODA (Discount Analysis Containing Optimal Decision Algorithms, since you asked) to help companies figure the real cost of airline deals by sorting through airlines' elaborate pricing and discounting landscape, enabling travel managers to assess the 'true value' of each travel option. This may not always be the lowest air fare.

Companies typically do route (or network) deals with several airlines whereby they get a cash rebate of anything up to 40 per cent if they hit a certain 'seat/miles' or market-share target. Such deals may include upgrades and other perks. What DACODA does is to monitor daily changes in the market (in terms of fares, capacity and frequency) and select the best option for each journey. This may be to fly with airline A today, but switch to airline B tomorrow.

'We're talking about incremental savings of 10 to 19 per cent over and above the 40 to 50 per cent discounts with airlines that we've already negotiated for them up front,' Rosenbluth says. 'We saw one instance where we could have in a three-week period saved a company $5,000 by selling them $69 seats with one carrier just opening up between two city pairs. But that would have meant they would not have met their volume hurdles for another carrier and would have given up a $500,000 check. That's all part of DACODA.'

But the harder an agency works at getting you the best deal, the less commission he earns. And how do you know how much money he's saving you anyway?

'We've already benchmarked what they're paying through their travel patterns and we also pick up what is the lowest air fare and then DACODA uses that plus all the negotiated fares; then we split the incremental savings,' Rosenbluth says. 'If a corporation spends $10 million a year in travel we typically take our 9 per cent commission – $900,000. Since DACODA most likely will be saving 20 per cent, that spend by the corporation is now only $8 million. We take the $2 million that is saved and split it, so we end up having a greater return for saving them money. And it gets rid of that conflict of interests that's at the back of everybody's minds.'

Once DACODA has selected the optimum flight, the booking is taken over by Trip Monitor – a 'robotics' programme that searches for the lowest available fare right up to the day before departure. This aims at beating airlines at yield management. It's a kind of star wars with computer playing computer.

Airlines use variable pricing to fill their planes at the maximum revenue or 'yield' – offering low fares if you book some time in advance, becoming more expensive at the peak booking period, and cheaper again near the time of the flight. Trip Monitor keeps going into the airline CRS, checking the fares and automatically cancelling and rebooking at a lower fare. So even if you booked originally at a high price, you can end up paying less.

'You can access all this through what we call Automated E-res,' Rosenbluth says. 'Someone only needs to put into their PC who they are, where they are, where they want to go, and when they need to be there, and if they want a car or a hotel, and our computer will take all that, find the lowest air fare, and send back the confirmation, or a spread of options, to the desk-top of that individual.'

Help for small-business budgets

Independent and small-business travelers face a daunting paradox. On the one hand, they are often frustrated at not being able to profit from the service and expertise that travel agencies offer major corporate customers: on the other hand, they find it hard to exploit the expanding galaxy of 'agentless' travel services in cyberspace. It's OK to say 'shop around'. Every self-respecting travel agency has a home page these days. But unless you have a tame 12-year-old to surf the Internet for deals, where do you find the time?

What the small-business traveler wants is a person at the other end of a phone who knows him and understands exactly what he needs – even if he isn't quite sure himself – and the skill and motivation to provide it. It's not enough for somebody just to pull up your 'personal travel profile' on the screen.

Few business travel agencies will talk to you – let alone open a credit line – if your travel spend is less than $100,000. But who needs to stand in line behind someone booking a holiday when you're trying to buy a business ticket? Yet there are nearly one million companies in the United Kingdom that spend less than £50,000 a year on business travel.

Business travelers in small companies often do the arranging themselves – when you have, say, one secretary for several people in the office. But they tend to be much more savvy, experienced travelers, much closer to the bottom line. There are all kinds of on-line systems that enable the independent traveler to select the best deals and then go down to their travel agency or book direct. But it puts the burden on the traveler to shop around. All that technology will do is give them more information at their fingertips – it's time-consuming. Small-business travelers still rely on their travel agency.

35

Fortunately, some travel agencies are addressing the challenge with dedicated small-business units, typically a phone-in service based upon a corporate card or personal charge card.

Hogg Robinson Travel in London has a small-business unit independent from its main corporate travel management service.

Adam White, business travel development manager at Going Places in London, says: 'If you're coming on the phone and spend, say, a minimum of £10,000 a year, we'll give you up to 45 days' credit and put you through to a dedicated business travel unit with the same array of our negotiated air fares and hotel prices.'

A.T. Mays, a sister company of Carlson-Wagonlit Travel, based in Scotland, set up a small-business unit in July 1995 called Business Direct, which allows companies with a travel spend less than £50,000 a year to connect directly by phone with one of a team of four people. Travelers then qualify for A.T. Mays' special rates including those of its own consolidator Airsavers.

Jill Henderson, head of sales at A.T. Mays in Glasgow, says: 'I can say to you confidentially that you will only ever have four people looking after you who understand your business. It generally tends to be the traveler himself or herself who calls us rather than a secretary, so they know what they want and can conduct the business far quicker. What we're trying to do is to get back to people, that old-fashioned quality, through efficient use of technology.'

Melody Goodman, at Gray Dawes Travel in London, says: 'We've developed a telephone reservations centre in Colchester for small-business travelers. What we recommend is credit card payment for which we'll make available special fares, our preferred hotel rates and access to our 24-hour helpline service. We have an "agentless" reservations service via e-mail. But we find it's quicker for somebody to pick up the phone and say, this is what I want, rather than trying to find the right bit on your computer to do it.'

Rosenbluth International in Philadelphia, the third-largest travel-management company in the United States, offers the small-business traveler the same negotiated air fares and hotel rates that the major corporate customer enjoys – either at a local agency or through a Rosenbluth 'IntelliCenter' located in a low-cost area such as Fargo, North Dakota.

'Whatever the size of the travel budget, it depends on the comfort level of the client,' says Liz Joseph, manager, corporate communications at Rosenbluth in Philadelphia. 'Some companies love the idea of being serviced through Fargo – it costs them less than an on-site facility. Or else they might want an on-site. Sometimes they want an on-site service here in Philadelphia. But we handle many small accounts here in Philadelphia, and it can be the most cost-effective plan since it costs them less than through an on-site office. We find that small-business travelers typically ask for fast turnaround; ticket delivery; quick last-minute changes; and lowest possible fares.'

An advanced 'agentless' travel system is E-Res, developed by Rosenbluth for major corporate clients, whereby travelers can plan and make reservations from their laptops or office PCs. You can book flights, hotel rooms and car rental on 'real time' without having to wait for an e-mail message to be queued to an agency for action and e-mailed back to you. Corporations can 'model' factors such as travel policies and priorities and the system comes up with the optimum choice.

Rosenbluth has a version of E-Res for small-business clients. This factors in Rosenbluth-negotiated prices for clients who do not have their own negotiated rates. You can dial up direct on your PC or through the Internet. You can find Rosenbluth at www.rosenbluth.com.

Then there are 'niche' agencies like Imperial Travel Consultants, with just one office, in Montreal (www.login.net/imperial),which specializes in saving money (as much as 50 per cent) on first- and business-class tickets for 'sophisticated' travelers around the world.

'Clients contact us by phone, fax or e-mail,' says Dave Miller, Imperial's president. 'The six-hour time difference to Europe works to their advantage as we are open till 11.30 pm Paris time. Since we only deal with first and business classes, we have the time and expertise to devote to this type of traveler. Our turnaround time is the same day.

'Originally, our clients were individuals or small companies. But since the recession, medium-sized companies in Europe have started to work with us. Large corporations are more interested in management reports than saving money.'

WEXAS International, a travel club in London, runs a phone-in service for its 37,000 members, a quarter of whom live outside the United Kingdom. Membership starts at £40, for which you get expert advice and a raft of travel discounts and other benefits. Gold Card members get extra services such as an emergency hotline, ticket delivery by courier and collection at airports. Members are primarily professional people, doctors, lawyers, teachers and small-business travelers, who use the service for both business travel and holidays.

WEXAS International
Tel: (44 171) 581 8761; fax: (44 171) 225 1099

Second-guessing your travel agent

Not every business traveler wants to be a travel expert. Delegation, after all, is the key to effective management. It pays to keep travel agents on their toes by testing them with your own information and asking the right questions. But second-guessing your agent takes time away from your own business. What we really need is a person at the other end of a phone who knows us and understands exactly what we need – even if we're not quite sure ourselves – and the skill and motivation to provide it. Booking online is fine for straightforward itineraries. But whatever happened to personal service and creative travel planning? And how do you know how much money your travel agent is saving you?

Scholefield Turnbull & Partners, a small business travel consultancy in London, claims to have the answer to these questions with a novel service called 'Travel Strategies' that 'guarantees savings of up to 25 per cent or no fee' on travel costs for the 10 to 20 most frequent travelers in a company, with no loss of comfort and convenience. The fee is 25 per cent of the savings made.

It sounds like a 'win–win' deal. These are incremental savings over and above those that may be achieved by your travel agent. But there is no need to disturb that relationship. STP sets up the itinerary, then passes it to the incumbent agency to issue the tickets.

Travel Strategies emerged from two pilot schemes with leading Wall Street financial services group J.P. Morgan and BP, the petroleum and petrochemicals giant – both clients of American Express. STP had said: Let us handle the travel arrangements for your most frequent fliers, and we'll save you money without upsetting existing travel patterns and preferred airlines, with all the flexibility you need. But we don't want the account; we're not big enough to handle it anyway.

Chris Turnbull, a partner of STP in London, says: 'The key to what we're doing is having a small team of people who know fare structures inside out, paying them well and locking them in with a bit of equity, so that the client has the continuity of a regular travel consultant asking him the right questions. That's the only way it can work: a conversation with the traveler. We encourage the traveler to explain what his diary looks like for the next 12 months. We never look at an itinerary in isolation.

'The traveler might say, "Well, I've got to go to South Africa twice, the States three or four times, plus a trip to the Middle East or Far East." So, if they are going to South Africa, we'd ticket a North American trip on the end of that ticket and save about 40 per cent.

'A classic example: the fare from New York to Johannesburg is exactly the same as the fare from London to Johannesburg – and you'd logically fly through London. So if someone plans to visit all three cities within a year, we'd issue a one-way ticket from London to Johannesburg, then a second ticket that reads: Johannesburg–London–New York–London–Johannesburg. So effectively, you travel the Atlantic free. You don't have to specify dates; you're still dealing with a full fare. What makes the saving is the combination of the bilateral agreement between the United States and South Africa plus a soft currency.

'Another oddity is that the business-class fare from Britain to Canada is about a third more expensive than the fare from Canada to Britain. In economy it's the other way round. What's interesting too is that although Scandinavian fares are high, because that's what the market can stand, fares from there to the United States are generally cheaper than they are from Britain; again because of the bilaterals.'

These are ways of exploiting the anomalies between fares at either end of a route (either because of currency rates or bilateral agreements between states) and 'fare construction' techniques under the International Air Transport Association's 'maximum permitted mileage' system. This allows you to travel up to 25 per cent more miles between two points at no extra cost or for a small surcharge.

Here are some examples of fare construction in business class:

 Back-to-Back Tickets. London–Sydney–London–Sydney (BA/Qantas) costs £6,987. This can be reduced to £5,938 by writing two tickets: London–Sydney and Sydney–London–Sydney, a saving of £1,049 or 15 per cent.

 Combination Tickets. London–Delhi–London (BA); London– Boston– London (American Airlines); London–Delhi (BA) costs £7,840.

Writing two tickets: London–Delhi and Delhi–London–Boston–London–Delhi costs £4,908, a saving of £2,928 or 37 per cent.

'We've calculated the maximum permitted mileage that allows the deviation to London,' Turnbull says. 'If it's, say, Delhi–Stockholm–Boston, you would calculate to see whether the maximum permitted mileage allows a stopover in Stockholm. If it does, you can surcharge proportionately from 5 to 25 per cent on the permitted mileage between Delhi and Boston. Suppose that to be 2,000 miles and going through Stockholm brings it up to 2,010 miles, you could still apply the Boston–Delhi fare plus 5 per cent; a heck of a lot cheaper than doing separate tickets.'

 Circle Tickets. London–Rio (BA)–Buenos Aires–London (Aerolineas-Argentinas)–London (BA)–London–Rio–Buenos Aires (Varig) costs £7,277. Writing two tickets: London–Rio–Buenos Aires and Buenos Aires–London–Rio–Buenos Aires costs £4,887, a saving of £2,390, or 33 per cent. These are two separate trips, 'exploiting substandard fares and currencies in South America by changing the point of ticket origination'.

'We compare air fare construction with whatever airline route deals the client has in place,' Turnbull says. 'Then we'll either hoist the white flag and say, your route deals are the best thing – if you're just flying between London and New York, for example. Or we'll say, we can save you more money by sticking a Tokyo trip on the tail-end of that trip to the States. This depends, of course, on travel patterns. We cherry-pick those travelers in a company whose itineraries are most conducive to our type of ticketing.'

All very well second-guessing a travel agent, but why can't they second-guess themselves by using the same fare-construction techniques?

'Lack of knowledge and experience and over-dependence on technology,' Turnbull says. 'Scripts are written into reservations systems and consultants have to follow that line. There isn't time, even if they had the experience and knowledge, to sit down and work out some of these angles. It's also having the confidence to ask the traveler daft things like, do you ever go to Dubai? Most agents expect to get about £1.5 million productivity per consultant. That means a lot of transactions. So these young people don't have time to think about it, even if they had the ability. Plus the traveler is dealing with a different person the whole time.

'What is important in our strategy,' he says, 'is that we cannot survive on cost savings alone – we have to service an account to the hilt. This means continuity, the same person, knowing the traveler's habits and phobias, being proactive in booking hotels and getting visas plus private bits and pieces. We have people at the airports who'll pre-empt offloading, try and get upgrades. Once people get used to savings, they're taken for granted. Unless you handle them well, clients could drift away.'

Scholefield Turnbull & Partners Limited
Tel: (44 171) 378 1788
Fax: (44 171) 407 4258
E-mail: TRAVEL@ST-P.PRESTEL.CO.UK

Traveling on the Net

Cyberspace has become the first stop on the itinerary of many travelers who now have access to a rapidly expanding galaxy of travel sites – airlines, hotels, online travel agencies, booking agencies – that allow you to plan and book your own travel simply by pointing and clicking with a mouse.

Behind the majority of booking sites is an airline-owned GDS (Global Distribution System) such as Sabre (American), Amadeus (Air France, Iberia, Continental, Lufthansa), Galileo (United, BA, Swissair, Alitalia) or WorldSpan (TWA, Delta, Northwest). There are GDS-owned sites – Sabre operates travelocity.com; Amadeus has amadeus.net; and WorldSpan is behind Microsoft's expedia.com.

It's often easier to make a booking than to be certain you're getting the best deal. Airline sites are biased towards their schedules, and prices and travel agency sites may show preference for certain carriers.

'So for the independent traveler, if you want the lowest fares you've got to do everything – wading through Internet sites and calling a travel agency, there's no one perfect solution,' says Ian Wheeler, key accounts director at Amadeus in Madrid. 'The lowest fare is the holy grail; fares and availability are changing all the time. So at any given moment that may not be the lowest fare. Check five minutes later, or five minutes earlier, and you might have got a better fare. You may find a low price, but it may not be available. And a lower fare is not always the best fare if it means you connecting four times on a journey. It's a trade-off between time, efficiency and choice. You'll get a more comprehensive selection by going through an agent.

'We've just brought to market a powerful fare-search tool called Value Pricer – a search engine that can select the best four fares that are available at any moment. You want to travel New York–Paris and have certain restrictions – like no way on Air India or only business or economy.

The system searches our fare database of more than 800 airlines, then hits our availability system, then returns the best four fares. At which point you can say – give me some more choices. The system will be available through some of our Internet-based products later in the year. But to be honest, it's such a valuable product that we're not sure whether to make it available for public use.' There has been a rapid increase in the number of people booking online in the last 12 months.

Online travel analysts, PhoCusWright in Sherman, Conn. (www.phocuswright.com/), expect Internet travel bookings to exceed $6 billion in 1999 and reach $20 billion by 2001. According to Forrester Research in Boston, consumer travel represented 42 per cent of all 1998 business-to-consumer Internet sales.

PhoCusWright predicts that Internet hotel bookings will reach $4 billion by 2001, with hotels gaining 5.5 per cent of all their bookings through the Internet in three years and 10 per cent within five years.

Some 46 per cent of business travelers now regard the Internet as a reliable way to make bookings, according to the OAG Business Travel Lifestyle Survey 1998 of 3,000 travelers in nine countries. But opinion is evenly split on the convenience of online transactions. The Japanese have the most faith in the Internet – 88 per cent of those having used it regarding it as reliable and convenient. The British are the most sceptical – only 3 in 10 of UK business travelers think it is reliable and only 2 in 10 think it is convenient.

Peter Yesawich, president and CEO of Yesawich, Peppardine & Brown in Orlando, Florida, co-publishers with Yankelovitch Partners of the *Business Travel Monitor*, says: 'In our 1999 survey in January, 28 per cent of business travelers told us they consult the Internet for travel information and 14 per cent have used it to book a business trip compared with 25 per cent in 1998 and 4 per cent in 1997 – a significant increase.

'We're about to see a fundamental change in the buyer–seller equation in travel because of the Internet. The power of the transaction shifts from the airline supplier to the consumer because the majority of people out there just want transportation as cheaply as they can get it – airline seats are becoming a commodity product – a scary thought for airlines. People are buying on price. The only way airlines can buy loyalty is by giving away miles.

'Airlines are using the Internet as a below-the-line marketing medium. You can log on to any of these airline sites, provide an e-mail address, and the airline will e-mail you on a Wednesday or Thursday night the unsold inventory – whether in first or coach – that you can buy at distressed fares for the following Friday or Saturday.'

European airlines are promoting themselves online using similar techniques, such as special fares, two-for-one deals and frequent flier incentives for booking through their sites. UK low-cost carrier, easyJet, for example, claims to be achieving 50 per cent of sales online, reducing costs for the airline and offering a saving of £1 per passenger for each one-way flight booked on the Web.

Travelocity (www.travelocity.com) caters to small-business and independent travelers. Its 'low-fare search' displays the three cheapest flights available when you enter city pairs and dates of travel. And www.lastminute.com offers eleventh-hour deals for services like plane tickets and hotel rooms.

Microsoft Expedia – www.expedia.com – has four sites, tailored to local needs: the United States, launched two years ago; Canada; Australia; and the United Kingdom. Germany is due to come online in June. Sites offer a flight booking service for published and discounted fares (updated every 30 minutes) hotel reservations and car rental.

Turner Broadcasting has a new site – www.cnntraveler.com – with hotel and general travel news.

Members of the International Airline Passenger Association have access to special rates at 14,000 hotels worldwide, 5,000 of which, from 20 major chains, they are able to book online in real time at www.iapa.com

'We launched the site in February 1999 to give members another way to make a booking,' says Steve Pinches, general manager of IAPA in London. It's just hotels at the moment: air fares are completely different. In the States, where it's nearly all domestic travel, straightforward point-to-point, airline pricing lends itself to online booking. But how on earth is the independent traveler on a 10-day trip to five destinations going to find his way around booking on the Web with all the different fares and conditions attached? It's better to pick up the phone and speak to someone.'

Other options for airline bookings are TravelSelect (www.travelselect.com) a bucket-shop site run by Globepost, one of the largest consolidators in the United Kingdom, which displays the cheapest available flights with conditions and allows direct booking with payment by credit card; and Travel Information Software Systems (www.tiss.com) linked to Sabre, which claims to offer the 'lowest airfares available on the Web' – although you cannot actually book flights.

Cheapflights (www.cheapflights.com), a UK site run by John Hatt, former travel editor of *Harpers & Queen* and owner of Eland, which publishes travel literature, claims 3 million page views a month, has no immediate plans to provide online booking.

'We will have a booking engine on our site, but only when they are good enough, but none of them are at the moment,' Hatt says. 'They are all flawed, for two reasons: they are still nowhere near user-friendly and frighten people off; and as a general rule, they don't carry consolidation fares.

'For my annual holiday to India, I would no more book online than die. I need a human being to shout at if anything goes wrong. And I need a human being to say, if you go a week later, it's half price; or there's a strike at Delhi Airport, so you'd better fly back via Bombay, I'll get you on the direct flight. No booking engine can cope with that kind of complication.

'But traveling point-to-point, if you know the airline you want to go with and you can see the price and they fax through a confirmation, then I would book online.'

Three kinds of booking systems

Shall we walk – or do we have time for a taxi? – a cherished remark overheard in Manhattan – is an apt metaphor when it comes to planning travel. Do we have time to surf the Internet or shall we just pick up the phone and call the airline or travel agent?

For many people the Internet is still more of an adventure playground than a serious way to plan and book a complex itinerary. Unless you have a tame 12-year-old to shop around for you, how do you find the time? Internet travel calls for patience and perseverance. Access to popular Web sites is often congested to the point where it can take forever to log on. And once you're there it can take several minutes for graphics to appear on screen and to wade past a gauntlet of ads and logos to what you need – even if you know where you're going. Then you have the problem (or doubt) of paying for the booking. Are you happy about sending your credit card details into cyberspace for anyone to intercept? And where and how are tickets going to be issued?

There are three main kinds of electronic travel planning systems: software that stores basic information – such as flight schedules and hotel prices – on your hard disk or CD ROM and allows you online access to view availability and make reservations; direct modem access to real-time schedule information and booking capability via the Internet; and customized 'Intranet' systems (closed systems using the Internet) whereby corporate travelers can plan and book travel from their laptops or office PCs. Corporations can 'model' factors such as travel policies and negotiated rates with airlines and hotels and the system comes up with the compliance with optimum choice – typically with the travel agency picking up the request either online or by e-mail and doing the ticketing, which these days might be ticketless. Such systems are often linked via proprietary travel agency software to independent sources of electronic flight information such as OAG, to a CRS/GDS such as Sabre, Amadeus, WorldSpan or Galileo, or direct to an airline reservations system. More than 300 airlines offer real-time schedule information and booking capability via e-mail either through software that you install on your PC or direct to a Web site.

But few companies are offering simple booking systems that are superior to picking up the phone. The key is speed and control. Companies should look hard at the cost and effort of installing a self-booking system, especially when booking travel is not your core business. Even if you put in something like Sabre Business Travel Solutions [www.sabrebts.com], which sells aggressively direct to corporations, it is not cheap when you consider training costs.

The Internet is fine for individuals – as we've seen there are some great systems out there, like Travelocity, operated by Sabre, and Microsoft's new Expedia site – but corporations need the speed of access that you get from an Intranet system, where there's no risk of a file server going down along the route to the site and you have ability to control what information travelers are seeing.

OAG has launched a new CD ROM product which combines its FlightDisk with more than one million flights and fares from more than 800 airlines with the OAG HotelDisk which lists around 10,000 properties around the world. This does not allow you to book. But it does allow you to customize your own travel requirements on a corporate Intranet which travelers can access from their PCs or laptops.

'Self-booking is very much in vogue, but there's a big difference between expectation and reality,' says Kevin Ruffles, group services director for Hogg Robinson Travel in London. 'From the travel agents' point of view it is fuelled by airlines' commission cuts and our subsequent need to drive down transaction costs. The reality is that you're moving some of the work from the agent to the corporation – linked, of course, to computer literacy. The issue is, how far does the corporation want their travelers involved in the travel planning and booking process?

'Self-booking will have a place at some point for parts of travel – straightforward point-to-point traffic where the traveler knows where he's going: like London–Edinburgh – point and click, book their ticket, go to the airport and off they go. No rocket science in doing that. In the United States, where all this is driven from, 85 per cent of air travel is domestic – straightforward journeys like Chicago–Denver. For complex international itineraries you still need a person who knows all the dodges of creative fare construction. That's what we're struggling with:

if we can use technology to bring costs down, let's do it. Does that mean no agent? Perhaps, for certain types of trip.

'Providing information on the corporate Intranet cuts the number of what we call "shopping calls" and enables us to staff up for transactions, or bookings. The issue with corporations is around the information, not the transaction.'

'We're seeing a very rapid sea change – a hurricane – in the role of travel agents, who see a decreasing revenue as airlines reduce their distribution costs by capping commission and selling direct to corporations and travelers: agents are losing their mystique of being travel experts, the only thing they need to be involved in is the actual ticketing,' says John Stephenson, managing director of Travelcom International in London, whose Empower 21 system comprises a suite of travel management functions – from budget control to expense-reporting, travel planning and booking via the Internet. 'Travel agencies, by promoting self-booking, are putting the spotlight on themselves: they're realizing that now they're charging management fees they've got to add value. Corporations need to capture travel information – especially details of where and how much they are spending. This data belongs to the company, not the travel agent. The way to get the best travel deals is to control your information.'

Travelocity (www.travelocity.com) operated by Sabre (American Airlines) is one of the best interactive sites on the Internet aimed at small-business and independent travelers. It offers schedules for 700 airlines, 37,000 hotels and 50 car rental firms in 70 countries with online booking. You can collect tickets from a travel agency of your choice. Online bookings can be held for up to 24 hours and only charged if you decide to travel. Its 'low-fare search' displays the three cheapest flights available when you enter city-pairs and dates of travel. 'Between 30 and 40 per cent of travelers are corporate executives accessing us from the workplace,' says Ned Booth, product manager for Travelocity in Dallas, Texas.

Frills to fit your needs: traveling à la carte

There are times when the most welcome sight in the world is someone holding a card with my name when I come through immigration – especially at a strange airport after a long flight. Or to see the inside of an airport lounge where you can suffer in comfort during an impromptu three-hour wait for a delayed connecting flight, while lesser mortals are stranded in the main concourse.

This is what you can expect, of course, when you travel first or business class. Many airlines offer premium passengers limo transfers (typically between a 30- to 50-mile radius of the airport at both ends), executive lounges, both on departure and arrival, telephone check-ins, advance seat assignment and priority boarding. You get a wider seat with more legroom, a lot more personal space than the folks in the back of the plane, pre-takeoff drinks and gourmet cuisine even if it never lives up to the poetic promise of in-flight menus or ads in the glossy magazines.

That is great if you can afford it. But you're not about to get a free lunch. All these frills have ended up in the price of the ticket. First class can cost twice the price of business class, which in turn costs up to four times more than full economy and 20 times more than the cheapest excursion ticket.

Travelers are faced with a stark choice. Do they pay top dollar to stretch their ego as well as their legs and a raft of frills that they may not want? Or do they save a ton of money rejoicing in the exquisite misery of cattle-class?

It's all or nothing. But why shouldn't travelers be able to mix and match amenities and services according to their needs by traveling à la carte? Why should business travelers have to pay for frills they do not always need? And why shouldn't leisure travelers be able to buy frills when they need them?

I would like a limo to take me to and from JFK Airport in New York and certainly to meet me at Jakarta or Lagos airports; in Singapore I'll take a cab; in Brussels or Amsterdam, I'll take the train. I would be happy to pay for a departure lounge in Hong Kong and an arrival lounge at Heathrow, where I can get my act together in the morning after a long-haul flight. And hold that 'welcome bottle of champagne' and give me instead an early 9 am check-in in London or a 7 pm late checkout in Singapore.

Airlines have got their branding (and pricing) out of sync with the reality of travelers' needs. This is because they assume that travelers fall into two monolithic groups – business travelers with expense accounts (front of the plane) and leisure travelers (back of the plane). We are not expected to stray from our pre-ordained role in the spurious findings of 'lifestyle' surveys. Never mind that some business travelers have tight budgets and some leisure travelers like to splurge.

People travel in different modes, depending on the purpose of the trip and where they're going. Some corporate travelers have deeper pockets than others and style and mode of travel may reflect status and company culture. Individual and small-business travelers typically have an overwhelming need to travel parsimoniously. But for merchant bankers and currency traders or high-powered consultants charging out travel to clients, comfort and convenience may be the overriding concern. ('Can you get me on the 9 am Concorde, an aisle seat in the front cabin?')

Travel mode often dictates choice of airlines and hotels and class of travel. Are you trying to combine business and pleasure? Road warriors may sometimes switch modes on the same trip for 'business extension' weekends with their partner. Business travelers become leisure travelers on vacation or even package tourists when traveling to unfamiliar places.

It may also depend on how much flexibility you need. Are you buying? Are you selling? Or fact finding? Are you visiting clients or local colleagues? How far can you plan in advance – to attend a conference, for example? Do you need to work in the hotel room with state-of-the-art information technology? Or entertain? Or just need a bed for the night? Which is why people often choose different hotels in a particular city on different occasions.

How you choose to spend your time in the air may depend on your mode – office mode, dining mode, relaxation/entertainment mode, or, indeed, a bad mode. On the morning flight out when you are wide awake, you may want to work; coming home, you may want to relax or sleep.

Thus, traveling west during the day, when you're going to drop into bed anyway when you arrive, you might opt to fly economy on a cheap ticket – especially if you can target an off-peak flight with an empty seat next to you. For a fraction of the difference between economy and business class, you could afford to upgrade to 'gourmet class' with an abundance of sandwiches filled with high-rent items like smoked eel or salmon, a pound of beluga caviar and perhaps a thermos of cold vichyssoise. Traveling east, you might want to invest in a sleeper-seat in business-class and forgo dinner.

There are ideas out there for à la carte travel. Four Seasons Hotels and Resorts came up with 'Gourmet Meals to Go' for departing guests 'to replace the limited options of airline dining'. The programme was launched in 1996 at the Four Seasons in Beverly Hills, in response to 'repeated requests from guests wanting to take popular dishes with them'. The service is available at Four Seasons properties in Bali, Dallas, Houston, New York, Newport Beach – and London. Meals are packed in 'bio-degradable mini-suitcase boxes'.

Caterers and hotels around the world have taken up the idea. The Dorset Square and the Covent Garden hotels in London provide take-out breakfasts for early-morning flights. The five-star Milestone in Kensington, London, offers 'lunch to go' picnic boxes with such fillings as smoked salmon, ham, cheese and pickle; crudités with cream cheese, fresh herb and onion dip; rotisserie chicken with tossed salad; fresh fruit salad; and banana and pistachio nut muffin.

A decade ago, the Canadian airline, Wardair, offered quality at reasonable prices, with a single standard of cuisine and service throughout the plane and a 'Big Seat' option. No matter how much you paid for your ticket, you could trade up to a Big Seat in the front of the cabin for around 50 Canadian dollars. Alas, Wardair, in spite of a loyal following, was subsumed about 10 years ago by Canadian Airlines. But it's an idea whose time may have come – again.

Why can't airlines introduce a modified Big Seat option? They could, for example, install 12 large, reclining seats in a separate cabin at a basic price that might include priority boarding and advance seat reservation, but you would need to buy your own food and beverages and pay for a lounge if you needed one.

Hotels could do likewise by selling a standard or 'deluxe' room and enabling you to pay extra for amenities like early check-in, late check-out, use of the health club and business centre.

Packaging à la carte travel is an unrequited business opportunity. I don't mean package tours. But for agents to help travelers tailor services and amenities to their mode of travel – depending on why they're going and where they're headed. Perhaps they could be looked after by an 'invisible' hand, a 'virtual' courier, using the latest information technology to smooth out the seams every step of the way.

Don't pity the package tourist

Why can't business travel be more like a package holiday? I don't mean in the sense of being herded as a group on a preordained itinerary (though that can have its attractions if you move from 'traveler' to 'tourist' mode on a short 'business extension' or holiday), but in having a courier to shepherd you through every phase of the trip, scanning information on flight delays and traffic conditions and ready to alter arrangements if needed. This is the notion of 'seamless' travel. All you should need to worry about is getting on with your business. Business travelers want to manage their business, not their travel.

The ultimate in seamless travel would be beaming in executives by satellite. Next best is your own corporate jet with limos and acolytes at either end – the ease, flexibility and comfort of private travel. You choose the airport. You drive up to the steps of the plane. Client cancels a meeting; palace revolution back home; inclement weather. No problem. You are in control. Great for heads of states, diplomats or tycoons. But the great majority of road warriors are not in control of their trips. And loss of control is the main source of travel misery.

Travel tends to be fairly smooth when you are moving through the air or over the ground; most problems occur at times in between — waiting for a taxi, checking in at the airport, waiting in the lounge, or disembarking at the other end. When schedules go awry and the seams come apart, travelers are thrown back on their resources. Great to be wined and dined at 35,000 feet. But what if the plane is three hours late or diverted to another airport? Who is going to smooth out the seams? What travelers need is a 'managed' business trip, being looked after every step of the way by an invisible, a 'virtual' courier. The 'courier' would need 'real time' information about each travel segment and all the seams between them plus the ability to provide an optimum schedule and alert the traveler to changes in the event of delays.

This is already possible with information technology. The problem is that airlines and other suppliers market only specific travel segments. None – except package-tour operators – is willing to accept responsibility for the traveler throughout the whole journey.

Business travel agencies now call themselves 'travel management consultants'. But travel management is about travel planning, and management of budgets and travel policies. A good travel agent can plan and book complex itineraries, but the service usually ends as soon as the trip begins.

Airlines do smooth out many of the seams for high-yield premium passengers, with limos to the airport from home or office, 'fast-track' facilities at airports and a hierarchy of executive lounges. VIPs and CIPs are met by 'special services' reps, fed and watered, and shepherded through customs and immigration. But this is well short of total journey management.

Airlines claim that code-sharing with alliance partners provides seamless travel. The idea is that you can check all the way through on a complex itinerary with a sheaf of boarding passes. So that if you miss a connection, someone will be waiting for you at the gate and figuratively take you by the hand.

Code-sharing sometimes takes the form of 'double designator', whereby one airline sells seats under its own code in another airline's cabin. We can expect to see several airlines sharing the same plane with their own fares, flight attendants and standards of comfort and service.

This leads to the concept of the 'virtual' airline. Airline seats are becoming a commodity. Who needs to own aircraft and infrastructure when you can 'brand' your own block of seats with your own cabin attendants and catering in someone else's plane?

Meanwhile, my vote for the 'Seamless Travel' award for the millennium goes to Airbus Industrie for suggesting that airlines pamper high-yield customers by installing air-conditioned cabins in the luggage holds of A-340s. Each cabin could be provided with beds, bathrooms and butler service. Perhaps, for an extra charge, the airline might deliver a container to your home or office, transport you to the airport and load you on to the plane.

'Good news, sir! We're pleased to offer you an upgrade from first class to air freight.'

Suiting the flight to the traveler

Just as I am sounding off about the airlines' crass assumption that business travelers are monolithic – by failing to recognize that people travel in different modes with different needs, motivations and priorities, depending on status, corporate travel policy, why they're going and where they're headed – here comes Air Canada with a programme to identify different types of traveler and address their specific needs.

The programme echoes, to some extent, my plea in another chapter for traveling à la carte – allowing people to mix and match amenities and services. Why should travelers in business class have to pay top dollar for frills they may not always need? And why shouldn't business travelers condemned to economy be able to buy frills when they need them?

Rupert Duchesne, senior vice president international at Air Canada in Montreal, says: 'It was clear to us a couple of years ago, that the business travel market was segmenting. Hotels, car rental firms, banks, and other service businesses, were recognizing different customer needs. We did a basic piece of research among our business customers and found that the needs of each segment were fundamentally different. We were surprised, for example, at how many flew economy – which taught us a lot about what we need to do with the economy product.

'The structure we've got now –although it's still early days – is really to take each group of business customers and give them what they want. It can be something as simple as an upgrade or as expensive as a concierge service. And make sure we make that available to that person and not to somebody else who doesn't need it. We can't afford to spend everything on everybody. A typical airline gets 65 per cent loyalty from its best customers, meaning that 65 per cent of the time they choose you and the rest of the time somebody else. You only have to raise that loyalty four or five points to make a very big difference to your economics and to their travel experience.'

Marc Trudeau, senior director, customer loyalty and product development at Air Canada, says: 'We sent out 15,000 questionnaires to business travelers across the entire network; we got 9,000 back and we tabulated about 5,000. We forced people to put a value on things like lounge access, quality of food, in-flight entertainment, not so much by asking them if they'd be willing to pay more for this, but implicitly making them choose between packages that included or excluded certain elements.'

Air Canada defined four distinct types of traveler, reflecting the different habits and mind-set between North American travel (typically, same-day or one overnight) and overseas travel:

 Executive Suites: The top 20 senior executives in a corporation. They are high-income, highly experienced travelers, who fly almost exclusively business- or first-class (Air Canada, like many carriers, has a combined first-business-class called ExecutiveFirst) and enjoy elite FFP status. Typically, 50 per cent of their travel is within Canada; 30 per cent trans-border, and about 20 per cent trans-Atlantic or trans-Pacific. These folks expect serious recognition, the red-carpet treatment. They hate using electronic booking or automatic check-in – expecting a concierge to meet and greet them along the way. They're not interested in discounts or upgrades; but do appreciate a companion ticket.

 Border-Hopping VPs: Senior corporate managers who make about two trips a week, almost exclusively short-haul. They typically fly full-fare economy, so they are hungry for upgrades and access to lounges. They are status- and time-conscious; they love everything high-tech – booking through the Internet; automatic check-in; electronic tickets; in-flight phones and faxes, laptop power points. They seek productivity on the road, not a relaxing experience.

 Globe-Trotting VPs: Senior executives who fly first- or business-class to Europe and Asia and enjoy elite FFP status. Typically, 70 per cent of their travel is overseas. But they comprise a relatively small group ('several thousand – that's about it'). 'With this group, it's the in-flight experience that makes the difference: you can do almost anything on the ground and it doesn't count for much,' Duchesne says. 'It's small details in the air – being able to eat when they want, choose their entertainment, use their laptops on the plane...'.

 Corporate Masses: Middle-management executives in large companies who typically fly full-fare economy. They aspire to be 'first among equals' and seek 'perks and recognition'.

One way that Air Canada supports the à la carte idea is by giving travelers the option of buying access to lounges for 300 Canadian dollars a year. 'We are piloting a "concierge" service for certain passengers who are booked on international flights out of Toronto,' Trudeau says. 'The concierge will check business-class reservations and make sure that all à la carte requests have been looked after. They will greet the passenger at the check-in area, iron out any problems and do all they can to support and assist them.

'We're coming closer to what you might call "travelgraphics" as opposed to psychographics in defining customer needs. Things like how often people travel, how sensitive they are to price, where they're going, job characteristics, how many years they've been traveling, linked with FFP membership, creates a different mind-set and a different level of expectation. For example, getting someone to use online booking tools like the Internet can have a big impact on profitability: you can save 8 to 12 per cent on agency commission right there.'

OK, but what's in it for the traveler?

'I could argue that these people are looking for the convenience that these tools provide,' Trudeau says. 'We don't have it yet, but it could be that if you know what you want, sign on to make a booking and identify yourself, you might get a better price, a 1,000 more FFP miles, or some other benefit tailored to your needs.'

What type of traveler are you?

Are you an enthusiastic, adventurous, reluctant or hesitant traveler? These are four archetypes revealed in a survey commissioned by Inter-Continental Hotels & Resorts of 6,000 travelers based in North America, Asia-Pacific, Europe, the Middle-East and Africa.

 Enthusiastic Travelers (34 per cent of the sample) love to travel and see new places. They find it enriching, a great cultural experience and an opportunity to meet new people. They look for 'high quality surroundings and quite like to be pampered with personal attention' during their stay in hotels. They are more likely to be from the Middle East or Asia-Pacific, younger than average, female, infrequent travelers, conference delegates or traveling on leisure. They take on average 5.8 trips a year and have stayed at an average of 2.4 hotel chains.

 Reluctant Travelers (18 per cent of the sample) say that travel is boring and a necessary evil: they find the experience more stressful than enriching. They want to get the whole thing over with quickly, don't particularly want exciting hotels and much prefer to choose one they've stayed in before. But they usually travel frequently, tend to be male and aged 40 or over. Reluctant travelers take an average 5.8 trips a year and have stayed at only 2.4 hotel chains.

 Adventurous Travelers (19 per cent of the sample) enjoy both the challenge of overseas travel and the cultural experience – they like to go out of the hotel to explore and like hotels to be different, giving high priority to efficiency but not luxury. They are more likely to be European, male and aged between 31 and 40. They take an average of 6.8 trips a year and have used 2.7 hotel chains on their travels.

 Hesitant Travelers (29 per cent of the sample) seek the reassurance of traveling with their own national airline, hardly ever leave the hotel and regard personal attention and recognition as important. They choose hotels for their consistency and tend to return once they find one they like. On average, they tend to be American or from the Asia-Pacific region, have used 2.7 hotel chains and take an average of 6.7 business trips a year.

What travelers want from hotels

Business travelers' needs and priorities have changed over the last five years and will change even more in the future when it comes to choosing a business hotel. They require much more these days than a quiet, spacious room with high safety standards and service. They see the room more as a high-tech 'command centre' from which they can manage their business and communicate with clients and the office. Recognition will still be important but it is reward that will increasingly motivate travelers in future. Top three loyalty programme perks are free upgrades to better rooms; free weekend leisure stays for two; and the opportunity to earn airline miles.

Mike Stajdel, senior vice president, sales and marketing, Inter-Continental Hotels and resorts, says: 'More and more, travelers want control over their journey, air travel as well as the hotel experience. They want to be able to do business in their room at the time they choose and have food – and a wider choice of dining – when they want to have it. They want flexibility, being able to check in and check out when it suits them and to choose the kind of reward that is appropriate for this particular trip.

'What we're picking up is that no two trips are necessarily the same: there can be one trip where I need full support facilities in the hotel for meeting clients or entertaining; another where I need to be in touch back and forth with my office, so I prefer to do that by e-mail out of my room. One trip may be a quick overnight, so I just want to be able to get in and out fast; or I might have a longer stay, some associates I'd like to invite up for a drink, therefore I need more space, perhaps a suite.

'What surprised us is that in-room business communications facilities have become top priority in choosing a hotel. We didn't realize the extent that this was happening. Travelers in the past used business centres, now they want to do the work themselves, especially e-mail. When all things are equal, loyalty programmes may influence choice of hotel. It is not the main criterion: location and ability of the hotel to satisfy my needs are always coming up first.'

American Express travel trends

An American Express 'Year 2000 Travel Trends Survey' of 360 corporate travelers at the Association of Corporate Travel Executives in Malaga, Spain, and at the World Travel Market in London in November 1999 revealed:

 The number of international business trips will increase by 29 per cent in 2000 – with a third expecting to make more than 15 trips during the year.

 Sixty-nine per cent worked more than they expected in 1999 and 86 per cent expect to work the same or longer hours in 2000. However, despite the pressures and time away from home, 70 per cent enjoy traveling regularly on business.

 Fifty-one per cent frequently use airport lounges, 30 per cent airport meeting rooms, 12 per cent showers, and 7 per cent video-conferencing facilities.

 Travelers are increasingly reliant on technology and the Internet while they are on the road. Ninety-two per cent use a laptop while traveling. Forty-four per cent have used the Internet to book a business trip this year, while 69 per cent expect to do so in 2000.

 Eighty-seven per cent say it is essential for hotel rooms to contain a modem, fax and Internet access. Two-thirds believe hotel rooms will evolve into 'virtual offices' next year.

Forty-nine per cent regularly browse the Internet to research holiday destinations for prices and availability for flights, hotels and car rentals. However, 60 per cent of them say they will continue to book vacations through a travel agent. A fifth book hotels online, 17 per cent book late bargains and 15 per cent book flights.

 Increasing work demands are changing leisure travel habits. The annual summer vacation is being replaced by more frequent weekend breaks as work commitments force executives to spend less time away from the office. A third say they take a vacation primarily to relax and unwind, with less than a quarter choosing to holiday with family and friends.

Is your journey really necessary?

People often ask with awe or pity: 'Handing out all this advice on travel, you must travel an awful lot.' I do make occasional forays afield – about once a month – mainly to reassure myself that business travel is a pretty miserable, often degrading experience. But the truth is that I spend more time on the phone than on the road and probably make fewer trips than most of you. Not that I don't enjoy meeting people, but it's often hard to justify time away that I could otherwise have spent sitting at my keyboard staring into space.

It's a question of productivity as much as budget. I can have twice as many meetings in a day on the phone than schlepping around Paris, London or Manhattan – not to mention the time and energy it takes to get there and back. What's more, I don't have to buy lunch.

Phone meetings are necessarily more focused than face-to-face encounters, when you can keep the conversation short if not always sweet. You miss the eye contact, the forensic handshake and, of course, the social dimension – although 'virtual reality' video conferencing threatens to reveal it all. But how much reality can you bear?

I have developed close tele-relationships with people I never expect to meet – avoiding the risk of mutual disenchantment. This is down to the exceedingly intimate nature of the phone. You can acquire more information in listening to what people are saying and how they're saying it than you do from watching for visual clues. Paradoxically, psychologists say, it's easier to tell if someone's lying to you on the phone than face-to-face. But if you really mean what you say, you're going to sound more convincing. The telephone is a confessional medium, because it allows you to talk to somebody without distractions. You are focused entirely on them. People often find it easier to deal with intimate or difficult topics.

In my corporate days, I would stick my head round my boss's door the night before, and say: 'Tom, I'm in Paris tomorrow. Jean-Pierre wants some help on the marketing plan.' 'Okay, fine, where can we reach you?'

There may have been times when I really wanted to discuss the marketing plan, or maybe I just wanted to get out of the office for a couple of days. Maybe I just needed a heart-to-heart with Jean-Pierre on the implications of George's successor in the latest management reshuffle back at the corporate Kremlin in Broken Springs, Colorado; or a field trip with the sales manager. We got the business done. And I like to think we never short-changed the company.

These days, I am less debonair, because – like most independent and small-company business travelers – travel costs are my bottom-line. But there are times when you feel you have to get away. The social drink, the impromptu meeting, can be pure gold. It's nothing you can quantify; it's intuitive; gut-feel; keeping faith with serendipity. Who, for example, goes to a conference to listen to the presentations? It's networking that counts. Or the chance of bonding with your boss or other colleagues for an extended time. To go or not to go. That is the question.

It's a big question. American Express estimates in its latest (October 1998) biennial Survey of Business Travel Management that US companies will spend $175 billion on travel and entertainment in 1998, around 12 per cent more than 1996. Travel and entertainment is still the third largest controllable expense, after salaries and data processing. This reflects record price increases for air fares, hotel rooms and car rentals, in what is still a seller's market.

At the same time, companies are taking more control of travel budgets, with international business travelers making fewer trips of longer duration, according to the OAG Business Travel Lifestyle Survey 1998. The amount of time spent away has risen by a quarter to an average 45 nights a year from 37 in 1997. Only 12 per cent of trips involve no overnight stay, suggesting more cautious and careful travel planning.

But travel management at most companies is more concerned with book-keeping – travel policy, the cost of the trip, who can travel in what class, getting the best deal from the travel agent and suppliers – than with its purpose. Few people are looking at travel management in the 'management' sense. Why are we making this trip? What are we going to achieve? Can we do business some other way?

'Intuitively, we believe that a high percentage of business travel is unnecessary. The challenge, however, is how to identify it,' says Hal Rosenbluth, president and CEO of Rosenbluth International in Philadelphia. 'We don't believe that people travel because they want to; we believe that they travel because they feel they must to achieve certain goals. But do they?'

Rosenbluth – in partnership with the Wharton School at the University of Pennsylvania and a sample of 'five or six significant corporations' – has embarked on a research project aimed at finding out why business people travel and how and why people choose to interact the way they do. The goal is to help corporations reduce unnecessary business travel and provide a better return on investment for the trips they do take. 'Travel avoidance' options might include video conferencing in its various forms, tele-conferencing or the old-fashioned phone-call as part of the solution. Initial findings are due by the second quarter of 1999.

'If the chief executive or chief financial officer walks into your office and says, cut travel by 20 per cent, you want to be able to manage where you do that,' says Danamichele O'Brien, vice president and chief travel scientist at Rosenbluth. 'If he knew more about where travelers' return on investment was, he might say, only in this area, this department. The last thing you want to do is keep your best sales or relationship managers off the road – you may want to have them double up. Or if they're going to San Francisco, maybe they should continue to Japan, because your pattern is that two weeks later they will be going to Japan anyway.

'Another way to look at it is: You spend 10 million a year on travel, you accomplish so much, you spend 15 million and you accomplish nothing more. Getting the best return on your 'interaction' expense may enable you to keep your budget at 10 million and achieve twice as much.

'There's also the 'opportunity cost' involved in traveling to Asia when you might be doing something even more productive. There's always an opportunity to do something else. What's the trade-off?'

It's fairly easy to quantify travel productivity for sales people or line managers, but what about staff people? Do companies have this kind of information?

'The information is there somewhere; but not under any specific heading – it might be in the travel or finance department, human resources: there are all kinds of ways to get at it through surveys and focus groups,' Rosenbluth says. 'But the T&E budget can be the driver, forcing corporations to quantify the productivity of all travelers, whether staff or line.

'The point is that when somebody calls to make a reservation, they'll get the lowest fare and a whole bunch of options including when to avoid travel, along with alternatives, and when and how to increase it.'

I don't know how much Rosenbluth is spending on this research. But I'll give you my 'business interaction management' strategy for free. Decide who you really need to meet and get them to visit you.

'Virtual conferencing': an alternative to travel?

If you've ever felt that stepping off a long-haul flight into a business meeting is a form of virtual reality (couldn't we have done this on the phone?), here comes Rosenbluth International – second-largest travel management company in the world, with real virtual reality in the form of 'virtual conferencing' called TeleSuite, developed by TeleSuite Corporation, which it is offering corporate clients as an alternative to business travel.

TeleSuite claims to achieve what video-conferencing has always promised but never delivered. Participants appear life-sized and have the illusion that they're in the same room, which means you can behave naturally and don't have to change the way you normally communicate. What's more you don't need a Space Invaders helmet.

'Ultimately, we are in the business of connecting people,' says Danamichele O'Brien, vice president and chief travel scientist at Rosenbluth International in Philadelphia. 'Virtual travel is the next logical step for our business. TeleSuite allows us to connect our clients from point A to point B in a shorter amount of time. As we've seen in all business practices from overnight delivery to e-mail, this era is about time compression – allowing people to do more – faster.

'Don't leave home is not typical advice from a travel company, but if it makes sense for our client, we recommend it. Virtual conferencing, video-conferencing or PC-based conferencing will not replace travel, there will always be a need to be somewhere in person. Just as the fax machine and postal service co-exist, so can virtual travel and actual travel. What we're creating with TeleSuite is virtual airlines. It may allow people to make three trips instead of five, or travel the same amount and just speed up their business cycles.'

Scott Allen, vice president corporate communications at TeleSuite Corporation in Dayton, Ohio, says: 'We set out with IBM Global Services and NEC Technologies to design a new video-conferencing system that didn't have a roll-about monitor with a camera sitting on top. Normally, you can only have your head life-size on a monitor, and if you see someone moving around, their image is very jerky.

'We wanted people to feel they were in the same room, like sitting across the desk, not just because they are life-sized and make eye contact with you, and the voice is coming from their direction, but because they're standing on the same carpet in your office, with the same wall-covering, the same decor. We have built what you may call a virtual environment.'

Picture this. Take a conference room with a circular or oval table. Then chop the room in half right through the table and put a 100-inch high-resolution screen down the middle and pull the rooms apart 100 or 1,000 miles and connect the two halves with a very high bandwidth cable. So that when the screen illuminates, you see the other half of your table completed as an image drawn on the screen with participants from the other site sitting around the table – like in a normal room.

The idea is you make a call saying you want to use the facility at such and such a time. A booking is made with the various TeleSuite locations involved and half an hour before the conference the locations are automatically connected, the lights come on, the screen is illuminated, and you just walk into the room and engage the other participants face to face, just as you would in a meeting-room down the hall.

'We are right now facilitating a 29-city meeting for IBM to train people to use a new software program,' Allen says. 'Rather than flying everyone in for a three-hour training session, the instructor in one location walks around the room giving the presentation and writes on a light board. That's an example of how companies are using TeleSuite to replace travel.

'Of course it would be chaotic if 29 locations tried to communicate one with the other. But we have done up to six meetings that are fully inter-active; it's just that participants need to be self-disciplined and not all speak at the same time. But you can have the illusion of being in the same room with up to three sites.'

The TeleSuite conference room is a modular design that can be set up as a room within a room at corporate locations. TeleSuite has 17 locations in the United States including public locations available for hourly reservations at the Waldorf-Astoria, New York; the Capital Hilton; the Atlanta Hilton and Towers; the Beverly Hilton, the San Francisco Hilton and Towers; and the San Jose Hilton and Towers. Cost is around $300 an hour. 'We expect to have our first international locations in Paris, London, Tokyo and Frankfurt by the first quarter 1999,' Allen says.

There is growing demand for video-conferencing in Asia. The Hyatt Regency Osaka claims to be the first hotel in Japan to have satellite tele-conferencing facilities, via Global Vision Network connected with 37 other venues in the Asia-Pacific region, with links to the United States and Europe.

Tele-conferencing via satellite provides one-way vision, two-way sound and is most suitable for point to multi-point applications. For example, a training seminar or marketing meeting in Japan can be broadcast to other sites and questions can be fed back via IDD phone lines. Similar facilities are available at Park Hyatt Tokyo, Grand Hyatt Hong Kong, Grand Hyatt Seoul, Grand Hyatt Taipei and Hyatt Suajana in Malaysia.

The Park Hyatt Tokyo claims to be the only hotel in the capital providing video-conferencing 24-hours a day, in an arrangement with Face-To-Face Communications in Tokyo, with an average eight video-conferences a month. A recent link with the Grand Hyatt Hong Kong allows you to conduct a one-hour video-conference with up to 10 people at each site for 120,000 yen – less than an undiscounted round-trip economy fare between the two cities. The hourly charge from the Grand Hyatt Hong Kong is 75,000 yen. And it costs around 87,000 yen to link up with the United Kingdom or France.

Kate Burchill, a Hyatt spokeswoman in London, says that video-conferencing is mostly used for monthly strategy sessions and troubleshooting, client presentations, training sessions, and interviewing candidates for jobs.

Video-conferencing is less about saving money on travel and more about global teamworking. It enables people to be brought in to meetings who might not normally attend if they had to travel – for example, senior executives or specialists,

'What we hear from our customers is that the interaction between video-conferencing and business travel is much more complex than it might seem,' says Dave Hooker, marketing director in London of PictureTel Corporation, a Massachusetts-based video-conferencing company. 'Yes, there are instances where companies have systematically turned to video-conferencing as a way of cutting business travel. But many users find that it is complementary to travel. For example, with an increasing trend towards globalization, the managing director of a company based in one country can hold daily meetings with managers in other countries. In this kind of situation travel is simply not a viable alternative.'

PictureTel claims that 49 per cent of Fortune 1000 companies currently use its video-conferencing technology.

Picture-Tel International
Tel: (44 1753) 723 000
Fax: (44 1753) 723 010

Rosenbluth International
Tel: (1 215) 4539
Fax: (1 215) 977 4826

TeleSuite Corporation
Tel: (1 937) 836 9995

VCON Videoconferencing
Tel: (44 1628) 829 555
Fax: (44 1628) 829 777
E-mail: sales@vcon.co.uk
Web site: www.vcon.com

Lifestyles in the skies

So what else is new? This is my usual jaded response to most business travel surveys, which allow you to prove pretty well anything you want, rediscover the obvious or confirm cultural stereotypes. What I look for these days is a good read with a few predictable insights that might second-guess my own prejudices.

All this is provided by two surveys: the IATA (International Air Transport Association) Corporate Air Travel Survey 1999 and the 1999 OAG Business Travel Lifestyle Survey.

The IATA survey reflects the views of more than 1,000 frequent travelers from 10 countries: France, Germany, The Netherlands, Britain, Canada, the United States, Australia, Hong Kong, Japan and Singapore. The OAG looks at attitudes and behaviour among 3,000 business travelers in Britain, France, Spain, Italy, the United States, Canada, Japan, Hong Kong, Singapore, Australia, Brazil and Argentina.

Both surveys show that, despite constrained travel budgets road warriors are making more trips (21 a year on average) involving more nights away in hotels (48 nights a year). More than a quarter of the IATA sample made between 16 and 50 trips in the past year, and 2 per cent of travelers more than one trip a week. Europeans have overtaken North Americans as the most frequent travelers for both short- and long-haul trips, while Asia/Pacific residents travel less often but over longer distances.

According to OAG, North America is the most popular destination (accounting for 17 per cent of all trips) followed by Asia (16 per cent) and Western Europe (15 percent). Fewer than 10 per cent of all business trips are to Eastern Europe, Africa, the Middle East and Central America. One in five trips made by the Japanese is to the United States or Canada.

Corporate travel policies are far more likely to restrict class of air travel or hotel rather than choice of airline (giving free rein to mileage junkies). This is reflected in a steady migration from premium cabins to the back of the plane. IATA reports that the majority of short-haul business travel (68 per cent) is in economy class, while just under half (46 per cent) of travelers say that they usually fly in business class on long-haul trips and only 4 per cent in first class. Europeans have traded down the most, with 45 per cent traveling in economy on long-haul, compared with 39 per cent in 1998 – a 15 per cent increase. Asia/Pacific travelers are most likely to fly in economy on short- and long-haul trips, with less than 30 per cent of them traveling in first or business class.

The search for cheaper airfares has become more intense over the past three years. In 1997, 55 per cent of travelers bought full-fare tickets, compared with 38 per cent in 1999. Not just in economy. Nearly 35 per cent of travelers now travel on discounted business-class tickets (through consolidators or corporate route deals with airlines), compared with 22 percent in 1997. Paradoxically, more travelers are flying on full-fare tickets in first class – from 37 per cent in 1997 to 65 per cent in 1999. Andy Hayward, author of the IATA survey, says: 'I think this is because airlines like British Airways, Singapore Airlines, Cathay Pacific and Virgin are better able to justify the cost of first class fares with the new generation of sleeper seats and proper beds. When it comes to moving down the back of the plane, carriers such as Singapore Airlines, Cathay, Malaysia and Qantas have revamped their long-haul economy cabins in the last 12 months with more legroom and better seats with lumbar support and head and foot rests.'

Familiarity with the Internet is growing at a spectacular rate. IATA reports nearly two-thirds of respondents (63 per cent) using the Internet for flight information (50 per cent more than in 1997), but only 17 percent have used it to book trips – mostly for straightforward point-to-point travel. However, 51 per cent expect to be using the Internet for making travel arrangements in five years' time. Along with Americans, the Japanese are avid users of the Internet.

OAG finds that 60 percent of travelers now regard the Internet as a reliable way to book flights. But while 56 per cent say it is cost effective and convenient, 40 per cent say that it will never be a substitute for travel agents, especially for complex itineraries.

Forget the food and in-flight entertainment, it's schedule, a reputation for safety and punctuality and frequent-flier programmes that count most when choosing an airline, according to the IATA and OAG surveys – although to varying degrees.

According to OAG, Singaporeans, Italians, Brazilians and Argentines put safety above schedule and convenience, while the French rate safety as less important than getting a cheap seat. Predictably, FFPs are still the big turn-on. OAG says 8 out of 10 travelers now say that frequent-flier membership affects their choice of carrier – Americans and Australians in particular, along with two-thirds of Europeans.

Delays are the omnipresent concern when traveling on business, whether the trip is short or long haul – 52 per cent of IATA respondents in 1999 compared to 36 per cent the previous year.

Both surveys report that 'air rage' – aggressive or abusive behavior in the air – has become endemic. A quarter of IATA respondents witnessed such behaviour in the past 12 months; nearly 4 out of 10 of the OAG sample witnessed 'verbal or physical abuse in the past year' and 2 per cent of them have had flights diverted as a result. More than half of these incidents involved verbal abuse of cabin staff. Drunken and disorderly conduct, illegal smoking and gratuitous sexual advances were also causes of trouble.

A more tolerant attitude towards hand baggage would cause 4 in 10 business travelers to switch airlines, according to OAG. Europeans are more uptight about this than anyone else. But the number of travelers facing baggage challenges at check-in grew to 23 per cent from 20 per cent last year.

Despite a stereotype of high-flying executives slaving over a laptop screen or business papers during a flight, most business travelers spend half of their time in the air reading for pleasure or sleeping. But only 14 per cent of their time is spent watching movies or listening to music. The more frequent the fliers, the more likely they are to work – especially North Americans. Asia/Pacific travelers work the least and watch in-flight entertainment the most. The Japanese are especially prone to napping during the flight.

Three-quarters of OAG respondents call their offices and two-thirds call home at least once a day. A half of all travelers e-mail the office at least once a day and 1 in 10 more than three times a day. Residents of Hong Kong and Singapore are the biggest office e-mail addicts. Asians call home less than other travelers, with 14 per cent of Japanese never calling, though they claim to e-mail their loved ones more than three times a day, only slightly less than American travelers.

Sizing up the value of business class

When I started traveling by air in the mid-1960s there were only two classes on the old narrow-body planes: first and economy. And there were only three types of fare: first, full economy and excursion. What's more, there were only two types of plane: empty or full. If you could get a row of seats in economy to stretch out and sleep, you were in paradise.

First class was a golden ghetto for the chief honchos and seriously rich. Everyone else flew economy – which wasn't as grand as business class today: you had to pay for drinks and headsets, but the food was OK and you had enough space to stretch your legs. It was, shall we say, democratic. You might find yourself chatting to a captain of industry, a diplomat, an aircraft salesman, a honeymoon couple or, perhaps, an ambiguous lady with a certain charm. There was much scope for social congress.

Life became more complicated when business class emerged as a third cabin in the late 1970s. The idea was to reward business passengers paying the full economy fare on the new wide-bodied planes with a separate cabin away from holiday folk who might have paid two-thirds or less for their tickets. There are now more economy fares than possible moves in a game of chess.

Flying has never been cheaper. In the summer of 1960, the round-trip economy fare from London to Sydney was £264 (£3,520 in today's money). Similarly, a return fare to New York in 1960 would have cost more than seven times the cheapest discount ticket.

Cheap fares came about through 'open skies' in North America, Europe and on most transatlantic routes – which allowed airlines to set their own fares and compete with charter carriers for holiday passengers.

Larger planes meant that they had more capacity. Better to fill the plane at whatever price than take off with empty seats. The bad news is the growing gap between business class and economy. While the premium cabins become ever more opulent – and expensive – economy has become cattle-class.

Virgin Atlantic reinvented the two-class system in 1985 with its Upper Class – first-class service and comfort at business-class prices – and Middle Class (now called Premium Economy) for people paying the full economy fare. You get a bigger seat and a separate cabin with a bit more attention but the same food as economy. Upper Class became the concept for the early 1990s as several airlines abandoned first class for a more spacious business class. Continental Airlines, which combined first and business class into BusinessFirst, was followed by carriers such as Air Canada with Executive First, KLM with Business Class and TAP Air Portugal with Navigator Class.

Business class today has far surpassed first class in the 1970s, with sleeper seats, limo transfers at both ends, departure and arrival lounges, separate check-in, and a raft of in-flight amenities, from electronic headphones and multi-channel video to satellite phones and power supply for laptops. Space, in the form of seat-width, leg-room and angle of recline, is the prime issue in the airlines' battle for the hearts and minds of business travelers.

Delta Air Lines raised the stakes with BusinessElite in its new Boeing 777s with a new all-singing-all-dancing ergonomic seat with 60 inches of leg-room and 'more recline than any other international airline' in 2-2-2 configuration, eliminating the dreaded middle-seat. It comes with 160 degree recline. It comes with five electric motors for 'lumbar and full leg and thigh support', six-way adjustable headrest, a 'battery-saving EmPower system' for laptops, a personal reading light, a telephone, and a swivel tray table that enables you to leave your seat before you've finished your meal.

'Comfort and personal space to work or sleep is what people want most,' says Stephan Egli, vice president Atlantic-Pacific at Delta Air Lines in London. 'By offering a clearly superior product, more like first class than business, we hope that people will switch their loyalty to Delta because of significantly greater comfort, not so much because of frequent-flier miles. Although we're not increasing the number of miles required to upgrade to business class – 25,000 miles one-way on the North Atlantic – we aim to increase our yields with a higher share of full-fare business passengers.'

More to the point for travelers is the growing premium between business class and economy. Business-class fares on the North Atlantic have risen by about 25 per cent over the past two years, while discount economy fares have fallen by 10 per cent. For example, the round-trip London–Los Angeles business-class fare is £4,508, compared with £1,200 for full economy and £200 for an excursion fare.

So it's not surprising that travelers are moving to the back of the plane as companies try to cut down on travel expenses. The American Express Global Travel & Expense Management Survey of 611 leading corporations worldwide, published in April 1999, finds that economy-class fares account for 72 per cent of all business travel, compared with 24 per cent for business class. Fourteen per cent of corporations do not permit business-class travel.

The choice is stark. Do I pay the cost of a small cottage in Normandy to stretch my ego as well as my legs in a fully reclinable ergonomic seat with 60 inches of leg-room? Or do I save a ton of money by cramming into a seat designed for vertically challenged circus performers with a meal-tray that I can't get down over my stomach if the guy in front puts his seat back?

Some airlines are addressing the dilemma by upgrading economy – but not enough to encourage too many premium passengers to move down the back. British Airways, for example, is coming up with new 'sci-entifically designed' seats with 'contoured back and side lumbar support' and adjustable head- and foot-rests and 'ear flaps' to stop you falling into your neighbour's lap.

Full economy fare is the worst buy in the sky, unless you're using it tactically to upgrade. If you've got to sit in the back, you might as well shop for the cheapest discount fare, savour what you're saving, and if you have to change your plans, just throw away the return coupon and buy another ticket.

Virgin Atlantic's Premium Economy is a successful compromise. You pay less than a third of the business-class fare. London–New York, for example, in business class is £3,244, premium economy, £1048, £310 for a 28-day excursion ticket and £169 for a Megasaver.

'Premium Economy was our response to the last recession five years ago,' says Paul Moore, a spokesman at Virgin Atlantic in London. 'Then, as now, travel managers were saying, you can't fly business class but you can fly economy. We're seeing a significant number of business travelers in economy as well. The vast majority are motivated by price. London–New York for less than £150 return means you can make 10 times as many trips as you could otherwise. It's a means to an end.'

Matthew Davis, manager of the purchasing management group at American Express in London, says: 'Corporations are cutting back by reducing the number of trips and class of travel. But at the same time they're doing more route deals with airlines in business class. We're seeing a significant increase in the number of special fares from airlines. Amex has special fares for long-haul destinations averaging 50 per cent discounts on published business-class fares and 60 per cent off economy fares, with no restrictions except that you'd be stuck on the same airline. The published round-trip business-class fare London–New York is £3,164. We could sell you a ticket for £1,388.

'Travel managers are getting tough. You can fly business class if you use our preferred carrier, with the route deal we have in place, or else you fly economy. That helps compliance with the travel policy, which in turn helps to save money. Six to seven hours is the normal threshold. You can't fly business class to New York, but you can to Los Angeles. In Europe, it's still hierarchical to an extent. But that's changing, driven by US companies. A lot of corporations now allow frequent travelers to fly business class, everyone else economy. Or business class to certain destinations, such as Eastern Europe where security and safety is a factor.'

'There is a perception that travelers are downgrading because of high fares,' says Pieter Rieder, vice president for Europe at Rosenbluth International in London. 'The reality is that most corporations are still allowing people to travel business class on long-haul but only on carriers where they have route deals.

'This could be around 40 per cent off the published fare – especially if you make a one-stop journey with a foreign carrier via its home hub, rather than fly direct. That kind of saving makes business-class travel acceptable to corporations. Typically, out of Northern Europe, where you're paying higher fares, you could save up to $2,500 on a round-trip to the United States with a route deal on a non-national carrier. Individuals can save almost as much.'

Getting most out of your mileage

You've spent thousands of dollars and heaven knows how much management time piling up frequent-flier miles. You thought you'd played your miles right by routing yourself from New York to Paris via Anchorage; charging everything to your credit card at one mile per dollar – international calls at prime rates; otiose car rentals; expensive duty-free bargains – and stayed in your least-favourite hotel for the sake of triple points. And now that the time has come to redeem those hard-won miles for a dream holiday with your family, the airline has the chutzpah to tell you that that destination has been dropped from the programme, there's a blackout for the dates you want to travel, or that while revenue seats are available, there are no seats left for frequent fliers.

You might have known that there's no such thing as a free flight. 'Planning award travel is similar to planning ordinary paid travel,' says FFP guru Randy Petersen. 'But just different enough to make you crazy. This is because programmes have different rules about redemption procedures, transferability, and blackout dates. On average, airlines set aside about 10 per cent of their seats system-wide for frequent fliers.

'Part of the problem is supply and demand. In the last two years, award redemption has grown by some 50 per cent, but the number of seats has not grown accordingly. So supply and demand is a factor, and so is bad timing.'

Most airlines impose blackout periods for frequent-flier awards during major holidays; some prohibit all award trips on some routes during peak travel seasons, such as flights between Europe and North America in summer. Airlines have brought in stiff new rules that make it harder to earn miles by raising award levels along with stricter time limits for redeeming them. Some airlines are putting the squeeze on infrequent fliers by closing the account – even with 20,000 miles of credit – if you haven't flown within the last 18 months. It's almost as easy to lose miles as to earn them. Few frequent fliers these days cherish thoughts of retiring as peripatetic mileage millionaires.

Airlines are raising the hurdles because of the meteoric rise in frequent-flier membership and the contingent liability if everyone cashed in their miles at the same time. There are about three trillion miles floating around the system.

Not that Armageddon is imminent: pundits reckon that out of 644 billion miles earned in 1998, only 280 billion were redeemed.

Here are some ways to avoid frustration when you try to redeem FFP miles:

 Plan your trip as far ahead as possible, as award seats fill quickly, especially in first and business class. Award seats on most airlines can be ticketed 320 days in advance. Have several dates and times in mind when you call to book your flight. You will have the best chance of redeeming your award if you fly midweek (Tuesday or Wednesday are most propitious) and avoid major holiday periods.

 If seats are not available, ask to be put on the wait-list. Check often for cancellations by calling as early in the morning as possible, when newly available seats are posted to airline computers. Call the airline once or twice a week, especially 60 days or closer to the time you want to fly.

 Try booking different routes, because non-stop flights tend to fill up faster; suggest departure from another city; or consider flying into one city and back from another if you can get seats that way.

 Most airlines offer award tickets with no blackout dates and no seat limitations, but at a price – typically, double the miles required for a normal award ticket. But it may be the only way to go.

 Consider buying a ticket and using your miles for an upgrade to a premium class with a firm reservation. (Not all FFPs allow upgrades – especially from an excursion fare – a key factor when choosing a programme.) Between North America and Europe, upgrades from economy excursion fares typically require 40,000 miles on most carriers. Even though the value of mileage required for an upgrade can exceed the cost of an economy excursion ticket, it may be the most practical way to trade mileage for comfort – and an assured reservation. It may be worthwhile buying a more expensive ticket in order to use an upgrade.

Flying long-haul, don't spend miles on an upgrade from economy to first, just upgrade to business class. Few airlines outside North America allow you to use miles for upgrades. And not all upgrades work the same way. What really counts in a programme is the ability to upgrade from any published fare.

 Many airlines refuse to give mileage credit on consolidator tickets, or allow you to use them for upgrades with FFP miles. Given that such tickets can save you around 40 per cent on published first- or business-class fares, this may be an acceptable trade-off. But it's worth asking your travel agent for a more expensive consolidator ticket that does allow you to earn and redeem mileage.

 A general rule: redeem your frequent-flier miles for expensive tickets, not cheap ones. If all stratagems fail, you may be better off buying a cheap ticket for your vacation and saving your mileage for another trip. (Figure that each FFP mile is worth 2 cents.) Or use your miles to cover hotels, car-rental and other services. Staying free at a resort hotel could save you more than if you had redeemed those miles for an award flight. Or else exchange miles for adventure trips on hot-air balloons or merchandise that you could pick up cheaper at a discount store.

Hotel loyalty programmes: points or perks

Perks or points? Do I need recognition or free stays? That is the question frequent travelers are asking when they sign up for a hotel frequent-guest programme (FGP). Many road warriors prefer added-value benefits such as room upgrades and other frills – especially recognition as an 'honoured guest' by getting to shake hands with the front office assistant manager – over points they may never cash in for free stays, or airline miles they don't need. Frequent-guest programmes, like airlines FFPs, have elite levels of membership whereby you progressively pile up perks and privileges the more times you stay – or the more money you spend. Elite members earn points or miles faster than ordinary frequent guests.

The next question is, what do I need most, hotel points or airline miles? At most hotels you can't have both: you have to choose between points and miles at check-in. Notable exceptions are Hilton and Westin which allow 'double-dipping' whereby you earn both. FGP points are obviously a smart choice if you're saving for a free night, because it's easier, cheaper and faster to get a free night through a hotel programme than through an FFP. Airline miles are the way to go if you fly more than you stay. Many airline FFPs do not offer hotel awards.

Your strategy may depend on your travel patterns, how often you travel and how far. Will most of your stays be in the same city or with the same hotel chain? Will you be staying one or two nights or five nights or longer? Do you just want a bed for the night or to use the hotel to entertain or as an office away from home?

Hotel programmes work well for people who make a lot of short trips – an hour or so each way – and spend a major part of their lives in hotels. Air journeys are often a fleeting part of the travel experience. You can put up with sardine class on the red-eye if you can enjoy the perks when you arrive. It makes sense – as with FFPs – to sign up in the programme of any hotel you stay. But it pays to focus on earning elite status in one, or FFPs.

Some factors to consider. Does the hotel have participating properties in the places where you travel most or where you'd most like to redeem? Do you seek special recognition, perks or free stays? Do both points and miles count towards elite status? Can you earn, redeem or exchange points/miles with FGP partners? Will all your hotel charges earn points, or just what you spend on your room? Will you be assured a priority reservation or room upgrade? How easily can you get room upgrades? How important is a free breakfast? Or access to the executive floors and concierge lounge?

The price of success: are mileage plans losing their lustre?

Frequent-flier programmes are probably the most successful marketing idea of all time. Since American Airlines introduced AAdvantage 16 years ago mileage counting has become an addiction with an estimated 150 million travelers (including 40 million Americans) signed up worldwide.

According to OAG, 9 out of 10 business travelers are FFP members. The more they travel, the more schemes they belong to, on average 3.5. Among Americans, half belong to five or more schemes.

Although some way behind schedule and convenience, FFPs are hugely influential in choosing an airline. More than three-quarters of all business travelers say that programme membership influences their choice of carrier on a given route, often in defiance of corporate travel policy. Americans and Australians are most likely to succumb to the blandishments of FFPs. The Japanese appear to be the least susceptible, although 6 out of 10 Japanese travelers admit to being swayed by membership.

The very success of FFPs may lead to their demise – at least in their present form, according to pundits. FFPs are under threat from all sides. Pressure is mounting from governments, which view FFPs as inimical to fair competition, especially in view of the concentration of major airlines in major alliances; leading companies who argue that while FFP perks make life on the road a bit more comfortable for road warriors, frequent-flier awards should belong to the company not the individual, that they inflate fares and encourage employees to make unnecessary or circuitous trips – often at the highest fares – to amass lucrative bonus points; airlines, which now owe travelers as many as two trillion miles, are placing more and more restrictions on earning miles and award redemptions, such as expiration dates, blackout periods, and 'capacity control', whereby only a few seats are available on each flight for award travel; while upgrades – one of the most sought-after benefits – are only given to full-fare passengers; tax authorities, who view FFPs as 'benefits in kind' are looking at ways to tax individuals and restrict allowances that companies can claim against air travel if they allow their executives to keep FFP miles earned while traveling at company expense. And travelers themselves who have seen the value of their hard-earned mileage diminish substantially within the last couple of years, and given the complexity of the programs, with a maze of mileage thresholds and partnerships, have become frustrated, asking, is it all worthwhile?

While membership of FFPs remains popular, there is confusion among travelers about their true benefits, according to the latest Carlson Wagonlit Travel business travel survey conducted by Mori in the United Kingdom. Although British Airways Executive Club is considered to offer the best rewards in terms of points gained per trip, 30 per cent of respondents were uncertain as to which FFP offers best value.

'I believe only about 30 per cent of business travelers use their FFP miles,' says Richard Lovell, executive vice president of Carlson Wagonlit Travel in London. However, FFPs should not be judged by miles alone. Perks such as lounges, automatic upgrades and tender loving care are the rewards at 'elite' level for 'very frequent fliers'.

Airlines are trying to reduce the high cost of running FFP schemes by concentrating on high value travelers – how much you pay is beginning to be more important than how many miles you fly – and offering fewer benefits to less frequent travelers. They are also bringing in more non-airline partners – such as credit card, retail goods and phone companies – to help pay for the schemes.

Mike Platt, director of commercial affairs at Hogg Robinson Travel in London, says: 'A major threat to FFPs is the airlines themselves. Airlines are now calling into question just how necessary it is to spend at least 3 per cent of the value of a ticket in funding FFPs at a time when there is enormous pressure on them to reduce distribution costs. Especially when corporations are doing more and more deals with airlines, such as route discounts or business-class upgrades for some executives, and dictating to their travelers which airline they must fly. As the main travel decision moves more towards the corporation than the traveler, airlines are asking whether they still need to incentivize individual travelers. Why should the airline pay twice?'

'FFPs are a cost to airlines, but I don't think any carrier would want to do away with them unilaterally because they are such a brilliant marketing tool,' says Betty Low, editor of *Business Travel World*, a trade magazine. 'It's more than brand loyalty. The personal name records that these programmes have generated are magic – a complete fix on the profile of who's using them and the opportunity to build a direct relationship with travelers.

'I think you have to make a distinction between the "managed" traveler and the "unmanaged" traveler. If you're an airline which has signed a contract with a corporation, you want to do everything you can to make sure that everyone obeys corporate travel policy; if you don't have a contract you want people to subvert travel policy and fly with you.'

Enter the tax man in the form of a landmark case in Canada in which the incomes of two executives were reassessed to take account of free airline tickets they had received; the court ruling that the value of free tickets was their market value on the relevant flights rather than the incremental cost to the airline of filling what would otherwise have been an empty seat. The Canadian ruling reflects recent moves in Sweden and Germany to brand FFP awards 'illegal inducements' when offered to business travelers. Swedish travelers are now liable for tax on awards earned on company business and later redeemed for leisure travel. Swedish employees must inform the company of any FFP award: the company then informs the tax people.

The German government has imposed a 2 per cent tax on FFP awards exceeding a value of DM 2,400 a year. Lufthansa responded by offering to pay the tax above this sum for its Miles & More members. Meanwhile, some 20 large German companies including Metallgesellschaft and Siemens have joined Swedish companies, such as Electrolux, Volvo and Saab, in their clamour for airlines to abandon FFPs or award benefits directly to them.

Most airlines refuse to give FFPs to corporations. Exceptions are Virgin Atlantic, Asiana, Turkish Airlines and China Airlines. Lufthansa has a corporate programme for the United States but not elsewhere.

The Inland Revenue in the United Kingdom has no plans to tax FFP awards because under present 'benefits in kind' rules, it is hard to establish the 'cost to the provider' and in any case is not worth the cost of collecting the tax, according to Lynn Simpson at the Inland Revenue in London. But the rules could change under the new government.

'If FFPs become a taxable benefit, the bubble will quickly burst,' says Kevin Watts, secretary of the Business Travel Liaison Group in London, which represents 25 large corporations spending around £500 million on air tickets alone.

Stelios Haji-Ioannou, chairman of rapidly growing no-frills airline easyJet in London, is campaigning against FFPs as being inherently corrupt and distorting the market. EasyJet's in-flight magazine carries an open 'memorandum' to the 'CEOs of all FTSE 100 Companies' to ban the collection of FFP miles – which is the case for government employees in the United States, the United Kingdom and Sweden.

'Low-cost airlines cannot afford to give FFPs – that's why we are low cost,' Haji-Ioannou says. 'FFPs are a bribery system; and like any bribery system you have to convince people to do things that they wouldn't otherwise have done. Air fares could be reduced by at least 10 per cent if FFPs did not exist.'

Virgin Atlantic has introduced a novel corporate loyalty programme called flyingco for small and medium-sized companies whereby both the company and the individual earn frequent-flier benefits. Companies can earn flyingco miles when they book full-fare business-class and economy tickets, while, at the same time, travelers continue to earn personal Freeway miles. Company awards include free flights, upgrades, limo transfers, lounge passes, Gatwick and Heathrow Express rail tickets and Eurostar tickets. Anyone in the company can use an award.

London–Hong Kong (one way) earns 3,594 and London–New York earns 1,960 flyingco miles (933 and 519 miles respectively in discount economy). Free flights start at 7,500 flyingco miles; upgrades, 17,500 miles; limo transfers, 10,000 miles and five lounge passes, 15,000 miles.

Mileage junkies will welcome the new (sixth) edition of Randy Peterson's *Official Frequent Flyers Guidebook* – 600 pages of detailed information on more than 100 airline, car rental, charge card and phone company programmes, which have grown so complex that few travelers understand the myriad options, elite levels, special offers and partnerships that have developed over the years.

The first section – Navigating Frequent Traveler Programs – includes a guide to airline alliances and helps you determine which programmes are best for your type of travel, including the class you usually fly or aspire to, such as free flights to the places you want to go on business or vacation, the ability to redeem miles for upgrades, companion tickets, threshold bonuses or ongoing promotions throughout the year, plus how to manage your programmes. The second section – Comparisons at a Glance – helps you compare how quickly you can achieve elite-level status in the hierarchy of very frequent travelers who enjoy access to lounges and free upgrades. It shows you the fastest way to earn miles and points, bearing in mind that more than 30 per cent of all FFP miles are earned through airline programme partners, such as affinity credit cards, hotels and car rentals. Plus strategies for redeeming miles and points – how to avoid blackout dates, expiration dates and capacity controls, and checking out last-minute award sales offered on the Internet. Tables show how many miles you need to claim flight awards (and upgrades) by airline, route and class of travel.

Sections three, four and five explain individual airline, hotel and charge card programmes.

The Official Frequent Flyer Guidebook, sixth edition, is available from:

Frequent Flyer Services
4715-C Town Center Drive
Colorado Springs
Colorado 90916-4709
Tel: (1-719) 597 8880
E-mail: airpress@insiderflyer.com

Perks for top fliers

The watchword 'shackle me with chains of gold' applies to corporate high fliers whose loyalty is rewarded with fat bonuses and stock options, insurance and retirement packages along with a fancy title, reserved parking space and a corner office with signed prints and a tobacco plant. Plus use of the corporate jet when the chairman's not using it for Gleneagles.

Airlines have devised similar diabolical schemes to reward 'high yield' business travelers with 'very-frequent-flier' (VFF) status. The idea is that you progressively pile up perks and privileges with the more miles you fly, rising through a hierarchy of 'elite' levels, depending on whether you reach silver, gold, platinum or diamond or beyond.

VFFs earn miles faster than ordinary run-of-the-mill frequent fliers (bonus miles every time you fly) and get more liberal upgrades, waived blackout dates or capacity controls when you come to redeem miles, waiting-list priority, preferential seating, 'dedicated' reservation and help lines, extra baggage allowance, access to lounges whatever class you fly and, perhaps most valuable of all, recognition and tender loving care when things go wrong.

Loyalty is not measured in miles alone, but in how much revenue you bring the airline. Few airlines outside North America allow you to earn miles on any published fare or allow you to use miles for upgrades. Typically, European and Asian carriers only give miles on fully flexible fares.

I hear a lot of emotional talk from people about what level they have reached in their FFP, taking extra trips to retain their gold card status. Maybe you're downgraded a tier because your job or travel pattern has changed.

The more sophisticated programmes are starting to recognize people who influence travel decisions as well as those who actually travel, modeling profiles through the database, assessing your value to them and tailoring awards/benefits and communications to your specific needs. We're almost talking about a one-on-one relationship.

Airlines like Swissair, Lufthansa, and Cathay Pacific have been doing this for years through their VIP clubs, long before frequent-flier programmes were invented – the flip side to Groucho Marx's 'I wouldn't want to belong to a club that would have me as a member'.

Membership by 'invitation only' was highly valued and carried a lot of prestige. The ultimate status symbol in those days was to waft into a VIP lounge with a green boarding pass stuck in your top pocket. These days, VIP clubs are more democratic but just as valuable.

Focus your mileage on one or two carriers and aim for at least the first level of VFF status, which typically requires 25,000 to 30,000 actual miles flown in one year, although some airlines allow short-haul travellers access to elite status based on flight segments rather than miles.

Read the fine print. Miles earned on partner airlines, hotels, credit cards and car rentals may not count. Some FFPs count qualification by calendar year; others calculate the year from your first credit flight.

Save money by flying around the world

There's an ineluctable logic to flying right round the world if you already need to go half way by buying a round-the-world (RTW) ticket, which can save you up to 40 per cent on the cost of a regular round-trip in first, business class or economy. If you're flying, say, from London or New York to Tokyo, or Los Angeles to Sydney, you might as well keep going, stopping off at half a dozen places along the route. It's a great way to combine business and pleasure.

Pan Am introduced the first RTW flight in June 1947 with a Lockheed Constellation flying west from New York, taking 13 days to visit 17 destinations in 11 countries. The airline started the first RTW promotional fare in 1978. Other airlines followed suit, but as none of them had a sufficiently extensive route network they were forced to team up in order to remain competitive.

But not every business traveler wants to be a latter-day Magellan. A good travel agent can construct partial RTW fares which enable you just to circle destinations in the North or South Pacific from Europe or North America; or a round-trip three-quarters of the way round the world, say from London through the United States, on to the Far East and back again, by using a combination of airlines and discounted one-way 'sector fares'. Sector fares are normally valid for a year and can be open-dated. They can be used to add on to RTW itineraries or to extend a normal round-trip to an Asian destination such as Tokyo by flying, say, Tokyo–Auckland–Hong Kong–Tokyo.

However, there are stricter conditions for RTW fares than for normal round-trips. You must travel in a continuous direction with no back-tracking (you are sometimes allowed side-trips; or you can buy them as add-ons) and you are not allowed to stop over more than once at any place. You must book the first leg from 14 to 30 days ahead – depending on the airline involved; thereafter, you can usually change flights as often as you like and can change your routing for a nominal charge. You must make at least three stopovers (which you'll probably need anyway!). Typically, you're allowed two free stopovers in Asia (such as Singapore or Hong Kong), two stops in the Pacific (Auckland, Sydney, Honolulu), and three within North America. You can usually buy additional stopovers for about $80. You must stay away at least 14 days, but tickets are valid for one year.

There are scores of itineraries, prices and airline combinations. A typical routing might take you from Europe, through the Middle East to the Far East and on to North America via the North or South Pacific.

There are two types of RTW fare: airlines' standard itineraries – either at published prices or discounted through consolidators – and customised fares constructed for a particular itinerary, which might be a mix of published and discounted fares. Prices range from less than $1,500 in economy (with four stopovers) to $7,500 in first class for a choice of 470 destinations. A northern hemisphere RTW, which will take you to Hong Kong, Singapore, Bangkok and Tokyo, is typically about 30 per cent less expensive than a southern routing to destinations in Australasia and the South Pacific.

You can buy RTW tickets in most countries, though prices will vary. If you're based in New York, for example, the answer might be to buy a round-trip to London, and start your RTW trip from there. You could then make a subsequent trip from New York to London on the last coupon of your RTW ticket and fly back to New York on the return coupon of your round-trip ticket – maybe making use of local air passes to do business across Europe. It always pays to check the local currency price of an RTW in main cities along the route you wish to travel.

One thing to bear in mind when planning a RTW trip is that some parts of Africa, South America and the Caribbean are not as well served with flights as North America, Europe, the Middle East, India, and Asia. A good way to include South America in a RTW itinerary is to make a side-trip from Los Angeles, San Diego or Miami. From Miami you can buy a round trip to places like Buenos Aires, Santa Cruz, Sao Paulo, Montevideo or Asuncion for less than $800.

Circle Pacific (CP) fares are a good alternative to full RTW fares if you want to make extended visits around the Pacific Rim. In the North Pacific, you can stop in places like Beijing, Tokyo, Taipei, Hong Kong, Bangkok, Ho Chi Minh City, Jakarta, Manila, and Bangkok; South Pacific stops might include Sydney, Auckland, Fiji, or Tahiti. Rules are similar to RTW fares.

travelers based in North America who make at least one trip a year to Europe and one to Asia should consider buying a round-trip ticket from London to the Far East via the United States. The idea is you fly to London the first time and use such a ticket to return to the United States, stop over at your home city, take a round-trip to Asia, and stop over again at home. You then have up to 12 months to return to London and start all over again.

Thus you have the equivalent of two round trips from the United States: one to Asia and one to Europe – saving a ton of money either economy or business class.

But premium fare tickets bought in the United Kingdom are more expensive than in other countries. A first- or business-class ticket costs about £1,000 less in Rome; £1,300 less in Bangkok and £500 less in Hong Kong. You must buy and fly from the same place.

The art of shopping for RTW deals is first to decide where you must go, then where you might want to go, and when. Be realistic. Think what you can achieve in the time available. There are countless ways to save money by combining separate trips on the same ticket. All you need is a desktop globe and a good travel agent.

Examples of round-the-world fares from London

Business class

1. London–Bangkok–Melbourne–Sydney–Fiji–Honolulu–London
    £2,526 (Olympic Airlines & Air New Zealand)

2. London–New York–Chicago–Seattle–Tokyo–Hong Kong–Bangkok–Singapore-Bali–London
    £2,949 (Star Alliance: United Airlines, Air New Zealand, Thai)

3. London–Harare–Perth–Melbourne–Christchurch–(own arrangements)–Auckland–Los Angeles–Toronto–London
    £3,139 (One World Explorer: British Airways, Qantas, American Airlines, Canadian Airlines)

4. London–Copenhagen–Delhi–Bangkok–Penang–Hong Kong–Tokyo–Honolulu–Los Angeles–Miami–New York–London
    £2,984 (Star Alliance: SAS, Thai International, United Airlines)

Economy class

1. London–Bangkok–Sydney–Los Angeles–London
   £700 (Garuda and United Airlines)

2. London–Bombay–Singapore–Melbourne–Christchurch–(own arrangements)–Auckland–Fiji–New York–London
   £1,010 (Global Explorer: Qantas, British Airways and American Airlines)

3. London–Harare–(own arrangements)–Johannesburg–Perth–Sydney–Tahiti–Los Angeles–(own arrangements)–Vancouver–London
   £1,004 (Global Explorer: Qantas, British Airways and American Airlines)

4. London–Singapore–Bali–Darwin–Brisbane–Auckland–Fiji–Raratonga–Los Angeles–London
   £988 (Escapade: Singapore Airlines, Ansett Australia, Air New Zealand)

5. London–Rio–(own arrangements)–Santiago–Sydney–Alice Springs–Cairns–Bali–Singapore–(own arrangements)–Bangkok–London
   £998 (Global Explorer: Qantas, British Airways and American Airlines)

From Trailfinders (44 171) 938 3444; www.trailfinders.com; August 1999. These fares are only a guide.

6. Oriental Escapade: Business Class from £3,143/Economy from £991 with Singapore Airlines, Air New Zealand, Ansett Australia. Allows you to visit Indo-China and the South Pacific island of Raratonga and throughout Australia and New Zealand.
   Sample routing: London–Hanoi–(own arrangements)–Ho Chi Minh City–Singapore—Bali–Darwin–Sydney–Auckland–Raratonga–Los Angeles–London.

7. African Escapade: Business Class from £3,137/Economy Class from £995 with South African Airways, Ansett Australia, Air New Zealand. A great way to include South Africa.
   Sample routing: London–Cape Town–Johannesburg–Perth–Melbourne–Sydney–Auckland–Tonga–Los Angeles–London.

From Wexas International, tel: (44 171) 581 8761; fax: (44 171) 225 1099.

Air passes offer bargains

Flying around North and South America, South Africa, Australia and Asia has never been cheaper – cheaper, that is, for overseas visitors who have had the foresight to purchase an air pass before they left home. They are rewarded with the best bargains in air travel.

Air passes originated in the United States following deregulation in 1978. Over the years, the variety of options worldwide has increased enormously and rules have been relaxed, which makes them a viable option for business travelers.

All the major US and Canadian carriers offer air passes for travel on their domestic networks. If you plan to visit more than three cities within North America on business or pleasure, an air pass can save you as much as 70 per cent on the regular fares.

North American air passes are only sold to overseas visitors possessing round-trip tickets on scheduled flights and must be bought before leaving home. Most airlines require you to fly either with them or a national airline of the country you start from in order to buy their air passes. You may have to pay a supplement of $100 or so if you fly with a foreign carrier. The big no-no is that you cannot fly with another US airline.

Typically, your air pass is valid for 60 days from the first day of use. You normally buy it in coupon form, one for each flight sector of your itinerary. Sometimes each connecting flight counts as one coupon. Most passes have a minimum of two or three and a maximum of 10 coupons. You must specify your itinerary in advance but only the first sector needs to be pre-booked; you can leave flights open and change the date and time of travel. You may be able to change your routing for a penalty of around $50.

Choosing an air pass is a matter of deciding which airline best serves the cities on your itinerary. You can't go far wrong with passes from United, Delta, American and Northwest, because of their extensive networks. Prices are much the same: three coupons will cost you from $350. Expect to pay $75 to $100 for each additional coupon.

North American Air Passes

To qualify you must be a non US/Canadian resident and have an international ticket into and out of North America. Some airlines such as Delta, United Airlines, American Airlines and Continental stipulate that you must be traveling on a return transatlantic ticket to qualify for their air passes. Others, such as Southwest Airlines, America West and USAir, are more lenient and will allow you to qualify for their air passes if you are traveling on a round-the-world ticket.

Southwest airlines – Freedom Pass

Flights can be pre-booked or left open. You cannot make bookings more than three months in advance.

Prices per coupon:

- the same or adjoining state £45;

- Western £69 (between any two points in the West);

- Eastern/Central £69 (between any two points in the East or Central areas);

- Anywhere $99 (for anywhere else).

You can purchase an unlimited number of coupons. One transfer is permitted per coupon. All flights must be on Southwest Airlines. Residents of the United States, Canada, Mexico, Guam, Bermuda or the Caribbean region are not eligible for this pass.

USA West

This pass covers Alaska, Northern Mexico, and US states including Washington, Nevada, Montana, Idaho, Wyoming, Oregon, California and Arizona. (Valid for travel on Alaskan Airlines and Horizon Air. Minimum two coupons, maximum 10 coupons.)

Costs: $99 per coupon for travel within Continental USA, Canada and Alaska; $149 per coupon for travel to/from Continental USA, Canada, Alaska, Mexico and to/from Sun Valley, Jackson, Wyoming and Calgary; $199 per coupon for travel on a through flight between Alaska and Mexico.

America West

All flights must be on American West Airlines. Coast-to-Coast: two coupons for £187 (about $299). Only a trans-Continental one-way can be used on this pass. System Wide Pass: two coupons for £237 (about $379), additional coupons for £44 (about $70). Only one trans-Continental round-trip is allowed. (Valid for travel throughout United States and Canada on the America West network.) Only one stopover allowed in each city. One coupon required for each flight. If, for example, flying from New York to Los Angeles requires a change of plane in Phoenix, this will cost two coupons. America West's main hubs are Columbus, Ohio, Las Vegas and Phoenix.

American Airlines

A three-coupon pass starts at $409. You must have return transatlantic flights on American, British Airways or Virgin Atlantic.

Asean Air Pass

For economy travel on international and domestic sectors within Brunei, Indonesia, Malaysia, Philippines, Singapore, Thailand and Vietnam. You must have an international ticket originating outside the Asean region on Royal Brunei, Garuda, Malaysia Airlines, Silk Air, Singapore Airlines or Thai International. Not valid for Asean nationals.

Each coupon costs $90 – minimum three coupons, maximum six coupons. You can only stop twice in any city.

Visit Indonesia Pass

Valid only on Garuda flights. You must buy at least three coupons at $100 each.

Japan Air Pass

Available only on Japan Airlines domestic flights. Can be used in conjunction with any international carrier. You must buy at least two coupons (maximum five coupons) at 12,000 yen each. Advance purchase 14 days, maximum stay, two months.

Amazing Thailand Pass

Valid on Thai domestic services. Costs about $180 for four coupons – additional coupons, about $50.

Prices from Trailfinders
Tel: (44 171) 938 3939
Web site: www.trailfinders.com

Europe by Air Pass

Visitors to Europe can travel on 17 participating regional airlines for $99 per flight plus tax to 115 cities. You must buy at least three coupons. Passes (not available to European residents) are sold in Australia, Israel, New Zealand and the United States; e-mail: www.europebyair.com

Gulf Air Pass

A Middle-East regional pass for overseas visitors. For $45, you can fly Bahrain–Doha or Dubai–Muscat; for $90, you can fly Bahrain–Muscat, Doha–Muscat or Abu Dhabi–Doha.

Seeking a welcome for women travelers

When I first wrote about the problems facing women traveling on business, it was a story of harassment, humiliation, loneliness, discomfort and danger. It was more to do with attitudes: women didn't ask for special treatment, just the same service and respect as their male counterparts.

And there were signs that the travel trade was promising to change its more egregious practices, such as bawling out room numbers in a hotel lobby; assuming that a woman and man checking in together want a double room; or asking a woman to prove she is a registered guest when ordering a drink in the lounge, or giving the wine list or check to a woman's male guest.

Today, it seems, little has changed – according to the result of a survey conducted recently by Total Research Corporation of Princeton, New Jersey, reflecting the views of 217 frequent women travelers in the United States and 136 in the United Kingdom. Even though women now account for a growing proportion of business travelers – 40 per cent in the United States and more than 20 per cent in the United Kingdom – they say they are still not getting a fair deal on the road. They still face indifference and disdain – if not rampant sexism – by airline, hotel and car-rental staff. Women believe they receive inferior service because of their gender, and many choose room service in hotels because they feel intimidated.

Personal safety is an overriding concern among 91 per cent of respondents:

 'Airlines should make more secure arrangements for women travelers when planes are delayed or arrive very late at night'.

'Car-rental companies do not escort women to their cars in unlit parking lots'; 'Men have a better chance of an upgrade'; 'Cabin crew and check-in staff are more respectful to men'; 'A drunk was pestering me but the cabin crew took no action'.

 'Hotels pay scant attention to giving women secure rooms away from stair-wells and elevators'; 'Women are made to feel uncomfortable in hotels bars and lounges'; 'Some hotels treat women as second-class customers'; 'Rooms are poorly equipped for females'; 'Carrying luggage on a business trip poses many problems'.

 'Airports should provide a security presence at taxi/shuttle pick-ups late at night and ensure well-lit, secure parking lots'.

A majority of the women surveyed say they are short-changed on service and amenities with 66 per cent saying that men are treated better – especially by female staff.

Many women say they would like an offer of help when stowing carry-on bags in overhead lockers and when walking long distances between airport gates and terminals. Men don't like having to walk long distances at an airport carrying heavy luggage – women hate it. 'In hotels, rooms should be designed so there is a socket within hairdryer's reach of a mirror and windows can be opened and still be secure; there should be proper ironing facilities, decent lighting, light and healthy food and a comfortable armchair in each room.'

What's needed to put things right is more an improvement in attitude than amenities. More than 70 per cent of respondents say that travel companies would see an increase in their business if they catered directly to women business travelers – 72 per cent say they would be more loyal to an airline and 85 per cent more loyal to an hotel that addresses their needs.

All airlines receive low image and performance scores, mainly because of 'rudeness and lack of help from staff and the perception that men get preferential treatment'. On a scale of one to 10, the top airlines in terms of 'perceived quality' are Virgin Atlantic (7.29); Swissair (6.90); Lufthansa (6.82); British Airways (6.60). But performance scores were at least one point lower in each case.

Hotels rated best on perceived quality versus performance are: Four Seasons (8.46/7.20); Westin (7.34/6.27); Marriott (7.27/6.29); Hyatt (7.15/6.2). UK respondents rated Sheraton (7.27/6.85); Marriott (7.12/6.29) and Radisson (7.03/6.59) most highly for image and performance.

Car-rental firms score thus: Hertz (6.89/5.51); Avis (6.61/5.39); National (6.32/5.13) and Europcar (6.14/5.27).

David Dower, marketing director of Total Research in London, says: 'I was worried that we'd end up with a whole set of obvious results. I'm not surprised that security comes through as the big issue. What is surprising is the strength of the message. There's a mind-set among airlines, hotels and car-rental firms that they're delivering what women travelers want: but the reality is they're not: they do not understand the special needs and concerns of women. We're getting very low scores coming through in terms of perceived quality, much lower than for samples of male and female business travelers. Typically, the top airlines have scores of 8 out of 10. But BA scoring only 6.6 among women is a significant difference. Only 18 per cent of people say that airlines make special efforts to cater for women travelers. I think that's a fairly damning vote.

'I don't know how many airlines, hotels and car-rental firms have said, let's go out and look at women travelers. But if they haven't, the female population in a broader male/female survey is relatively small so the voice gets lost.

'There are some differences between UK and US respondents. UK women seem to have higher expectations – such as women should be allowed more carry-on baggage. UK women are more expectant of airlines doing something about it all than Americans. There's a slightly stronger message from the United Kingdom. Things are slightly less of an issue in the States.

'It comes down to improving attitudes towards women travelers, more to do with management, training of staff, than vast changes to infrastructure. Why can't women be escorted to their rental car at night? Or helped with hand baggage on the plane? How many hotels, when reviewing incoming guests, allow women a choice of room – not just allocating a ground-floor room or one at the end of a corridor. There's a lot of lip service to this in the travel trade. But this survey shows how little has been done.'

Angela Giveon, editor of *Executive Woman* magazine, says: 'The majority of women scuttled upstairs and made nests; they were prisoners to room service. If a woman was brave enough to come down to the restaurant, she was shoved behind a pillar and wasn't served for ages. Big-spending executives were regarded as hookers. Hotels could make a lot more money if they knew how to address this gender problem. But then if a woman goes in like a victim, she'll be treated like a victim.

'So we invented something called Facilitator, which started off with networking in hotels – bringing women down to meet and eat together.

We feature about 50 hotels in the United Kingdom and Europe that are prepared to go that extra mile to be woman-friendly – special parking places, for instance – where staff are trained to avoid the worst nightmare scenarios.'

'I think hotels are wising up to single women travelers – special floors with concierges and not shouting out your room number,' says Patricia Yates, editor of Holiday Which? magazine in London. 'Most businesswomen are well able to take care of themselves because that's how they've got the position they're in. Hassle on the streets? Well, apart from Rio I've never found it particularly intimidating or threatening. If you retain your competence and say no, most men will back off. It's not physical, it's just hassle. Maybe I've just been lucky, or foolhardy. Safety applies to men as well as women. You mustn't think the world's against you. Things happen. Yes, you can walk into a hotel with a man and they try to put you in a double room; that's just an embarrassment, no more than that. A friend of mine hosting a business dinner was outraged when they gave the male guests the priced menu and her the unpriced menu; and they were very unsure about letting her taste the wine.

'I traveled business class recently to India – BA on the way out, United on the way back. United were really good, treated me as someone special. BA really snapped at me – a moment's hesitation in choosing the meal. She said, "Talk to me!" My male companion didn't get any of that. That's the area I have personally encountered, the "what are you doing here?" type of thing.'

Victoria Mather, travel editor of Tatler magazine in London, says: 'I don't particularly worry about security. But I think a woman who is nervous about traveling probably shouldn't stay in one of the great big mid-range hotels – they're too anonymous, nobody knows you. Go somewhere with a good concierge who can keep his eye on you. You have to be forceful and assert yourself as a woman, so that they don't put you in a broom closet. Room service is good nowadays. My idea of utter complete heaven is being alone in a hotel bedroom.'

For details about Facilitator, call Terry Spencer on (44 181) 420 1210.

Total Research
Tel: (44 181) 263 5200
Fax: (44 181) 263 5222

Tips for women travelers

Choosing a hotel:

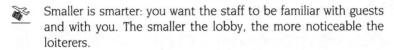 Smaller is smarter: you want the staff to be familiar with guests and with you. The smaller the lobby, the more noticeable the loiterers.

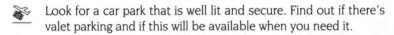 Look for a car park that is well lit and secure. Find out if there's valet parking and if this will be available when you need it.

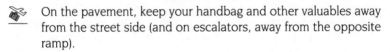 On the pavement, keep your handbag and other valuables away from the street side (and on escalators, away from the opposite ramp).

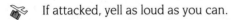 If attacked, yell as loud as you can.

Room Rules:

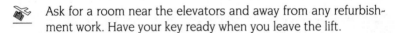 Ask for a room near the elevators and away from any refurbishment work. Have your key ready when you leave the lift.

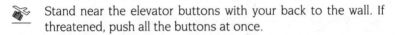 Stand near the elevator buttons with your back to the wall. If threatened, push all the buttons at once.

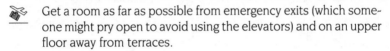 Get a room as far as possible from emergency exits (which someone might pry open to avoid using the elevators) and on an upper floor away from terraces.

Make sure the door has double locks – one of which is a dead bolt – and a peephole. Bring along a rubber door stop for extra security, or ask the hotel to provide one.

The PLEASE MAKE UP THIS ROOM sign tells everyone you're not there. Call housekeeping instead.

Put expensive clothing on hangars under other garments. Thieves usually take what they see.

Lock valuables in the front-desk safe.

Travel Savvy:

- Use covered luggage tags with your office, not your home address.

- In public lavatories, use the corner cubicle.

- On overnight flights, keep an eye on your valuables. When you go to the lavatory, take your purse with you.

- Talk to female flight attendants and passengers on the plane about the safety of your destination.

- Don't exit a taxi until you're sure you've arrived at your destination. Pay while still in the vehicle so that you can be sure you've received the proper change.

- Stay close to your valuables when passing through airport security.

- If you place your carry-on bag on the floor when sitting in a restaurant or other public area, put your foot through the strap; don't leave it loose.

- Tear your name and address off magazines before leaving them on the plane. Why announce to the world that you're away?

- Renting a car at a strange airport, consider hiring a taxi to lead you to the main road. Never use an unmarked taxi.

- Rent a mobile phone or bring your own. Put the police number on speed dial.

- On the road, if someone tries to get your attention or your car is bumped, don't stop until you arrive at a well-lit and busy area. Alternatively, stay in the car and blow the horn until someone comes to your aid.

- If suspicious about 'phony' police, don't open the window but hold your license against the glass.

- In your car, keep items out of sight (especially maps and guidebooks). Be cautious of hatchbacks, as they leave your luggage in plain view.

When possible, park so you won't have to back out. It makes for a speedier departure.

Street Smarts:

Study your map before going out; once on the street, use a pocket-size guidebook to avoid looking like a tourist. Ask the concierge or female employee to mark any dangerous areas on your map.

Dress down.

Loop a money belt around yousar belt loops so that if anyone cuts it won't fall from your waist.

Avoid jewellery. Even a chain that's fake gold can be ripped off your neck.

Be wary when getting off a bus, a train, or an escalator; that's when pickpockets tend to strike.

Carry just one credit card and photocopies of important documents. Divide money for small and larger purchases so you don't have to expose a wad of money. Become familiar with foreign currency before you have to use it.

Have tips ready for porters and doormen.

Use prepaid phone cards instead of carrying your card number.

Ask the concierge to make any restaurant reservations, and have him or her say 'Please take care of our guest, she's coming alone and will need a taxi home.'

Should a car start to follow you, turn immediately and walk the other way.

Cross over the road to avoid anyone threatening or suspicious.

Ask directions from families or women with children.

Source: *Safety Points for the Female Traveler*, Red Carnation Hotels.
More tips for woman travelers can be found at www.redcarnation
hotels.com

Meetingmanship

Try to phone anybody these days and the chances are you'll get an earful of the xylophone version of Greensleeves, or a low-fi rendering of The Four Seasons by the Muzak Symphony Orchestra. Then the doom-laden words: 'He's in a meeting. I can't disturb him.' Or the pompous: 'He's in conference.' Yes, yes, our cheque is in the mail.

Of course, it all depends what you mean by 'meeting' or 'conference'. Some executives are perpetually in meetings, it seems, when you want to get hold of them. This can mean almost anything. Either they are nattering with their secretary, or someone else's secretary, on another line, in with the boss, gone for lunch, not back from lunch, gone for the day, trying out their new waterwings in the company think tank, or truly engaged in motivating the troops at a cost-effective little resort on the Costa Extravaganza. You may be passed from one voice mail to another or else patched through to a mobile. Even if you do manage to speak in person and in real time, you may find that the guy you want is sitting across the aisle from you in business class, on the way to the same conference.

Meetingmanship requires a strategic and tactical approach, depending on whether you're talking conferences or meetings. Conferences differ from meetings, mainly because they are occasions when you are talked at rather than talking among, if you follow. They come in several guises: from management development seminars, new product launches and sales meetings to association jamborees. (You even get conferences for conference organizers.) Conferences are a way of wasting everybody's time away from the office and form an integral part of 'Management by Absence'; while meetings are great way of wasting other people's time when in the office ('Management by Pre-emption'). Successful conferences and meetings are an end in themselves, rather than a means to an end. 'We are, therefore we meet.' Or vice versa.

They are also a good excuse for holding impromptu board meetings in the absence of a fellow director who wasn't able to make it to the conference, poor chap. ('Howard, we're sorry you weren't able to join us in Mogadishu.')

This is an egregious example of the 'invisible agenda' (somewhat similar to the 'invisible organization' within the company) whereby executives are able to meet and conspire in those invigorating after-hours sessions far from the daily pressures of the office.

Meanwhile, back in the office, there are many variations to this gambit. You have 'shadow meetings' (meetings within meetings) when a caucus, or a breakaway group, has its own meeting and subverts the official one ('Management by Destabilization'). A related gambit is to invite as many people as you can who have no interest whatsoever, nor any conceivable contribution to make, while excluding people you don't want, either by calling the meeting in their absence or simply forgetting to circulate their copy of the agenda.

The same goes for minutes. Minutes are best written before the meeting and circulated to a select few. They reflect what you have decided, rather than what participants said. In a refined form, this involves distributing 'minutes' to folk who thought they'd simply been chatting in your office, or while traveling. You can formalize any kind of discussion by calling it a meeting. ('Come in, Howard, we're having a meeting.' Or, 'You remember that meeting we had on the flight from Paris the other day?')

Keeping the initiative is the essence of meetingmanship. You need to consider where you're going to meet. ('The venue is the message,' as Marshall McLuhan might have said.) The approach might be casual: 'Your office or mine?' Or, 'I've managed to get the boardroom.' Or more authoritative: 'I've decided we ought to join the others in Cleveland.'

You also need to decide whether to turn up early – which may or may not involve changing the time at the last moment ('I thought we'd start early, Howard; I'll fill you in later' or late ('Sorry I'm late, Howard, would you quickly recap?') Or not at all.

Which tactic you use will depend on who is in the chair. Some meetings are leaderless when they start – a chairman emerging by dint of rank or strength of personality. A useful role is that of 'shadow chairman,' speaking, as it were, from the back benches. This is often done as a prelude to a meeting within a meeting. But perhaps the ultimate ploy is to chair a meeting consisting of your boss and other heavy hitters. Do this through a 'planned crisis', for which, of course, you provide a miraculous solution.

You may also need to decide whether to make your presentation on slides, an overhead projector or a flip-chart (this works well for brain-storming, when you control the meeting by selectively writing down what people say) or with your new Banana 2 laptop with expensive split-screen colour graphics.

Whether you decide to take notes – or ostentatiously not to take notes – may depend on the kind of 'statement' you want to make. A similar effect can be achieved at an international conference by using or not using the earphones for simultaneous translation. Or you might want to plug in your Walkman.

You must consider too whether to hand out copies of your presenta-tion before, during, or after the meeting or conference, and to whom. Tactics may dictate whether you adjourn for lunch, work right through, or send out for sandwiches.

Lunch meetings are still popular in countries like the United King-dom, Spain and France. But in the United States, any hint of hedonism these days is likely to invoke the combined wrath of Mammon and the shareholders: strictly a matter of putting the guilt on the gingerbread and avoiding gilt by association. I rang a business friend in New York on a recent trip. 'Let's do lunch,' he said. 'We don't need to eat.'

The ultimate conference style is to teleconference from a yacht cruising in the Caribbean. But telephone meetings have a unique sense of urgency and putative fulfilment, especially from an overseas subsid-iary. (The number one rule for business travelers is never to do business in the country you are visiting, but always be on the phone to some-where else.) You don't have to buy lunch. And you can always get some-body to say you are in a meeting or a conference.

Making meetings work

You've spent a chunk of your budget bringing the troops to Hawaii, or some other sun-blessed archipelago, for this high-powered meeting to celebrate your new software product. And all has gone smoothly – the travel; the meeting logistics; the multi-media presentations; the gala dinner and the fireworks. Yes, it has been a great event; everyone seems fired up; congratulations to the meeting organizer. But are the troops properly prepared to go out and sell? Has the medium delivered the message?

The answer, as Sam Goldwyn might have said, is a definite maybe. For here comes Meeting Professionals International, a charitable foundation based in Dallas, Texas, with a study, 'Making Meetings Work: An Analysis of Corporate Meetings', which examined key success factors in sales meetings, management meetings and education-training meetings. It concludes that there is 'often a large gap between how senior managers and attendees view the success of a conference or meeting' and between expectation and fulfilment. While 85 per cent of senior managers think that their meetings are successful and 'are pleased with facilities and arrangements', they have concerns 'about what happens with the attendees after the meeting'.

'The focus is on what meeting planners should be doing to help management achieve its goals,' says Nikki Walker, a spokeswoman for MPI in Brussels. 'Traditionally, senior management has taken control of the content of meetings themselves and left meeting planners just to handle the logistics and making sure the equipment works. What we're saying is they should sometimes take the advice of professional planners on the content as well, to make meetings more motivational, more effective – avoiding some of the classic mistakes, like having sessions that drag on too long, and making sure that the corporate goal is actually being achieved.'

MPI plans to develop a 'benchmarking' system that rates 'proven success factors' to enable corporate meeting planners to develop their own 'gap analysis' of their company's sales, management or education meetings. 'The idea of a successful meeting must be expanded beyond "satisfaction" to the "achievement of corporate goals".'

In my corporate days, I would often gather my guys in some exotic place like Malta for a loosely defined 'marketing meeting'. (Or somewhere more austere, like Birmingham, depending on prevailing signals from the corporate Kremlin.) High on the agenda would be the 'hidden agenda' – now institutionalized as 'networking' – whereby Jürgen, Jean-Pierre, Marcello and Miguel could creatively convene behind the scenes. And plan future meetings among themselves.

Nowadays, the buzzword is 'cost-effective' – not just in travel terms but in achieving clearly defined goals.

'Meeting content needs to be addressed in a strategic fashion, not just an operational one, so you need to be asking your boss or client, "Why are we having this meeting? What tools will measure its success?"', says Vanessa Cotton, managing director of The Event Organisation company in London. 'The message is, let's plan the meeting and what we want to achieve and then we'll think about venues and hotels, hot food on hot plates and the colour of badges.

'A lot of meeting organizers think on a micro level – getting small things right. That's important; but getting the big things right means understanding the strategy and reinforcing that throughout the event, and how delegates will evaluate the event – whether it's value for time and money. A big part of that is how they get there and where they stay; not just their experience at the conference.'

'There's a definite feeling in organizations these days that time equals money and it's essential to get an efficient return on peoples' time invested,' Walker says. 'Making sure that speakers are delivering the message. That comes out over and over again in the MPI Survey. The traditional five-day company conference reduced to two and a half days. Europeans stick to European destinations to limit time out of the office and traveling time. A one-day meeting at an airport hotel in Frankfurt or Paris saves commuting time downtown.'

Meetings and conferences have become more purposeful and less glitzy; more of an investment in better times to come than a junket for times past. Meeting planners talk about getting the right balance between 'motivational values' and strategic and tactical 'imperatives'. A good conference, or meeting, is a catalyst, a means to an end rather than an end in itself. Objectives should be clearly defined along with a clear idea of how you measure success.

Manuela Ranzanici, meeting planner at Hewlett Packard in Geneva, says: 'People these days are very, very busy – they don't want to spend half a day or a whole day getting there. There's a tendency to start or finish over a weekend, taking advantage of APEX fares and weekend hotel rates – instead of arriving on a Monday and getting back to the office on a Thursday, it's starting on a Sunday and back in the office Tuesday night or Wednesday morning latest. Or start on Friday and go back on Sunday.

'I wouldn't say we have fewer meetings these days, but times are tough and there are budget constraints. Management is much more stringent on the need for objectives; everyone wants more for their money, more for the time they spend at any kind of conference. There has to be something for you there, otherwise you don't go. Outside speakers and delegates are very solicited these days: they don't only get invitations from us. Gap analysis should help make meetings better value, better focused, in a shorter time.

'What is coming up now is a trend for people who travel a lot to bring their family and kids along to a conference, depending on the programme; although they might have to pay for them. It is contradictory in a sense, but it's all to do with "new values" – "work–life" balance.'

Choosing the venue is sometimes the hardest part of organizing a meeting. If you have people from more than one country, you might plan to meet on neutral ground, such as a beach in Jamaica or the new conference centre in Hong Kong.

'Whenever the economy takes a lurch, companies adopt a leaner, meaner persona – steering away from, say, the French Riviera, which is excellent for meetings, but may give out the wrong message,' Cotton says. 'So they meet in The Hague, Berlin or Birmingham. But places like Rimini, just slightly out of season, are incredibly cheap. Then you need to think of communications – bringing people in, either as a group or individuals. That's why Copenhagen is so popular because it's got excellent communications with the Baltic States, the rest of Scandinavia and Northern Europe; so if you've got an American coming in, he's not marooned there and can add on another business meeting.'

If there's a recession, Cotton says, the meeting industry will be affected as it was the last time around. 'What companies have learned in the past is to keep talking, not only to their staff but their customers.'

What meetings are priority? 'Any meeting where key messages need to be communicated. If a company has a new licensing agreement and they want to communicate what that means their sales force or end users, that's a prime candidate for a meeting, or rolled into part of an existing meeting. What we might see decreasing is meetings as rewards. Incentives took a real hit last time.

'But meetings are also motivational tools, even if it's not an incentive programme. If you look at a Microsoft or an IBM meeting – volatile industries where they're all competing for the best personnel – their perception of the way internal meetings are held is important too. You don't want to be lavish, but you want to do things properly.

'When it comes to making meetings work, getting there and back and the hotel is part of the overall experience of the event.'

MPI Meeting Professionals International European Bureau
Tel: (32 2) 743 1544
Fax: (32 2) 743 1550
International Headquarters
Tel: (1 972) 702 3000
Fax: (1 972) 702 3070
E-mail: mpi@associationhq.com
Web site: www.mpiweb.org

Vanessa Cotton
Managing Director
The Event Organisation Company
Tel: (44 171) 228 8034
Fax: (44 171) 228 8034

Flights of fancy: rewarding high fliers

How do you reward high fliers who have got almost everything? Provide them with status, a fancy title, a corner office with a squishy visitor's chair, signed prints and a tobacco plant, and use of the corporate jet. Motivate them with money, such as big pay rises, bonuses and stock options, insurance and retirement packages?

Yes, yes, all that. And then what? You send them on an incentive trip with their fellow high achievers. Not just any trip, mind you. But, in the terms of the trade, 'an exceptional travel experience'. The idea is to take them somewhere and provide them with activities that they would not normally be able to buy for themselves.

I know frequent travelers for whom the incentive would be staying at home, but a growing number of companies find that expenses-paid trips are better than bonuses for motivating employees from salesmen to vice presidents, firing up dealers and honeymooning customers. Incentive travel is a booming market and has bounced back strongly from the last recession.

Ken Clayton, a London-based specialist, says: 'Companies are shy about revealing how much they spend because of the taxman. But you can say that it is the fastest-growing sector in the industry.'

'During the recession, budgets were cut and companies took fewer people shorter distances within Europe,' says Graham Povey, operations director of Capital Incentives in London. 'It now seems to have gone back to the way it was. People are looking farther afield again – America, the Caribbean are still popular. But Zimbabwe, South Africa – combining, say, Cape Town with Sun City, or Mauritius, terrific beach resorts – Dubai – are very popular.'

Patricia Conibear, European manager for the Hong Kong Convention & Incentive Travel Bureau: 'The old markets of North America and Europe are stable. The big growth is to and within Asia.'

Almost every meeting has an incentive, or reward aspect, if only to get people to attend. And incentive trips usually have a conference, a business element – even if it is simply the chairman doing a bit of flag waving.

Incentive travel should be an integral part of a marketing or sales programme to motivate participants to achieve predetermined goals. It is the reward for winners. You could say that a corporate meeting is a means to an end and an incentive trip is an end in itself.

Traditionally, the biggest users of incentive travel are the insurance and motor industries, which have legions of salesmen and dealers to inspire. Other big spenders are computer, electronics, electrical appliances, office and farm equipment, pharmaceutical and financial services firms.

There are four major trends: experimentation with more distant destinations, growth of individual travel awards, increased emphasis on the quality of the programme, and more companies including non-sales staff.

'The key to incentive travel is to give everybody the time of their lives, something quite different from what they could do under their own steam,' says Sydney Paulden, a London-based publisher. 'When it comes to destination, you could say that almost anywhere is the best place; it depends on the type of people you're trying to motivate. Unfortunately, there hasn't been enough research into exactly what stimulates people. You have to go by instinct – that is why experience counts for so much in this business.'

The perfect incentive destination is within the participants' horizon of appreciation, but beyond their horizon of expectation. Almost everywhere can be perfect. What is exceptional for one person or group may be run-of-the-mill for others. The important thing is to deliver what you have promised.

Every place can offer a wonderful time, but only a few have an image that will excite people while they're working nights to win. Most European capitals have a saleable image – London, Paris and Rome continue to be very popular. Groups are also turning increasingly to the Far East. Hong Kong, Thailand, Australia and New Zealand will excite people.

There is a need for more and more unusual and exciting travel programmes. When you have already taken your group on safari in Kenya or up the Amazon, then you have to go back to the old destinations and do it differently. It's a question of topping the act.

This could entail staying two nights in Paris then going into the countryside for three days: with a château visit, a barge trip in Burgundy, with hot-air balloons. Creativity comes in when you have continually to surprise people who expect the best. VIPs want to be greeted by VIPs. So in a foreign destination you may arrange to meet someone from the government – maybe even royalty.

'Creative travel is making things happen in a resort, even if people have been there before,' says an incentive travel guru. 'In Hong Kong they'll take you on a boat trip for dinner, then arrange for a pirate ship to raid it.' Presumably a new dimension to the tourist trap.

'Then in Vancouver, they'll take you by helicopter to the top of a glacier, where another helicopter has brought a marquee, and serve lunch. You can do the same in Bali on top of a volcano. There's virtually no end to it.'

'Surprise is absolutely essential,' Povey says. 'In New York we simply told people it was a gala dinner and to wear black and white. We hired a private room and outside caterers on the 38th floor of the Empire State Building decorated throughout in black and white. People thought it was absolutely incredible. We've had people fly into New Orleans, picked up in a fleet of white limos and escorted to the hotel with a police escort, sirens wailing. Just an unbelievable experience.'

Although incentive travel normally involves groups, it requires specialist skills. 'The trick with incentives is to make individual travelers feel like VIPs,' Clayton says. 'It's not like normal group travel or package holidays. You have to go to an incentive travel firm to organize both the incentive and the travel.'

This involves analysing objectives, structuring the programme, announcing it, and promoting it to participants. The incentive travel company will look after the whole thing, working with professionals on the spot – the destination management company.

Individual travel is getting more popular – the company rewards you with a trip and you choose the location. But in the trade it's not considered to have anything like the potency of a group trip, simply because part of the award is the recognition among the group that you're a winner. Companies might compromise by taking a group, say, to Paris and then giving individuals a Mercedes and signing privileges at selected hotels and restaurants.

I always dreamed of an even more informal approach. This is when the chairman says, 'Roger, you've done a great job. Why don't you and Fiona take off for a couple of weeks? Use the Gulfstream if you like. And there's a yacht in Fort Lauderdale...'.

Then you can really say you have arrived.

Taking your partners

'Next year, if you all do well, we'll go to Miami,' says the chairman at the annual sales conference. 'And if you do exceptionally well, you can take your partners.' At which an executive from the floor raises a hand. 'And if we do fantastically well, can we leave them at home?'

'Why do companies feel they have to include the spouse?' asks a journalist. 'It's humiliating; you're never treated like a human being in your own right.'

'Accompanying my husband to conferences is one of life's pleasures,' says a corporate wife.

'I'd never dream of taking my husband on a business trip,' says a consultant. 'I mean, what would he do?'

There you have it, an unscientific sample of views on the often vexed question of whether or not executives should take their spouses (sorry, partners) on business trips. It's a grey area of corporate practice seldom articulated in formal policies. The answer, of course, depends on the executive, his or her partner, who picks up the tab, and ultimately, the taxman. But it is an issue that can have a decisive effect on the morale and effectiveness of the long-distance manager.

Thirty years ago, when I first started traveling on business, life was fairly simple. If you were happily married, you'd take your wife along whenever you could. She would share the expense-account lifestyle and play the role of the corporate wife, dispensing carefully measured charm to the boss, and other arbiters of your commercial destiny, her place in the corporate pecking order clearly defined. On formal occasions, she might wear a hat.

Of course, a partner who is willing and politically aware can be a huge asset on a pilgrimage to the corporate Mecca, cementing relationships, or breaking the ice with potential customers.

'Never underestimate the social side of business, especially in countries with a strong tradition of hospitality,' says UK publisher William Davis. 'Business is about people as much as numbers, particularly at higher levels. Social contact gives people a chance to build personal relationships, and to discuss the merits of a proposal in an informal way. Couples are more likely to secure dinner invitations or to have their own invitations accepted. You can work as a team, following a pre-arranged strategy, and don't have to rush back home.'

On the other hand, an executive can easily lose commitment and cutting edge by taking a partner on a hard-nosed tour of the markets, which is why some companies require their people to ask permission, even if they pay themselves.

Absence may or may not make the heart grow fonder. But many a relationship has survived in spite of – or, perhaps, because of – prolonged or frequent trips by one of the partners. The 'honeymoon' effect when the traveler gets home has to be compared with the risk of a rival relationship on either side. Nature abhors a vacuum.

Enlightened firms recognize what is often a problem by offering the partner an occasional trip as a reward. It may be important for a frequent traveler to convince his or her partner that being far away on business is far from being a holiday, but a lot of pain and grief.

'More and more companies are coming round to realizing that there are advantages to having the other half along. It makes the executive's life a bit easier at home and is relatively inexpensive,' says Arthur Lyddall, former corporate travel administrator at Chevron in London and veteran travel consultant. 'Hotels these days charge much the same for a double as a single. Any company worth its salt will negotiate a special rate. And you can use spouse airfares: fly first or business class and you can often buy a half-price ticket for a companion traveling with you. Another angle is to ask the airline for a special conference fare to such and such a place. Whether you actually attend the conference doesn't matter. But I think what's really driving the trend towards spouse travel is free tickets and upgrades from frequent-flier programmes.'

Companies taking advantage of cheaper fares and hotel rates for conferences over a weekend find they can build morale among the troops by inviting partners at little or no extra cost.

Some companies involve partners in incentive travel. 'The partner helps to push the executive to achieve his or her targets if they know they're going to Monte Carlo as well,' says Merville Speirs, partner of Conference International in Monaco. 'If the other half is along, it makes for a much more sane and balance approach. It's the difference between dancing the night away and drinking the night away, which is what happens if you've got all men together.

'We had a nightmare experience with an incentive for the business unit of a company that didn't bring partners. It was an office party for three days. Not a good idea!'

These days, an 'accompanying person' is just as likely to be male as female. And few companies make a distinction between a legal spouse and a 'significant other'.

But women take a measured view of their hard-won emancipation. Wine critic Jancis Robinson says she enjoys having her husband with her. 'He has a better memory than I do and jogs my mind.'

Annie Redmile, a travel writer and consultant in London, says: 'Taking somebody with you on a business trip is always a problem unless they're actually involved in your own business. I'd rather enjoy myself with the man in my life when I'm relaxed – at home.'

Extending the pleasure principle

Combining business with pleasure always reminds me of that felicitous French custom, near the end of a meal, of asking for a little cheese to finish off the wine, followed, of course, by more wine to finish off the cheese...

Not that you have to look very far these days for an excuse to build a holiday on the back of a business trip. Or vice versa. Airlines, tour operators and hotel chains are all hard at work undermining the Puritan Work Ethic with a smorgasbord of special offers for the 'business extender', ranging from half-price hotel rooms (with 'welcome' fruit baskets, flowers, champagne and a 'personal thank you' from the assistant deputy house manager) to elaborately packaged mini-vacations (with 'gourmet' dinners, tickets to a show, golf and tennis), insidiously favouring double occupancy. There's something for most tastes and proclivities, from parachuting and falconry to competition ludo. One of the wackiest weekend breaks I've come across is a 'final fling' for divorcing couples (with an optional solicitor at the final dinner) at a hotel in Essex.

Clearly, the top priority for most business travelers is to get there and back as quickly and comfortably as they can. But the professional extender will typically stop over somewhere, take off the middle weekend, or add two days to either end of a 10-day trip for rest and recreation.

Successful business extension needs both a strategic and tactical approach. Look after long-haul trips and the side-trips will look after themselves. You could describe the ideal extension as a kind of planned surprise getaway – the paradox is that thoughtful preparation can lead to impromptu discoveries.

First plan your long-haul itinerary for opportunistic stopovers. If you are flying business or full economy you may be able to earn a free airline package, say, in Madrid or Copenhagen, as a reward for flying through those hubs. Or combine a money-saving point-to-point fare on the way back with multiple stops on the way out. Always point out how much you're saving the company. ('In that case, Howard, you may as well take Fiona along.' Or, 'As long as you're in Hong Kong, Howard…'.) Piggyback as far as you can on expenses, and then take off with a local air pass or series of excursion tickets.

Extending within Europe can involve some tricky management decisions. Let's say it's Friday in Vienna and your next appointment is at 9 am on Monday in Paris. So do you fly home to Zurich tonight, or stay in Vienna? You'd have a chance to unwind, see something of the city for a change, or work on your expense account if you felt especially creative. Or you could fly to Paris and spend the weekend there, maybe bringing your 'significant other' for a surprise treat.

Whatever you decide, there's always the risk of becoming a victim of your own flexibility. Back at headquarters in Broken Springs, Colorado, they are plotting to dislocate your schedule. A weekend's golf – or, heaven forbid, a carefully wrought assignation – goes down the tube with a request for you to be in Munich on Sunday. In these days of instant communications, it's hard to go missing (although I have been known to check out of my hotel with the red message light still blinking).

Professional extenders never permit business to interfere with pleasure. The secret is pre-emptive planning. You make sure that whatever pre-trip (or mid-trip) crisis occurs, you are included out. One way is to plan your own crisis: 'Charles, I'll have to miss the emergency budget meeting; it's absolutely crucial I meet Karl in Frankfurt Friday… We can always talk on the phone.' Two crises are better than one. So sandwich your golf break between two 'inviolable' business meetings. Should you need to go off the air for opportunistic reasons, invoke a 'field trip'. ('Charles, Sven wants me to check out the crayfish stocks in the north of Sweden.' Or, 'Charles, you know this is the first time anybody has actually talked to our customers on the French Riviera.')

An (almost) sure-fire way to prevent an extension being scuppered at the last minute is to make complex APEX bookings that can't be changed without extreme penalties. A friend of mine in Ireland has developed this technique into an art form. Whenever he flies to Paris on business, he saves his company money by coming down to the Côte d'Azur for the weekend for a change of pollution. I've never understood the legerdemain, but we all enjoy his extension (and expense account).

On Friday evenings at Nice Airport, crowd-watching is good value when the flights from Paris arrive. There are groupies and weekend wives, a gaggle of executives on their way to lubricate a conference in

Monte Carlo, machos in designer dungarees and ambiguous ladies with impatient poodles. On Monday mornings, the first flight to Paris is filled with suntanned executives who seem not quite to have decided whether they are on business or pleasure.

I can think of worse kinds of identity crisis.

Chartering a flight to freedom

Charter a Cessna Citation 11 executive jet from London to Strasbourg and back at £1,500 an hour and it will cost you around £3,500; hardly a steal when you compare it with the round-trip business-class fare of £420. In purely cash terms it only makes sense if you take half-a-dozen colleagues along.

But leaving at 7.30 am, you would arrive in 70 minutes, faster than a scheduled flight and be back (if you must) in time for lunch. Take in Maastricht and Vienna on the way to Strasbourg and you can still return the same day. This will cost you about £6,000, but there is no other way you could do this.

Similarly, leaving home at 6.30 am on a day-trip from London with meetings in Berlin and Lyon, you could be back at your office in central London by 3.30 pm. This would cost £8,250 for a seven-seat Learjet compared with a scheduled ticket of around £1,000 plus a mandatory one-night stop in Lyon, not getting back to London until 2.30 pm the next day. But with two people on board, the difference between charter and scheduled is £5,750; with four people it goes down to £3,250 and with six it goes down to £650. But you have saved eight desk-hours for every person on board. This means that two executives worth, say, £1,000 an hour for their company have 'given back' or saved £16,000 for the company in management time.

A two-night trip from Madrid to Baku and Billund and back in a 6/7-seat Learjet 35A costs $42,000. Or a four-day trip from Aberdeen to London, Tbilisi, Baku and back to London in an 8-seat Hawker 125 will set you back £26,000.

You may never justify the cost of a business jet by how much you save in airline tickets. It comes down to how much you value your time and the opportunity to take trips that you couldn't otherwise, and to run on your own schedule – especially for forays into Russia or Africa. Plus the lack of stress, being able to work or relax, hold meetings with associates in privacy, and the blessed freedom from the misery of megahubs. (There are 600 or so airports throughout Europe where a jet can land; only about 170 are served by scheduled airlines.) What price do you put on that?

'If you can save a working day for three executives each earning £100,000 a year, you've more than justified the cost of chartering,' says Tony Mack, chairman of Air Partner, Europe's largest charter broker. 'If each executive is worth, say, six times his or her salary to the company, that values him or her at £3,750 a day. So the saving to the company would be more than £11,000. This is the same logic that justifies a taxi. Otherwise, everybody would go around by bus.'

David Savile, managing director of Air Partner, says: 'If you were to sit in our office and watch our ops board, what you would see on a day in day out basis is people who take aircraft away with eight people on board for road shows and things like that.

'Take an itinerary like London–Paris–Geneva–Vienna–Copenhagen–Edinburgh–London. I could get that done in a day and a half. You leave London at 7 am on day one, have an hour's presentation in every city and an hour for your transfers and still get back to London by midday on day two. The absolute minimum by scheduled airlines if you caught every connection would be three and half days, more like four and half. You've saved two days for every person on the trip – 120 hours. If every person is worth even £100 an hour, you've delivered £12,800 of extra value to the company. With an 8-seat jet the itinerary I've just given you will cost around £16,000. Scheduled flights would cost £1,400 per person; but you have two extra nights away. So for eight executives charter comes to the same cost as scheduled before you've even started talking about the 128 executive working hours you've saved.'

Charter is a booming business. Air Partner reported a turnover of £52 million for 1998, an impressive and significant increase on the previous year – £40 million – and £35 million in 1996. The company arranges more than 5,000 charters a year for about 500 clients worldwide. Hunt & Palmer charter brokers had a turnover of more than £20 million in 1998.

'It's not just mega pop stars and fat cats off to check their swimming pools in Athens who charter corporate aircraft,' Savile says. 'The fact is that today almost 10,000 business jets and a further 10,000 turbo-jet aircraft – like King Airs – are flying a combined 9 million flight hours a year around the world. That means that every working day there are some 35,000 flight hours being completed.'

Modern corporate aircraft are safe, fast and comfortable. A Learjet 60 cruises at 35,000 feet, reaching nearly 600 mph. The so-called 'big irons' have a range of 5,000 miles and can fly from London to Chicago at 650 mph and 45,000 feet – faster and higher than a 747 and well above the weather and commercial flights. They include corporate icons such as the Falcon 900, Gulfstream IV and Canadair Challenger RJ, which carry 12 passengers in supreme comfort along with 20 pieces of baggage. They have big, stand-up cabins, separate from the crew, and all mod cons with fully reclining sleeper seats, a video system, computer ports, two-way fax and satellite phone, along with two pilots, a flight engineer and a cabin attendant. You may find more electronic wizardry than on the flight decks of the latest Boeings and Airbuses.

Two new super-long-range jets designed to fly 6,500 nautical miles non-stop are set to raise the stakes. The latest Gulfstream G-V and the Canadair Global Express are powered with twin BMW Rolls-Royce BR710-48 turbofans that power these beasts to speeds of Mach 0.8 and to cruising altitudes of up to 51,000 feet.

'There are two Gulfstream G-Vs available for charter right now,' Savile says. 'Within the first month of the first one arriving back in April 1998, we did a charter using its full potential: non-stop London–Johannesburg; then on to Rio – an 11-hour sector over water; then from Rio up to New York; and then New York–London.'

Chartering involves a basic decision whether to go with a piston engine, turbo-prop or jet – depending on comfort, speed and price. You may find a piston engine quite adequate for trips such as Versailles–Rheims, Innsbruck–Vienna, or navigating the vineyards in Alsace or Burgundy.

A Piper Chieftain carries up to eight people and would cost around £900 for a trip from the London area to Deauville. However, piston-engined aircraft (or air taxis) are mostly unpressurized – which means they cannot fly above 10,000 feet and if there is a lot of low cloud it can be bumpy. Farther afield you need the speed and comfort of a turbo-prop such as the pressurised Beechcraft King Air 200 or a jet. The King Air costs about £750 an hour compared with about £400 for a Chieftain, but higher hourly costs are offset by shorter journey times. Horses for courses.

Charter is not only the perfect solution for getting from A to B but can also be used with scheduled flights. Fly from London to Zurich with BA or Swissair, then charter an air taxi or a helicopter to get you somewhere remote, like Davos or Gstaad.

Helicopters are relatively slow and expensive but come into their own for short distances of up to 150 miles, especially when you want to stop off at several places – such as visiting building sites or stores around the country. Fly to Manchester, say, and charter a helicopter from there.

Most charter operators charge on a basis of hours flown, from the time the plane leaves its home airport until its return, plus overnight expenses for the crew. (You might be asked to pay for time overnight when the plane is idle, or unless you fly at least two hours a day. This is negotiable; compare it with the cost if it flies back empty and returns – either the same plane or another – to pick you up.)

Companies – and travel agents – are now looking at the 'total travel' solution and charter may be part of that. How else do you get from Yellow Knife in Canada to Florence except by a combination of scheduled and charter? People fly out to Hong Kong on a nice scheduled carrier, then charter a business jet and fly around China for a week. Some journeys you just can't do by conventional means.

'Much more is expected from executives these days; jobs are combined, departments rationalized, whole layers of management removed, and geographical areas stretched quite unreasonably,' Savile says. 'But with, say, 50 hours a week to work, something, somehow has to give. Most of the people we deal with are highly stretched. If you say to them, look, would it help if we can give you two extra days a week, they're going to jump at it. We are selling time: we're giving time back.'

Air Partner Plc
Tel: 01293 549 555
Fax: 01293 536 810
E-mail: charters@airlondon.com
Web site: www.airlondon.com

Hunt & Palmer Plc
Tel: 0171 580 8991
Fax: 0171 636 3604
Web site: www.huntpalmer.co.uk

The route to a good deal

It helps to know the ropes to secure both the right aircraft and the best deal.

Do

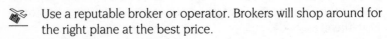 Use a reputable broker or operator. Brokers will shop around for the right plane at the best price.

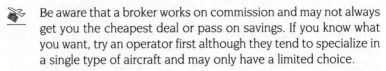 Be aware that a broker works on commission and may not always get you the cheapest deal or pass on savings. If you know what you want, try an operator first although they tend to specialize in a single type of aircraft and may only have a limited choice.

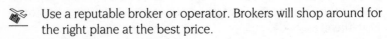 Make sure you know what you are trying to achieve and communicate this to the broker/operator. Is cost, speed or comfort paramount? Do you have bulky luggage? What about catering?

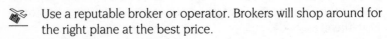 Get a map showing the 2,000 or so airports in Europe. Remember that jets can use only 500 to 600 and half will be closed at night. Check customs facilities.

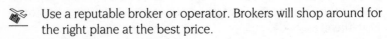 Ask for alternative quotes. Prices on identical routes may vary by up to 30 per cent. Ask what prices include: one or two pilots? Cabin crew? Is there a positioning charge to get from where the plane is to where you are?

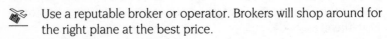 If quoted for a flight of an hour or more in a piston-engine plane, ask for costs for a pressurized turbo-prop. Instead of a turbo-prop for a three-hour flight, what about a jet? Higher cost per hour may be offset by greater speed. For up to 150 miles, get quotes for helicopters and a piston-engine plane.

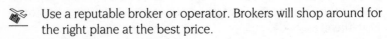 Ask how prices are worked out. Usually you pay for actual hours flown from the time the plane leaves its home airport until its return, plus overnight expenses of £200 to £400 for the crew. Problems can arise if you want to spend two nights away, involving three days' utilization of the aircraft.

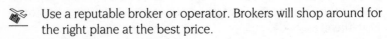 You might be asked to pay for time overnight when the plane is idle. This is negotiable: compare it with the cost if it flies back empty and returns to pick you up.

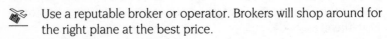 Decide how many are in your core party and how many can travel if there is room. One extra person could mean paying another £1,000 for a larger plane.

Do not

 Shop around between brokers. Most inquiries are filtered around the market and you will lose credibility.

 Use brokers or operators who are not members of a trade association (such as the Aircharter Brokers' Association, 44 171 836 7971).

 Assume you know the best aircraft or route. Say where you are and where you want to get to; you may be able to fly closer than you think.

 Think of charter as a perfect solution for getting from A to B; it may be best in tandem with scheduled flights.

EuroAirport as a regional hub

Swissair's introduction of a non-stop service between Basel, Switzerland, and New York (Newark) in December 1998 was welcome news to business travelers who can now make fast onward connections through a small, user-friendly airport to provincial cities like Bilbao, Nuremberg, Dresden, Toulouse, Nice, Marseille, Valencia, Friedrichshafen and Rostock.

There are also flights to major cities such as London and Berlin, but often to business airports like London City and Tempelhof, a short cab-ride to the city centre. In addition, there are connections to megahubs like Heathrow, Charles de Gaulle in Paris, Amsterdam and Frankfurt – if that's where you really need to go.

The six-times-weekly service is by Swissair Airbus 310 (42 business-class and 143 economy seats) as a code-share with Delta Air Lines and Crossair – Swissair's regional subsidiary – which is developing an extensive 'hub and spoke' network through Basel.

Newark–Basel is the first of a dozen similar 'long, thin' services (that is, with sparse traffic) that will be operated in Crossair colours on routes such as Basel–Buenos Aires/Atlanta/Mexico City/Charlotte, NC – what I call regional long-haul routes. Crossair ultimately plans to acquire a long-haul fleet of 12 upgraded Boeing 767s to serve these routes.

Book a flight to Basel, Switzerland, or Mulhouse, France, and you'll arrive at the same airport – EuroAirport Basel–Mulhouse–Freiburg – right at the border between Switzerland, France and Germany in the Upper Rhine Valley.

Four million people live within 60 minutes of the airport, which is 6.3 miles (10.1 kilometres) from Basel; 16 miles (25.7 kilometres) from Mulhouse and 46 miles (75 kilometres) from Freiburg in the south-western corner of Germany. Zurich will be 45 minutes away when a new highway is completed.

EuroAirport, 50 years old but in the process of expansion, served nearly three million passengers in 1998 (around 40 per cent each from France and Switzerland and 20 percent from Germany) with 12 airlines currently offering more than 45 scheduled flights to 92 destinations in 25 countries. Such carriers as Air France, British Airways, Sabena, KLM and Lufthansa serve 36 cities in 20 countries from EuroAirport.

Bypassing the megahubs

Crossair plans to develop EuroAirport as a regional hub for people who wish to travel between, say, Nuremberg and Bilbao, or Dresden and Toulouse, thus saving time and avoiding the misery of changing planes at a megahub like Amsterdam, Brussels, Frankfurt, London, Paris or Zurich which give priority to long-haul connections.

Crossair's 'EuroCross' is a new strategy that provides 550 connections a day between 40 cities through EuroAirport with an expected connecting time of 20 minutes. The carrier aims to have 1,000 daily connections between 48 European destinations by 2000, including regional services from EuroAirport to such destinations as Warsaw, Budapest, Athens, Ankara, Bologna, Stockholm, Copenhagen, Glasgow, Oporto, Trieste and Moscow, as well as long-haul routes to North America and Asia.

Moritz Suter, president and chief executive of Crossair in Basel, says: 'We are seeing the biggest change in the history of Europe – the birth of a European economy with cross-participation of companies in other countries. The growth of business travel in Europe is huge, much bigger than the USA or Asia – airlines in the European Regional Airlines Association carried 60 million passengers in 1997, 11 per cent more than the year before. Crossair alone had a 30 per cent growth in passengers – 80 per cent of them business travelers. People are traveling like crazy to build the new Europe. They have to sit down with each other to discuss ideas and go and build those ideas. It's a huge thing we are doing.

'You see people today traveling on routes that never existed before – like from here to Birmingham and Birmingham to Hanover; Hanover to Bilbao; Bilbao to Munich; Friedrichshafen to Milan; or Toulouse to Copenhagen. The Crossair network would not have been possible 30 years ago. There's a huge need for more trans-regional links. My plan for 2003 is to have 55 planes making those connections. And when the new terminal extension is built here, passengers should never have more than a 10-minute walk from gate to gate.'

EuroCross flights arrive and depart in four co-ordinated waves: early in the morning, midday, afternoon and evening, enabling people traveling to and from most destinations in Europe to get there and back the same day. For example, Toulouse–Vienna via EuroCross is 2 hours 15 minutes faster than via Zurich; Amsterdam–Bilbao is 2 hours faster than via Paris; and Friedrichshafen–Birmingham is 1 hour 30 minutes faster than connecting in Frankfurt.

'If someone could fly point-to-point from Frankfurt to Palma at a suitable time, he would never go via EuroCross, or if someone in Nuremberg could save time by flying to Bordeaux via Frankfurt, he would not use EuroCross,' Suter says. 'But people will take EuroCross because it is faster and easier in many cases.

'We developed the EuroCross idea in 1996, but we only officially launched it in spring 1998 when we were able to link the destinations with realistic schedules. Let's say in Dresden we have the biggest market for Madrid. Then we schedule so that the gate for the Madrid flight is closest to that of the Dresden flight.'

Crossair flies to 82 European destinations (plus around 25 services on behalf of Swissair) with a fleet of 80 aircraft consisting of 33-seat Saab 340 turboprops; 50-seat Saab 2000 turboprops; and 97-seat Avro RJ jets. The company carried 4.7 million passengers in 1997 – 19 per cent more than the previous year – and made a net profit of 43.2 million Swiss francs (about $28 million). Small planes operating frequent flights on lightly traveled routes, and relatively high fares, are the key ingredients to Crossair's success. Round-trip fares from EuroAirport to London City, a 15-minute cab ride from the City, or to Heathrow, are around $1,000 in business class, $845 in economy and $190 discounted fare.

Crossair is what you might call a 'high frills' carrier. Riding the 33-seat Saab 340 Cityliner, for example, is the next best thing to a private plane. On short flights you're served regional specialties with wines to match, or open sandwiches of smoked salmon and cheese with Champagne from a real bottle.

The triangle where the frontiers of Switzerland, France and Germany intersect on the Rhine is the crossroads of ancient north-south and east-west trading routes, in use long before the nations were created. Alsace changed hands many times between France and Germany over the years – belonging to Germany from 1871 to 1918 and again from 1940 to 1945.

From the balcony of Moritz Suter's office at the airport, you can see the city of Basel to the south, St Louis in France to the north, and beyond that the German city of Weil-am-Rhein on the other side of the Rhine, and to the north-east Lörrach, in Germany. Mulhouse is to the north-east; to the north is Mulheim in Germany and Strasbourg in France.

The region had its genesis as a trading hub in 1226 when Bishop von Thun of Basel mortgaged his entire fortune to build the first bridge on the Rhine – the toll-house still stands in the centre of the old bridge. Merchant caravans from Scandinavia and northern Germany would come down through the Rhine Valley, crossing the river at Basel on their way south via the Alps to Italy; the silk caravans from China came up from the Balkans, crossing the Rhine here, and continuing on to Paris and London.

In the mid-19th century, railway engineers followed the old caravan routes: the night express from Stockholm to Palermo still crosses the Rhine at Basel – one of the most important railway hubs in central Europe.

Germany and France have train stations on Swiss ground in the centre of Basel. Modern highways follow the old routes from north to south and west to east, still crossing the Rhine at Basel.

The EuroAirport is an intercultural experience. It is built on French soil and run by a kind of public joint venture between France and Switzerland, with representatives from each country along with 'representatives' from Germany – a fast-growing sector of the airport's business.

There is a notional Franco-Swiss frontier within the airport, which apparently can be shifted depending on how many departure gates are needed on either side.

The Eurobar straddles the frontier; the same bartender serves on both sides. The Airport Grill offers entirely different menus, with prices to match, on the French and Swiss sides, with the food coming from the same kitchen. A three-course dinner with wine could cost $55 a person on the Swiss side, a third less on the French side.

Whether you use the French or Swiss side depends, of course, on where you're heading. (Each country has its own immigration and customs channels.) But it may be a good idea to compare taxi and car rental prices in French and Swiss francs. There are separate parking lots on each side.

If you're going somewhere in Germany, you can come out on either side. But the airport bus to Freiburg goes from the French exit. And a French taxi is likely to cost a lot less than a Swiss taxi. You may like the idea of taking a French taxi to Germany or Switzerland.

The airport on the doorstep

'The problem of providing a suitable landing platform for flying machines in large cities has always puzzled engineers', wrote the aviation correspondent in *The Illustrated London News* of 18 October 1919. A futuristic solution at that time was an elevated circular landing strip that would allow pilots 'to start and alight dead against the wind as they always must'. A neat example of lateral thinking, even if the thing never got off the ground. But finally, modern technology came up with a better idea: London City Airport, which handled 1.4 million passengers in the first half of 1999.

When it opened in 1986, London City was widely seen as a white elephant. Today it seems set to become a major hub in a network of similar city centre airports across Europe. There are currently 12 airlines operating high-frequency business services from London City to 22 European cities.

Traveling from London City is the next best thing to having your own corporate plane. The airport is built on the old Royal docks only six miles – about 15 minutes by cab – from the City, and it has already fulfilled its promise as a business traveler's dream. The airport is like one big executive lounge, with all the usual amenities, a state-of-the-art business centre with online financial information, car rental and a civilized restaurant.

You can check in 10 minutes before boarding and walk 40 yards to the plane. Fly from London City and you could arrive in Paris, Brussels, Antwerp, Bern or Rotterdam at the very time you would be boarding the plane if you had gone via Heathrow.

We're talking about the convenience and comfort of the old days – when flying was human and before airports had moved out of the city to the next county or beyond and become mega-hubs where you have to fight your way through endless shopping malls to the gate – but now it's with high-tech equipment. For example, the four-engine BAe 'whisper jet', said to be the quietest in the world, capable of landing on short runways in built-up areas; the Boeing Dash 9, the Dornier 328, the Fokker 50 and the 'third generation' turboprop, the Saab 2000.

What the business traveler wants is choice, convenience and comfort. This means the choice of a convenient airport as well as an airline. For short-haul flights in Europe between major hubs, actual flying time can be as little as 20 per cent of total travel time from door to door.

The City Centre Airports Association was formed in 1993 to promote the benefits of downtown airports. Members include London City Airport, Stockholm Bromma, Belfast City Airport, Berlin Tempelhof, Tel Aviv Dov Hoz, Toronto City Center Airport, Edmonton Municipal Airport, Detroit City, Kuala Lumpur City Airport, and Amerigo Vespucci in Florence. The Florence Airport, four miles from the Ponte Vecchio, handles about 1.5 million passengers a year. To get to Florence by air, one used to have to fly to and from Pisa – a 55-mile train ride away.

Bromma – four miles from the centre of Stockholm, compared with 24 miles for Arlanda, the main international airport – has service to Gothenburg, Malmo and Lidkoping in Sweden, Aarhus in Denmark, and London City.

Berlin Tempelhof (which has the shape of an eagle from the sky) was Europe's leading airport in 1938, handling a quarter of a million passengers a year flying to 78 destinations. Now superseded by Tegel as Berlin's main international airport, Tempelhof, a 10-minute cab ride from the city centre, has become a mini-hub with services to 25 destinations including Bern, Copenhagen, Geneva, Lugano, Luxembourg, Oslo, and EuroAirport Basel–Mulhouse–Freiburg, home hub of Crossair – the regional subsidiary of Swissair – which hopes eventually to start services between EuroAirport and Moscow City Airport.

Richard Gooding, managing director of London City Airport, says: 'The aviation scene in London has changed dramatically over the last five years. If you wanted to travel on business, it was Heathrow, take it or leave it. Today, the top six or seven destinations in Europe are served from all five airports around London: Heathrow, Gatwick, Stansted, Luton and London City.

'People have choices that they didn't have before. Not only choice of airport, but different types of carriers. Heathrow succeeds in many ways at being all things to all men, providing services across the spectrum from business to leisure travel; services at Luton are entirely focused on people who want value for money – low fares with no frills; then London

City focused on the upper end of the business market for people for whom time is invaluable.

'For the inbound market from the continent, we think we already are the airport of choice. I spoke to someone who had flown overnight from Singapore into Amsterdam with KLM, something like a 50-minute connection on the KLM UK service into here, and he was at his meeting in the City by a quarter to nine. He could not have done that by going via Heathrow.'

Gooding also serves as chairman of the City Centre Airports Association. The airports belonging to this group share similar characteristics: they are in built-up urban areas with short runways requiring steep approaches and face severe environmental, operational and planning restraints. Associate members include aircraft manufacturers such as Bombardier and Dornier, and ground-handling companies like Servisair. 'City-centre airports are characterized by aircraft of up to 100 seats, and quick ground handling,' Gooding says. 'We do achieve a very short corridor between your taxi and the plane. Small planes mean you can get on and off quickly.

'There should be a much wider range of aircraft, especially jets, capable of coming into city centre airports, such as the McDonnell Douglas MD-95, if it is ever built. We are trying to raise awareness with manufacturers that this is a growing market. Some of the newer models of the Boeing 737 and Airbus A-319 can almost make it. They need, say, another few yards of runway or are one or two decibels out on the noise requirement.

'There are dozens of other city centre airports emerging around the world. The new Sheffield Airport in Britain shares our philosophy, and there's Eilat Airport in Israel and John Wayne Airport in Orange County, California. All in high urbanized areas, close to where people want to get to.'

London City Airport currently serves 12 airlines flying to 22 European cities.

Amsterdam	KLM UK
Antwerp	VLM-Sabena
Basel	Crossair
Berne	Air Engiadina
Brussels	Sabena
Dublin	CityJet
Dundee	Suckling Airways
Dusseldorf	VLM
Edinburgh	KLM UK
Frankfurt	Lufthansa CityLine

Geneva	Crossair
Glasgow	Suckling Airways
Jersey	VLM
Lugano	Crossair
Luxembourg	VLM-Luxair
Malmo	Braathens/Malmo Aviation
Manchester	KLM UK
Milan	Alitalia
Paris	Air France
Rotterdam	VLM-KLM UK
Strasbourg	Air France
Zurich	Crossair

(July 1999)

London City Airport
Tel: (44 207) 646 0000
Fax: (44 207) 511 1040
E-mail: info@londoncityairport.com
Web site: www.londoncityairport.com

No-frills options grow

Nice Airport. My 8 am easyJet flight to Luton left from Gate 40. The British Airways 8.30 am flight to Heathrow was leaving from Gate 41. Head-to-head competition you might think. But it was no contest.

I had paid £98 for a mid-week, round-trip ticket. The cheapest comparable British Airways fare, allowing me to leave Tuesday and return Thursday, would have cost around £500. Both aircraft were Boeing 737s with similar seating (easyJet proudly announced that the plane – the latest addition to the fleet – was two days old!). And there seemed a similar mix of business and leisure travelers turning up for both flights.

That means I can make five round-trips on easyJet for the price of one Eurobudget economy ticket on BA, which carries some restrictions. And even a full house on an easyJet 737-300 is at least as comfortable as sitting behind the curtain (or in front of the curtain, for that matter) on BA. Nobody minds paying for drinks and snacks when you're saving that kind of money.

No-frills airlines like easyJet, which started services from London Luton in late 1995, the Dublin-based Ryanair, Virgin Express, based at Brussels, and BA's Go, its low-cost clone launched in May at Stansted, collectively serve more than 50 destinations – including most major business routes. No-frills is the fastest-growing sector of the airline industry in Europe, which, analysts say, could triple in the next five years. Mintel in its 'No-Frills/Low-Cost Airlines' report in February 1999 predicts that the sector will grow from 5.4 million passengers in 1998 to 15 million in 2003.

BA's 'if you can't beat them, join them strategy' with Go opened a Pandora's box institutionalizing the no-frills concept. Business people – especially independent and small-business travelers – have found in the last four years that, despite a few rough edges (easyJet does not assign seats, for example, which results in a mad scramble to get on the plane and stake a claim to the overhead bins), no frills is a great way to fly.

An American Express Business Travel Barometer survey of 270 corporate travelers in February 1999, showed that 40 per cent had used no-frills airlines in the last 12 months and 56 per cent planned to use them again soon. Two-thirds said they had no problem flying from secondary airports (such as Luton and Stansted, which is convenient for the City) that these carriers typically serve. The 1999 Carlson Wagonlit survey reveals that 78 per cent of business travelers are prepared to forgo frills for price. Many companies are rewriting their travel policies to mandate no-frills airlines on point-to-point routes in Europe. As the market matures, they are seeking to capture the corporate market. KLM UK launched its own low-cost clone Buzz on 4 January 2000 with services from Stansted to Berlin, Dusseldorf, Frankfurt, Lyons, Paris, Milan and Vienna.

You normally book a no-frills flight by phone or Internet (easyJet claims that 40 per cent of sales are online), thereby cutting travel agents' commission. But business travel agents these days tend to work on a fee based on how much money they save a client, so most are happy to recommend no-frills options.

The crucial challenge that no-frills carriers pose is not so much their low fares but their low one-way fares, which allow travelers a degree of flexibility at a fraction of the cost – breaking the convention that low fares in economy come with conditions (such as advance purchase and the Saturday-night stay nonsense) deliberately designed to frustrate their use by business travelers.

Mike Platt, international commercial director at Hogg Robinson BTI, says: 'A lot of small-business travelers are migrating to no-frills airlines, which have won a lot of business from companies located near their airports. Go, for example, has picked up a huge amount of business in the Midlands from people who used to come down to Heathrow. However, they are still hampered in that they don't always fly at the right times from the right airports and their tickets are not interchangeable. We're happy to book these carriers because we work with 70 per cent of our clients on a management fee basis.'

No-frills carriers tend mainly to compete with national carriers rather than among themselves. EasyJet, for example, considers BA, which flies most of its routes, to be its main competitor and Swissair out of its new Geneva hub to Barcelona and Nice – it competes with Go only between London and Edinburgh, Madrid and Barcelona. Go and Ryanair (serving 33 routes between Ireland, the United Kingdom and mainland Europe) compete only between London and Venice.

'Go is one of BA's main competitors,' Platt says. 'The strategy might have been that Go would become the leisure arm of BA, which could then focus with smaller planes and business-class seats for the corporate market. Unfortunately for BA, there's been a sizeable wastage of business travel migrating from BA to Go.'

Tim Jeans, marketing director of Ryanair in Dublin, says: 'Our view is that Go will be ceded routes by BA, which will ultimately withdraw from certain markets. For example, what on earth is BA doing, with its high costs, flying from Heathrow to Venice when Go can do it for them? BA has said that it's intra-European feed is losing money, and I think you'll find that BA will turn to a much more limited European network, focusing on business destinations from Heathrow, and ones that provide high-yield business-class transfer traffic to their long-haul network.'

Go has recently come out with two types of fare for its 16 destinations – 'flexible discount' requiring a five-day advance purchase with no changes unless you upgrade, but with no minimum stay, and 'fully flexible' fares 'at least 50 per cent lower than the full-fare economy price on a traditional airline'.

There's a separate hand-baggage check-in at Stansted and priority reservations for business travelers when you book by phone or online at www.go-fly.com/business.

Dominic Paul, head of business development at Go in London, says that about 40 per cent of passengers are traveling on business – and more than 80 per cent at peak business times, in the morning and evening, on routes like Copenhagen, Munich, Milan, Rome, Edinburgh, Lisbon and Madrid.

'We used to be allied to small-business travelers,' Paul says, 'but since we added higher frequencies – up to seven flights a day on our business routes – we're attracting more corporate travelers from companies like Marconi, Ford, Tesco, Glaxo Wellcome and Marks & Spencer. Plus a lot more small-and medium-sized companies, from one-man bands to 50 employees, who say they are traveling more – often on day trips – because of lower fares.'

easyJet offers one-way fares that allow you almost total flexibility. Fares rise up to three-fold as the plane fills up, a simple one-way fare structure that allows you almost total flexibility. The idea is that fares rise with demand – the antithesis of classical airline 'yield management'. What counts for easyJet is the total yield for a flight. This can mean that latecomers pay more for a round trip than an excursion fare on a conventional airline. But even if you pay the highest fare out, you may get the cheapest back. You can change your flight out for a £10 charge – although you may have to upgrade to a higher fare.

James Rothnie, spokesman for easyJet in London, says: 'Our concept is to sell the first seat on a flight three months in advance to a budget leisure traveler, who will sacrifice flexibility for a good price, and seat number 149 the day of departure to a frequent traveler on business. Typically, the spread of fares between Luton and Nice is between £39 and £129 each way. On the weekend of the Monaco Grand Prix when the demand exceeds supply, we might charge you £159 each way when BA might only be able to offer you business class for around £400 each way.' Rothnie has no hard data on how many business travelers fly with easyJet. 'But more than 50 per cent of our passengers going to Edinburgh are traveling mid-week for one night or less,' he says. 'Which suggests that they are on business.'

One-way fares allow you the flexibility to travel around Europe with different no-frills airlines – maybe in combination with high-speed trains. For example, Paris to London with Eurostar; Luton or Stansted to Barcelona with easyJet or Go; Barcelona to Brussels with Virgin Express; and Brussels to Dublin with Ryanair.

easyJet is launching more routes across Europe from its new hub in Geneva with flights to Nice, Amsterdam, Barcelona, Belfast and Madrid, with plans to establish hubs in Amsterdam and Paris. Go has new services from Stansted to Lyons and Zurich; Virgin Express now flies between Berlin and Stansted, Rome and Brussels.

Buzz is offering two types of fare: Done Deal, a restricted round-trip ticket with a minimum stay of two nights, no changes or refunds, but no advance purchase, and Open Deal, which, for up to twice the price, gives you total flexibility with a one-way ticket. For example, a round-trip Done Deal ticket from Stansted–Frankfurt costs £80–£140 compared to £125–£512 with Lufthansa; a one-way Open Deal ticket costs £120–£140 compared with £241–£267.

Tony Camacho, commercial director of Buzz in London, says: 'We've tried to keep things simple – and transparent. I don't think the no-frills sector has done itself justice by pushing silly "come on" fares. The great thing about no-frills, as easyJet has shown, is a basic product for a basic price, allowing people to buy the frills they need. We get this on KLM services. "I want to buy the flexibility, but I don't want your food or lounge, can't you make it a bit cheaper?" So we're offering people the option to buy food and drinks on board and in lounges, but not to build them into the price.'

Buzz
Tel: (44 870) 240 7070
Web site: www.buzzaway.com

easyJet
Tel: (44 900) 29 29 29
Web site: www.easyjet.com

Go
Tel: (44 845) 60 54321
Web site: www.go-fly.com/business

Ryanair
Tel: (353 1) 6097 800
Web site: www.ryanair.com

Virgin Express
Tel: (32 2) 752 05 05
Web site: www.virgin-express.com

Rail travel gathers speed

A rapidly expanding network of high-speed trains is setting the pace for travel within Europe. Speeds of up to 186 miles per hour (300 kph) have cut journey times by at least half between major cities, making the train often a faster way to travel from city centre to city centre than the plane – especially for journeys up to 350 miles (560 kilometres). You often don't think of flying unless you need to change planes. A flight time of one to one and a half hours (plus one hour at each end for city centre transfers and check-in) roughly equates to a rail journey of three to three and half hours. (On short-haul flights, flying time can be as little as 20 per cent of total journey time.)

But what counts most with rail travel is the quality of uninterrupted time from the moment you board to the time you arrive. And high-speed trains offer superb comfort especially in first-class with meals and drinks served at your seat and executive lounges at main terminals. Going by plane, the time is fraught and fragmented with all the steps involved – allowing more time than you need to get to the airport, checking in an hour before, hanging around waiting to board and struggling off the other end. Take your laptop and mobile phone and do a pile of work in peace.

It is no surprise that high-speed trains are said to capture 80 to 90 per cent of market share on a route if rail travel time is less than two hours and 50 to 60 per cent if rail travel time is between two and three hours.

While high-speed trains challenge airlines on short routes, there are synergies between the two modes of transport. Integrated air-rail links through high-speed train stations at major airports – such as Paris Charles-de-Gaulle, Amsterdam, Frankfurt, Brussels and Lyons – enable travelers not only to get to the city but to use high-speed trains to connect between long-haul flights and other cities, high-speed rail assuming the role of regional airlines.

'Fly/rail in Europe equals fly/drive in the United States,' says Bernard Frelat, president and CEO of the Rail Europe Group in Harrison, New York. 'Rail in Europe is the perfect answer to most people's needs. You don't need a car in a big city and you're not going to improve your performance driving from one region to another. You're much better off using the high-speed train network, then renting a car at the train station and dropping it back somewhere else.'

Eurostar – with high-speed services between London and Paris and Brussels (via Lille in Northern France) is a huge success – with travelers, if not investors – since it ran the first trains through the Channel Tunnel in November 1994. London–Paris is 3 hours and London–Brussels, 2 hours 40 minutes. Prices are pitched to compete with airlines. First Premium Class is interchangeable with British Midland business class tickets so you can fly out in the morning and take the train back. Or vice versa. First Premium passengers enjoy access to Eurostar lounges, late check-in, on-board drinks and meals and a free taxi when they arrive.

The Lille–Brussels high-speed line is part of a project to link Paris, Brussels, Antwerp, Rotterdam, Amsterdam and Cologne by Thalys (TGV) trains (a consortium of French, Belgian, German and Dutch railways). The journey time between Paris and Brussels is 1 hour 25 minutes (a new direct service from Charles de Gaulle Airport to Brussels from November 1999 takes 75 minutes); Paris–Amsterdam, 4 hours 12 minutes; Paris–Cologne, 4 hours 2 minutes; Brussels–Amsterdam and Paris–Cologne, 2 hours 40 minutes (soon to be cut to 1 hour 40 minutes). When all the high-speed track is completed to Cologne (2005), the Paris-Cologne trip will be cut by 50 minutes to 3 hours 10 minutes. A Paris–Frankfurt high-speed link should be completed by 2004, reducing travel time from 6 to 4 hours. There is an Anglo-French plan for a high-speed rail service between Heathrow and Charles de Gaulle.

The TGV travels at speeds up to 300 kph (187 mph) on dedicated track and around 225 kph on conventional rails. Paris–Bordeaux is under 3 hours; Paris–Nantes is 2 hours; Paris–Toulouse is 4 hours 30 minutes; Paris–Geneva is 3 hours 30 minutes and Paris–Zurich, 4 hours. An eastbound high-speed line to Strasbourg is under construction.

The first TGV (train grande vitesse) entered service between Paris and Lyons in 1981. The route now serves 6 million passengers a year (57 per cent of whom are traveling on business) with 23 trains a day taking just two hours to cover 462 kilometres. The current speed of 270 kph will be raised to 300 kph when the line has been upgraded in 2006. The train now claims 90 per cent of the market between the two cities. Upgrading to high-speed track beyond Lyons will bring Marseille within 3 hours of Paris by 2000. Eventually, Paris–Nice will be cut from 6 to 3½ hours.

The Italian Pendolino tilting train – which can travel faster around curves on conventional track – takes 4 hours 25 minutes from Milan to Rome (via Bologna and Florence). Florence–Rome takes 1 hour 35 minutes. A Rome–Naples high-speed service is due to start this year.

Deutsche Bahn (German Rail) runs its InterCityExpress (ICE) trains at speeds up to 280 kph. Hamburg–Frankfurt (via Hanover and Kassel) in less than 4 hours: another 4 hours brings you south to Nuremberg or Munich via Mannheim and Stuttgart. High-speed networks down the Rhine valley now link Hamburg–Cologne and Cologne–Munich with ICE trains. The Berlin–Hannover journey has been reduced from 2½ hours to 1½. ICE trains reach into Switzerland to Zurich and Interlaken.

Rudolf Richter, director of German Rail in London, says: 'We are testing a new generation of tilting ICE trains which can achieve high speeds on both new lines and track where no upgrading is possible. ICE 3 will be capable of 330 kph. If you want to get businessmen out of their Mercedes and BMWs you have to offer them comfort and speed. People used to fly between Frankfurt and Stuttgart: it's now 75 minutes by train: you can't beat this time by car. Frankfurt–Munich is 3 hours and 50 minutes; Hannover–Frankfurt used to be 4 hours by train; now it's 2½. People use the train.

'Our flagship will be a new line between Cologne and Frankfurt (about 300 kilometres) in 2001. This will follow the autobahn and cut the journey time from 2 hours 20 minutes to 58 minutes with one stop and a train every seven and a half minutes. You'll arrive at Frankfurt Airport, go down to the station in the new third terminal, which will be ready in 2001, straight into an ICE train.

'This is part of an integrated rail/air concept. Lufthansa is keen because they want to get rid of their domestic flights to have more capacity for long-haul. We have plans for a high-speed line between Berlin and Warsaw; and a line from Berlin through Prague to Vienna, which before the war was one of the main lines in Europe.'

Rail passes

A rail pass can save money for business or leisure travel. Choose from a dozen national and multi-country passes, typically priced on unlimited train travel in a given number of days. Eurail Pass covers travel in 17 countries (Austria, Belgium, Denmark, Finland, France, Germany, Greece, Hungary, Ireland, Italy, Luxembourg, Netherlands, Norway, Portugal,

Spain, Sweden and Switzerland). First-class travel costs from $470 for 15 consecutive days to $862 for any 15 days in 2 months. A EurailDrive Pass allows you to combine first-class rail travel with car rental – $359 per person for a compact car (unlimited mileage with free drop-off at selected locations) allows any 6 days (4 rail + 2 car) within 2 months + 5 additional rail + as many car days as you like for $80 a day.

The Europass gives you unlimited first-class travel in France, Germany, Italy, Spain and Switzerland from $348 for any 5 days in 2 months to $728 for any 15 days in two months.

The BritRail Pass for travel in England, Scotland and Wales has many prices and options – from $265 (second class) for 8 consecutive days to $510 (first class) for any 8 days in 2 months. A BritRail Pass 'N Drive starts at $358 (second class) for an economy car for any 6 days (3 rail & 3 car) within two months.

You can book through Rail Europe on any railway – from Ireland to Russia – through its Euronet reservations system at 700 travel agencies worldwide or online at www.raileurope.com. Bear in mind, however, that rail passes are intended for visitors and may not always be available to residents of the countries to which they apply.

Air/rail comparisons

Route	Rail Time	Air Time
London–Brussels	2h45m	3h
London–Paris	3h	3h5m
Dusseldorf–Amsterdam	2h30m	2h55m
Paris–Lyons	2h	2h15m
Geneva–Milan	3h45m	3h15m
Frankfurt–Munich	3h30m	2h55m
Frankfurt–Zurich	4h	3h
Milan–Rome	4h25m	3h5m

NB Air journey times include an hour at arrival and departure points to cover city centre transfers.

Keeping yourself fit for business

In my corporate days, we always got visiting firemen from Broken Springs, Colorado, to stop over at our subsidiaries in Paris and Milan for wining and dining. By the time they joined us at the European HQ in Switzerland to review the budgets, unfamiliar food and drink had taken its familiar toll. The idea was not to put them *hors de combat*, you understand, but just to loosen them up, keep them on the hop, so to speak, for the crucial slide show.

My come-uppance came in Oslo after a crayfish party (although I suspect the aquavit may have played a role) laid on by an unscrupulous distributor. Never check into a hotel without a phone in the bathroom.

The plain fact is that most business travelers are hit sooner or later by Gippy Tummy, Delhi Belly, the Katmandu Quickstep or Montezuma's Revenge, and a new one called Lenin's Revenge. According to Dr Richard Dawood, a physician in London who specializes in travel medicine, as many as a third of travelers become ill from gastro-intestinal problems when they are abroad – 30 per cent of whom are confined to bed, and another 40 per cent are obliged to change their travel plans.

Dawood, an inveterate traveler, is the editor of *travelers' Health – How To Stay Healthy Abroad* – which has become a classic since it was first published in 1986. The fourth edition was published in December 1999 by Oxford University Press. The book assembles 45 specialists, top in their fields, from several countries, who provide practical advice on the prevention and treatment of health problems, both exotic and mundane. They range from diarrhoea, hepatitis and malaria, to dental emergencies and gynaecological problems. Not to mention a host of minor upsets that can make life a misery, such as trouble with contact lenses, insect bites and sunburn. The book is both erudite and lucid, compellingly readable on how diseases are spread, what precautions to take, self-diagnosis, how to check that you're getting the right treatment and, in an emergency, how to treat yourself. A measure of its scope is that many doctors will discover how to treat diseases they've never even heard of.

The message is simple. There are teeming health hazards for the unwary traveler, especially outside North America, Northern Europe, Australia and New Zealand. But they are easily avoided if you take a few simple precautions.

Dawood says: 'The kind of medical technology that surrounds the affluent business traveler at home creates a false sense of security. People tend to delegate precautions. They tell their secretary to find out what they need and then go and get immunized. In fact, you are only protecting yourself against half-a-dozen diseases – hepatitis, polio, typhoid, tetanus, rabies, yellow fever, and cholera. Sometimes vaccinations are not mandatory, but that doesn't mean they're not important for your personal protection. "Here are your malaria tablets and be careful with food and water."

'People then think they've done all they can. After all, they say, we're going to the good hotels, we're not going to mix with locals, so we don't need to worry any more. Nothing could be further than the truth.'

A major hazard resulting from such ignorance, is that serious diseases can be missed or mis-diagnosed when you get back home. Malaria, for example can mimic the symptoms of other diseases – high fever, lassitude, headache, pains in the joints. The classic case is the traveler returning from Africa in winter and having malaria diagnosed as flu. Any suspicious fever should be checked.

Similarly, travelers need specific advice before setting off on a trip. 'Many intelligent travelers spurn advice because it often goes no further than a list of dos and don'ts and "consult a doctor if you get sick",' Dawood says. 'That's ridiculous. Even if you can find a doctor, it doesn't guarantee that you'll get appropriate treatment.'

Dawood recommends a pro-active approach to vaccinations by getting your basic shots in plenty of time and 'fine-tuning' at short notice, depending on your destination. 'It's no use turning up three days before a trip to the Ivory Coast for a yellow fever vaccination because the vaccine can be in short supply and it takes 10 days to get a certificate,' Dawood says. 'It takes two weeks to get good protection with the new hepatitis A vaccine.'

His book is 'prevention based' and divided up according to how diseases are spread. The first chapter deals with diseases caused by food, drink and poor hygiene: diarrhoea and intestinal infections, intestinal parasites, polio, viral infections and a nasty infection called Guinea worm, transmitted by polluted water. Seven pages are devoted to 'safe water'.

'With food and water hygiene, you have to learn what to look for,' Dawood says. 'You have to accept that a fly in a five-star hotel hasn't suddenly become clean. It just takes one fly to land on your food once.' What this means is choosing food that has been freshly and thoroughly cooked and served hot. Avoid salads that may have been washed in polluted water and prepared buffets (mayonnaise is a notorious source of salmonella food poisoning and Russian salad may be even more awful than Lenin's Revenge). What looks appetizing can be a poor guide to food safety. Local dishes, like curry, are often safer than Western food. Fruit should always be peeled. And above all, never drink unbottled water (make sure that the bottle is opened in front of you) and avoid ice in drinks. (I was assured at the Shangri La in Jakarta that the ice was made from bottled water – one test of a fine hotel.) I agree that a warm gin and tonic isn't much fun (it's called a Silver Slipper among aficionados). But brushing your teeth with duty-free malt whisky is not an undiluted disaster.

Then there are diseases spread by contact with humans, fresh water, sand and soil. These include tuberculosis (a re-emerging scourge), tetanus and biharzia. Dawood says he picked up 'creeping eruption', a type of hookworm that burrows under the skin, from a beach in Florida. (It is normally found in Asia and the Caribbean.) The advice is to walk barefoot on sand only below the high-water mark and to avoid swimming in lakes and rivers.

Twelve chapters are devoted to diseases, apart from malaria, that are spread by insect bites, yellow fever, dengue fever, sleeping sickness and a group of exotic nasties known as arboviruses.

The rest of the book covers pretty well everything from snakebites and altitude sickness to eye troubles and AIDS as well as the dangers of unsupervised snorkeling.

By this time you're probably off to join Hypochondriacs Anonymous (although even a hypochondriac can get sick!). The good news is that with sensible precautions, you can rest easy. Perhaps the greatest risk for a business traveler these days is to get back to the office and find that your PC has gone down with a virus.

Dos and don'ts

 Do visit your doctor before and after the trip – especially if you're going somewhere in Africa.

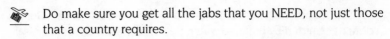 Do make sure you get all the jabs that you NEED, not just those that a country requires.

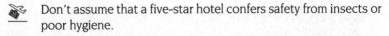 Don't assume that a five-star hotel confers safety from insects or poor hygiene.

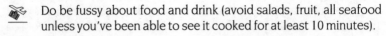 Do be fussy about food and drink (avoid salads, fruit, all seafood unless you've been able to see it cooked for at least 10 minutes).

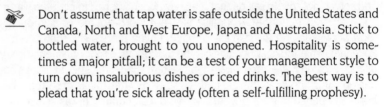 Don't assume that tap water is safe outside the United States and Canada, North and West Europe, Japan and Australasia. Stick to bottled water, brought to you unopened. Hospitality is sometimes a major pitfall; it can be a test of your management style to turn down insalubrious dishes or iced drinks. The best way is to plead that you're sick already (often a self-fulfilling prophesy).

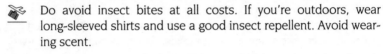 Do avoid insect bites at all costs. If you're outdoors, wear long-sleeved shirts and use a good insect repellent. Avoid wearing scent.

The growing menace of malaria

The day before I was due to leave for a conference in New Delhi, I took my first tablet of mefloquine (Larium), the latest high-tech drug for malaria. I'd left it too late to start with chloroquine, the conventional choice of prophylactic.

I never made it to the airport. The next morning I was struck down with vertigo, rapid heartbeat and something close to a panic attack. I sent a message that I could not give my speech at the conference. I put it down to stress, working late to prepare for the trip, and my usual paranoia.

I might have avoided acute embarrassment and recriminations had I known that I was victim of the side-effects of mefloquine, which range from sleep disturbances, hallucinations and anxiety attacks, to serious neuropsychiatric convulsions requiring hospitalization and which affect as many as 20 per cent of people taking the drug.

Anti-malarial drugs have a history of side-effects. But as malaria becomes ever more dangerous with new virulent resistant strains, so drugs for prophylaxis and treatment become more toxic. Business travelers, forced to choose between side-effects or catching the disease, are tempted to take a chance on short, last-minute trips to major cities in Africa, India and Southeast Asia – relying on insect repellent and air-conditioned rooms. Did I really need to worry about malaria on a quick trip to New Delhi?

Richard Dawood, a London physician who specializes in travel medicine and is editor of *traveler's Health* (Oxford University Press/Random House) says: 'Malaria needs to be taken very seriously; people can die within 24 hours of getting the first symptoms. Getting malaria is not a disaster. It's recognizing it and treating it; that's the real problem.

'I'm always a bit careful about people saying, "I'm just going to Delhi, I don't need to take anything." It doesn't turn out that way. Even in an urban situation like Delhi, you land in the rural outskirts. An air-conditioned taxi doesn't protect you. It only takes one bite. Malaria is a killer; it's too dangerous not to take drugs.'

And there is a big risk of misdiagnosis. 'About half of fatal malarial cases are misdiagnosed as flu,' Dawood says. The disease is not necessarily fatal, but early treatment is crucial.'

To complicate matters even further, some of the latest drugs may not be effective against ordinary, non-resistant malaria. It is possible to contract multiple forms of the disease simultaneously. So you may need to take a combination of drugs.

Drugs such as amodiaquine and Fansidar (a pyrimethamine-sulphadoxine combination) – routinely prescribed a few years ago – have been withdrawn as prophylactics because of severe side-effects, even death. Fansidar is sometimes used for treatment of malaria.

One hundred years ago, Captain Ronald Ross, a British military medic stationed in India, established that it was female anopheles mosquitoes that were spreading the malarial parasite as they feed on human blood. It was a monumental discovery that promised the near extinction of the disease, through insecticide programmes and prophylactic drugs such as quinine and later chloroquine, by the mid-1950s. By 1960 the World Health Organization was confident that malaria could be all but abolished, with about 4 million cases worldwide by 1980.

It didn't work out that way. Malaria is on the march again. The 700 scientists who met in Hyderbad, India, in August 1997 to mark the centenary of Ross's discovery, had little cause to celebrate. According to the latest WHO estimates, malaria kills up to 3 million people worldwide and attacks more than 200 million every year. In the next three years, WHO predicts a worldwide increase of 16 per cent new cases. That means that by 2000 there will be another 80 million cases.

Air travel means that around 20 million Western travelers are at risk every year. Even the United Kingdom now records about 2,000 cases a year from people who have been overseas, with up to 12 deaths. Almost one in every 100 visitors to sub-Saharan Africa gets malaria. An effective vaccine is at least 10 years away. But they were saying that 10 years ago.

High-risk parts of the world include sub-Saharan Africa, where resistance is also widespread; most of the Indian sub-continent; and large parts of South America, Cambodia and the Philippines.

Global warming adds a new hazard: the disease never quite left southern Europe, and it could be back in northern Europe in a decade.

Once it was eradicated in Azerbaijan: now cases have been reported across two-thirds of the country and in many parts of the former Soviet Union.

There are four types of plasmodium – the malarial parasite: *Plasmodium vivax*, P. *ovale*, P. *malariae* and P. *falciparum*. None of them is any fun. But falciparum is the deadliest, the one you are most likely to catch, especially in Africa where it accounts for 90 per cent of deaths (6 million Europeans visit Africa each year), and the one most resistant to drugs. One per cent of falciparum victims die, according to WHO.

Infected mosquitoes spread malaria as they feed on human blood. The parasites invade the liver and multiply before spilling into the bloodstream to attack red blood cells, where they multiply even more. When there is no more room, the blood cells rupture and the plasmodia burst out and invade more red blood cells. Infected blood cells become sticky and block blood vessels in vital organs. When the brain is infected – as in cerebral malaria – this can lead to coma and convulsions.

Dr Peter Trigg, a physician at the WHO malaria unit in Geneva, says: 'In virtually every country that has falciparum malaria there is some degree of resistance to chloroquine. But that doesn't mean that it is completely ineffective; it still has a role to play both in prophylaxis and treatment. We still recommend taking chloroquine plus proguanil (Paludrine) in India, Sri Lanka, Pakistan, parts of Bangladesh, parts of Afghanistan, some parts of Iran, also east of the Solomon Islands in the Pacific, Thailand, Malaysia and Indonesia. Of course, most tourist areas and major cities are not at risk.

'Mefloquine is the recommended drug in areas with high chloroquine resistance and high risk of infection – many countries in Africa, the Indo-China peninsula, Papua New Guinea and the Amazon basin. Certain areas, like the borders between Thailand, Burma and Cambodia, where there's a high degree of mefloquine resistance, we recommend doxycycline, a tetracycline antibiotic with anti-malarial action.'

Doxycycline needs to be taken with care. Swallow it well, or it may cause a nasty chemical burn if it sticks in the throat; it can cause vaginal thrush; a photosynthetic rash in sunlight; and can stain the teeth in children. It is not recommended for pregnant women.

'South-East Asia – Vietnam, Burma, northern Thailand – seems to be the area where resistance to drugs like mefloquine first appear,' Dawood says. 'Mefloquine is first choice for East and West Africa, parts of central India. Chloroquine alone is useful for Central America; chloroquine plus proguanil is useful for most parts of South America and parts of India and Sri Lanka, not all. Mefloquine is necessary for the Amazon region, parts of India and all of Africa.

'The latest drug is Malarone (marketed by Glaxo), a combination of proguanil and atovaquone. It is effective as a prophylactic and treatment for all types of malaria and seems to have few side-effects. The mefloquine issue will disappear as mefloquine resistance spreads and new options like Malarone become available.'

Dawood especially recommends Malarone for short trips because you don't need to take it more than 24 hours in advance to get protection; and you can stop taking it seven days after you get back.

The best defence against malaria, of course, is not to get bitten. Avoid being a soft target. If you are outdoors use an insect repellent containing at least 20 per cent of DEET (diethyl-toluamide) on exposed skin at all times – every four hours if you're sweating or running around. DEET comes in sprays, sticks, gels, cream and liquid. It can be impregnated into cotton clothing and cotton wrist and ankle bands. DEET will make mosquitoes fly away to bite anybody close by who is not protected. It's also a good idea to spray or soak clothing with permethrin insecticide. Permethrin kills mosquitoes on contact.

'The pregnant females need a blood meal to mature their eggs, so they have quite a powerful life-drive to bite you,' says Dr Peter Barrett at MASTA, a malaria advisory service in London. 'But they only bite between dusk and dawn; no daytime biting at all.

'DEET has been the gold-standard repellent since 1957: it works well; but there are problems. It's an extremely powerful solvent, so spill it on your camera or laptop and it can melt them. It is also quite toxic and causes a fairly high number of skin reactions from mild to quite unpleasant; so it's not a good idea with young kids. A new insect repellent has been developed from lemon eucalyptus oil that is just as effective as DEET but is much less toxic, with no solvent properties. Citronella oil is not nearly as effective as DEET or lemon eucalyptus oil.'

Barrett advises keeping your room free of mosquitoes at night by using a knock-down fly-spray or plugging an insecticide vaporizer into the power point. 'They work well as long as the room is not too draughty,' Barrett says. 'Mosquitoes are incredible at finding gaps or holes anywhere. So impregnate bed nets with an insecticide like permethrin. Sonic "buzzers" are useless.'

'The bottom line is to be aware of the risk and seek personal advice on a trip-by-trip basis,' Dawood says. 'It's the risk-benefit equation. There's a great deal of public information available. But there comes a point where the individual has to go and see someone to get the pills. This is the time for a frank discussion. You need to sit down with somebody and get some kind of risk assessment based on where you're going, what you're going to do when you get there, your own feelings and medical history.

'You may want to take a bit of a risk so as not to put up with even minor side-effects, which can ruin a business trip or a holiday. A lot of it is down to the individual. Somebody needs to put the evidence to the traveler in a reasonably balanced way. And the traveler needs to ask, "Doctor, what would you do?"'

For advice on malaria, contact:

Fleet Street Travel Clinic
London
Tel: (44 171) 353 5678

Malaria Reference Laboratory
Tel: (44 891) 600350

Malaria Unit
World Health Organisation
1211 Geneva 27
Switzerland
Tel: (41 22) 791 2111

Medical Advisory Services for travelers Abroad (MASTA)
based at London School of Hygiene and Tropical Medicine
Tel: (44 171) 631 4408
Faxback health briefing on premium line (0891 224 100) within United Kingdom only.
E-mail: www.masta.org/staying/index.html

The WHO publishes International Travel and Health (the *Yellow Book*).

United States Centers for Disease Control (CDC)
Tel: (1 404) 639 3311
or (404) 332 4565 for a fax briefing
Web site: www.cdc.gov/travel/blusheet.htm

Dos and don'ts

 Do avoid mosquitoes. If you're outdoors, wear long-sleeved shirts, preferably light-coloured, and use a repellent containing

DEET. Remember malaria mosquitoes bite mostly at dusk and through the night. Avoid perfume. Outside, sleep under an impregnated mosquito net. Inside, sleep with close-fitting window screens, or use an impregnated mosquito net. Spray rooms with knockdown insect repellent before going to bed.

Do seek expert medical advice on the best anti-malarial medication for the region you are visiting. Take the tablets for at least a month after you return.

Do whenever possible test anti-malarial drugs for side-effects in good time before your trip. Better to be sick at home than on the road.

Do take an emergency supply of drugs for treatment of a malarial attack. This is important for high-risk areas such as East Africa and the Thailand-Cambodia border regions.

Do take a self-testing diagnosis kit (like a pregnancy testing kit) which is specific to falciparum malaria. You put a drop of blood on a filter paper along with a drop of reagent and if you get a blue line you've got malaria.

Don't neglect flu-like symptoms after returning from a malaria region. These may include fever and chills, headaches, sore joints, diarrhoea, or just general malaise. See a doctor within 12 hours.

Don't pack your insect repellent in a checked suitcase. Carry a can or stick with you at all times. There's always a risk of mosquitoes on your plane and at the airport.

The ins and outs of travel in Eastern Europe

The names are daunting enough to start with – spin-off states from the former Soviet Union (the Russian Federation plus Belarus; Ukraine; Moldova; Georgia; Armenia; Azerbaijan; Turkmenistan; Kazakhstan; Uzbekistan; Tajikistan; Kyrgyzstan; plus Former Yugoslavia; proudly rejuvenescent countries like Poland; Bulgaria; Albania; the Czech and Slovak Republics; Rumania; and the Baltic States – Estonia; Latvia; Lithuania. All freed from communism but faced with their own problems and opportunities and growing in different ways and at a different economic pace.

'The area is so different within itself,' says Paul Colston, editor of *New Markets Monthly* in London, 'that a lot of people make the mistake of thinking of the former Soviet Union as being at the same level of development. The Baltic States, for example, have made the transition to a market economy very quickly, but if you go into the central Asian republics, it's almost like stepping back a century. You might take a tip from the Turks in the way to do business there: they're the most successful in the area with language overlaps. Brits and Germans are a long way behind.'

Traveling wisely and well in and around the region requires at the same time a keen sense of survival, an opportunistic eye, and, heaven knows, a capacity to appreciate, and enjoy. The trick for business travelers is to make the cultural and logistical leap. Things ain't what they are in the West.

'If you go in with a mentality that these people belong behind the Iron Curtain, you won't get very far. You've got to accept that you're

153

going into a different world – don't expect everything to be Western-ized,' says Colin Reeve, general manager, Central and Eastern Europe for American Express. 'The value equation is different in all these countries. There's a reason why a hotel in Moscow, for instance, costs you $250 when you can get one for $110. Westernized hotels set the standard. If you want clean, normal facilities, like a bath and phone, you're going to pay the price. You can get a hotel for $100 but you'll have unwelcome visitors in your room. The message is: don't try to cut corners and don't think you're going to save money. You won't.'

'It's no use being sniffy about the price of top-quality rooms in Almaty or Uzbekistan. There are plenty of Russians with 10 times as much cash,' Colston says. 'I remember five years ago, if you went into one of the hard-currency bars in Moscow it was 90 per cent foreign businessmen; today, it's the other way round – £6 for a glass of beer in what you would call an ordinary pub. But there are Russians who can afford this.'

Reeve says: 'These people really do want to serve you; but you have to be a lot more tolerant and a lot more patient. They are trying to learn, and it doesn't help if foreigners snap at them. They don't understand what they've done wrong: you have to have a higher level of patience – for lack of service, lack of understanding and lack of communication.

'And things go wrong. They don't see a need to explain that. If a plane's delayed for five hours, they don't get upset; it's no big deal.

'Everyone used to work for the state with a set of procedures and many still do. But if you take these people and privatize them, they will come up with amazing, creative solutions. In order to survive under the communist system they had to know how to get around the rules.'

Mary McDonagh, general manager of Worldmark, a specialist travel agency for Eastern Europe and the CIS, in London, says: 'Most times Russians will pick you up at the airport, and take you for dinner; Poles and Czechs are much the same – they're lovely people. Prague has changed beyond belief; it's not like being in Eastern Europe at all. I think Moscow will end up the same way in a couple of years.'

There is a social dichotomy in Boris Yeltsin's sub-utopia between those that have done well in the market economy, whether legitimate or mafia, and what you might call the dispossessed – retired people or black economy and disgruntled aparatchiks sometimes aggressively nostalgic for the *ancien régime*.

'Yes, some of these people maintain a public appearance of being pissed off, the doctors or teachers who moan that their state pay or pension has not kept up with inflation,' Colston says. 'But in reality, they're either moonlighting or daylighting. There is a middle class that isn't recognized, or doesn't recognize itself. The very fact that they sell more BMWs in Moscow than in Bonn shows that the very top elite is no longer just a small percentage: even in the middle ground, wealth is there, but not declared. Former communist bosses have become mafia chieftains.'

Best bet for traveling to the region is on a familiar Western airline. Lufthansa flies to 23 destinations in Eastern Europe, from Almaty to Zagreb; SAS offers 200 flights a week to the Baltic States; KLM flies from Amsterdam to Almaty, the Kazakstan capital; Austrian Airlines offers more than 100 flights per week to Central and Eastern Europe and Central Asia.

But many former communist bloc airlines now conform to Western standards. Malev Hungarian Airlines (which claims to have the youngest fleet in Europe) and Riair Riga Airlines (Riga–London; Moscow, Paris); Estonian Air and Ukraine International Airlines and Lot Polish Airlines have new Boeing fleets; Uzbekistan Airways operates Airbus 300s between Tashkent and London.

Charlie Hempstead, regional director, former Soviet Union, for OAG, part of the Reed Travel Group, in London says: 'The only time there's genuine concern rather than knee-jerk concern about safety is on domestic Russian services – international services between former Soviet states (such as Kazakhstan or Azerbaijan) by and large are not an issue; airlines flying between those republics are also flying somewhere in the real world. They've got maintenance arrangements with Western flag carriers. Russian carriers are turning towards Western manufacturers, which is bad news for Tupolev and Ilyushin – although there's nothing wrong mechanically with these manufacturers; the problem is how to get spare parts if something falls off.

'What we're seeing now in the former Soviet Union is around 400 local airlines (almost every city has its own airline sometimes with only one aircraft) which have split off from the old monolithic Aeroflot and still operate under Aeroflot codes.

'I don't think Aeroflot is unsafe – it has many Western alliance partners and has maintenance arrangements with Lufthansa – although service may not be up to Western standards. My advice is to use Aeroflot International or Transaero – a new independent Russian airline with modern equipment – whenever possible. The problem is that some ex-Soviet bloc airlines that have a bad reputation are punishing the rest. Aeroflot has swish lounges at Heathrow and Sheremetyevo. And their catering is done by Marriott.

'But be wary of carriers operating under Aeroflot (SU) codes within Russia. It is unlikely to be Aeroflot itself. The concern is in the back of beyond, in Siberia for example, where the problem is simply access to spare parts.'

Malcolm Timming at IMS Travel, a wholesale consolidator in London, says: 'Some companies, including The European Bank for Reconstruction and Development, won't allow their executives to fly on Aeroflot because of its bad reputation. But they can fly Air Moldova or Baikal Airlines, for instance, because they're no longer part of Aeroflot. But some of these newly independent states don't have the money, the resources to support an airline properly. On the other hand, Vnukovo Airlines, the largest Russian domestic airline based in Moscow, was the first Aeroflot division to operate the Tupolev TU154 jet on domestic routes. They have an unblemished safety record.'

Here are some tips for a successful trip:

 Choose a business travel agency with experience of the region and with its own local people or associates on the ground.

 Pre-book and pre-pay as much as you can before you leave – airline tickets, hotels, excursions and visits to the ballet or opera – to avoid hassle or black-market prices. And try not to change plans on the road.

 Arrange to be met at the airport – especially the first time – by a travel agency representative or local business associate who can steer you through the airport procedures. This should be a firm rule for women business travelers – who are still a rare sight in Eastern Europe.

 Check visa requirements at least one month before you need to travel. Your travel agent should be able to do this for you. Consider getting a duplicate passport so that you are able to travel while your visas are being processed. You will need visas for all countries in the former Soviet Union. In some cases you may need written support from the company you intend to visit. This in turn needs to be stamped by the Ministry of Foreign Affairs. A Russian multiple entry visa is valid for one year and enables you to make trips of up to two days in certain neighbouring republics without the need for a local visa. Visas are subject to actual regulations and political events. If your country has just expelled half-a-dozen diplomats for spying, you may find it hard to get your visa next week.

Check health warnings for the areas you are to visit. Russia itself tends to require little health attention but some of the remote states have recently suffered from bouts of diphtheria, typhoid and hepatitis.

 Face it: you'll pay top dollar. Don't try to save money or beat the system. 'Don't cut corners, you'll pay for them.' Safety and reliability are your prime concern.

 Check the airlines you'll be using – especially traveling within Russia. Look for carriers which operate Western equipment. Avoid airlines flying under Aeroflot (SU) flight codes – they may not be reliable or serviced to Western standards. (OAG flight guides have details.) Insiders recommend Aeroflot International (which serves five domestic routes between Moscow Sheremetyevo and St Petersburg; Novosibirsk; Yakutsk; Neryungri; and Khabarovsk in Siberia). Transaero Airlines (exclusively on Boeing equipment) has excellent safety and service standards on domestic and international flights – flying direct between Moscow and St Petersburg, and Frankfurt, Berlin and London (on a code-share with Riga Airlines, which is OK).

 On arrival ignore the airport taxi touts and go to the official taxi kiosk. 'They'll rip you off, but they probably won't rob you once you're in the car,' Hempstead says. The 35–40-minute journey from Sheremetyevo Airport to central Moscow should cost $40–50. (Budapest has good coach services into the city costing 600 florins compared to 2,000 florins for a taxi.) Never hail a taxi in the street – it could be dangerous, especially if you don't speak the language. Ask your hotel (or restaurant) to book a taxi or a chauffeur-driven car for the day. Rates in Russia and the CIS tend to be reasonable. Don't even think about renting a car.

 Confirm your onward reservations and get to the airport in good time. Airlines often close flights early no matter how many passengers have turned up. Planes sometimes take off with empty seats leaving booked passengers stranded on the ground.

 Count on a two-and-a-half-hour minimum connecting time between Moscow Sheremtyevo 2 – the international terminal – and Sheremtyevo 1 for domestic flights (they share the same runway but you have to drive half an hour on the public highway to get from one to the other). Avoid transfers between (and flights from) Moscow's other three airports (Domodedovo; Vnukovo and Bykovo) which may require a connecting time of six hours and a

$100 taxi fare. Some domestic routes are only served by these airports: but stay away if you can.

 Leave plenty of time in your schedule for things to go wrong – delays or cancellations (travelers' tales abound of flights simply abandoned for 24 hours, leaving passengers stranded at far-flung airports without explanation or help); confirm bookings and turn up at the airport with time to spare.

 Take plenty of small-denomination dollar bills. These should be clean, unmarked and have been produced after 1990. Travelers cheques can be hard to cash. Take a leading credit or charge card. Change money only when you need to and never on the black market. Phone cards are useful.

 Be streetwise. Dress down when possible; avoid conspicuous signs of wealth (which can invite hostility) and don't wander around or stray off the beaten track. Look as though you know where you're heading even if you're not too sure!

 Get a free copy of the Worldmark *Business Travel Guide – Eastern Europe and the* CIS, which gives basic travel tips to the Russian Federation and the 14 CIS countries plus 11 Eastern European states from Albania to Slovenia.

Worldmark Travel
Tel: (44) 171 799 2307
Fax: 171 976 7891

Worldmark Travel is a joint venture between Hogg Robinson Business Travel International in the United Kingdom and BTI Polska in Poland and Epic Travel in Russia.

New Markets Monthly (tel: 44 1306 877 111; fax: 1306 889 191) is a great source of business and travel opportunities in the former Soviet Union, Eastern and Central Europe.

Cover yourself with insurance

There are two fundamental rules when it comes to travel insurance: make sure it covers all that you need, and make sure that it is there when you need it.

The first depends on where you're going (traveling around your own region or farther afield), how important your trip is (will your business suffer if you miss meetings due to flight delays or missed connections, or if you become sick or have an accident?), what you may be carrying (business samples, documents, laptop, video equipment), and what you want to do (corporate in-fighting, bungee jumping, off-piste skiing or scuba diving).

The second means choosing a policy that delivers up-front with on-the-spot emergency assistance, financial and practical help. This should pre-pay or guarantee the full cost of medical expenses and arrange for repatriation, if necessary, by air ambulance. Never buy insurance that only reimburses you when you get home – you may not get home if you are refused treatment or not allowed to leave until bills have been settled. The same applies to personal liability and legal expenses.

It sounds obvious but it needs saying: read the small print on your policy. According to a recent American Express survey, only 32 per cent of UK travelers had read the small print of their policy documents. Not only may you find that you don't have the level of cover you thought, but that a claim may be invalid because you failed to follow the insurer's instructions.

The main point of travel insurance is protection against catastrophe. The art of buying it is deciding what catastrophe means in your case, and how much risk you are prepared to take. And always buy by benefit, not by cost.

The best buy for business travelers is a comprehensive annual policy that covers you for any number of trips – either within your normal travel patterns, say Europe or North America, or worldwide. (You can always take out additional cover on a per-trip basis if you go elsewhere.) But check how long you can stay away on any one trip – typically, from 31 to 91 days.

A comprehensive policy (costing from $150 to $300 a year) will offer a raft of benefits. These should include: medical cover (plus emergency repatriation and costs of traveling home for the walking wounded); hospital cash benefit; emergency cash; personal accident; personal liability; travel delays, cancellation and curtailment; loss of luggage, personal effects and money; loss or damage of business goods; and legal advice and expenses. Plus the cost of having a business partner or colleague flying out to replace you – for a critical meeting or an exhibition or conference.

Some policies allow for the cost of an emergency return home if you are burgled or flooded or a close relative is taken ill. More exotic benefits may include reinstatement of frequent-flier miles; loss of ski equipment or ski pass; even poor snow conditions (cost of traveling to another local resort, or a cash payment).

You may not need all of these benefits, but that doesn't mean you shouldn't have them – and they may come in useful. (You're unlikely to get a better deal by buying a tailor-made policy from an insurance broker.) But you may want to take out additional insurance to match your specific needs.

Do not travel without at least $2 million of cover for medical expenses – take $5 million for peace of mind. In North America, open-heart surgery with all the trimmings won't leave much change. Personal accident insurance for death, injury or disablement is a personal judgement: $80,000 is the top end of most policies. This is woefully inadequate if you are not already covered by a personal or company life policy. If not, take out additional insurance.

Look for personal liability cover of at least $3 million for legal expenses or damages for accidental injury to another person or damage to their property. This will not include liability for cars, motorcycles, watercraft or aircraft, where insurance is part of the rental cost. So consider taking out separate 'top-up' insurance, especially in the United States.

Ian Irvine at insurance brokers Campbell Irvine in London says: 'The business traveler needs the same type of comprehensive package policy as the leisure traveler. Except that under any travel policy there is a limited amount of personal baggage or belongings cover and a limit for any one article. So if they're traveling with samples or a $5,000 laptop, they need separate insurance – not under their travel policy. You're looking at a premium of 2 per cent of the value.

'Another important aspect – which we do include in our policies – is to make sure that if a person goes out on a particular contract and is taken ill, the insurer will pay for all the expenses of having someone sent out to replace them. Yes, you'll say it's perfectly obvious, but it isn't obvious to people who don't read their policies and, of course, 99 per cent of people never read their policies because they are so complicated.'

Most major credit card companies offer comprehensive business travel insurance. American Express, for example, has a Premier World-wide policy (costing around $280 a year) that covers the cost of a business colleague to replace you if you are sick or injured during a trip, plus around $60,000 for legal expenses in the event of death, illness or injury. It also covers you for up to $50,000 collision damage waiver when you rent a car in the United States.

Whatever the colour of your plastic, don't rely on automatic card insurance. It's unlikely to cover such crucial things as medical expenses and personal liability. 'You can divide credit card travel insurance into two clear categories,' Irvine says. 'Gold and platinum cards that offer, sometimes free of charge, a comprehensive travel insurance (although you do need to check the cover). And ordinary cards whose misleading literature leads people to think that they have travel insurance when they are only covered for personal accident while traveling on modes of transport for which they have paid with their card. This is the big con that the card companies use. You need to be fully insured all the time.'

Travelers accustomed to having unlimited third-party liability insurance may be driving into a legal minefield when they rent a car in the United States or Canada. You may only be covered for a negligible amount. Some states have limits as low as $10,000 for bodily injury and $5,000 for property damage. You only have to be involved in an accident with, say, multiple damage and injuries to risk bankrupting legislation.

Make sure you buy 'top-up' liability insurance. This will cost around $10 a day for $1 million coverage. Major car rental firms will offer this. Don't treat it as another come-on.

Start by assessing your needs and shop for a travel policy that best matches them. Check what cover you already have. Most people have enough life insurance, and corporate travelers are covered for life and personal accident through company plans. Then buy extra cover on a per-trip or annual basis. But before you buy, get the insurer to take you through 'What if?' scenarios. Make sure you take a copy of the policy with you and that you have a 24-hour hotline number.

PART 2

Traveling

Getting to the plane on time

Getting to or from the airport can be the most stressful part of travel. It's not so much the time it takes, it's the time you must allow. Some airports are easy: Geneva and Singapore are a short cab ride. Hong Kong, Amsterdam, Paris, Brussels and Geneva have reliable train services, Stockholm, you take the bus, JFK and Newark, you take a cab; some airports, like Jakarta or Lagos, you may need a little help from your friends. But usually there's not much choice. Few cities have more than two or three airports.

London has five – Heathrow, 15 miles (24 kilometres) west of London, which has the dubious distinction of being 'the world's busiest airport'; Gatwick, 28 miles to the south; Stansted, 30 miles north-east; Luton, 32 miles north-west; and London City, 6 miles from the City. Which airport you choose can depend on which part of London you are visiting.

A reliable way to get to Gatwick, Stansted and Luton is by train – 35 to 40 minutes from Victoria, Liverpool Street and King's Cross. London City, take a taxi.

Traveling to Heathrow, a metered black cab can cost £40 to £60 ($65 to $97) and take an hour or more depending on traffic. A 'minicab' or chauffeur service is your best bet. Airport Transfers (0181 691 3400) charges a flat rate of £22 to or from central London. Heathrow has an Underground link (an hour from Piccadilly) costing £3.50, convenient if you're headed somewhere along the line and an obvious choice for most travelers. But delays, breakdowns and endemic overcrowding have made it the subway from hell.

A cautionary tale. A post-prandial rush from Covent Garden in central London to Heathrow. A slow line at the ticket counter and no change for the self-service machines. A friend helps me out with a 'Zone 1' ticket to get me through the gate and on to the train. Pay the difference (about £2.20) at the other end you would think.

Not so. At Heathrow, I was fined £10 for not having 'a valid ticket for the entire journey'– with the implication that I was intent on cheating London Underground. The same fate awaits any hapless traveler who strays across one of the six fare zones without paying the correct fare. Buy the wrong ticket or change your mind on the way by getting out at Victoria instead of King's Cross, and you'll be fined £10.

What I should have done was get off the train at the point at which my ticket became invalid, bought a new one and boarded a later train. Unlike the Paris Métro, for instance, a fast, efficient, subsidized service, where a ticket costs the same no matter how far you travel, London Underground is one of the world's most expensive public transport systems, with the cheapest single ticket costing £1.30 – soon to be increased. The ageing transit system suffers from decades of underfunding and neglect. Trains are overcrowded and delays, breakdowns and fires are common. John Kenneth Galbraith was right when he talked about public squalor and private affluence.

One-day Travelcards (priced according to how many zones you need to cross) are the cheapest way of getting around. But you will need to buy a 'Ticket Extension' when traveling to other zones or connecting from a main-line station. Or else you'll be hit with a £10 fine.

London Underground has an information number 0171 222 1234. Customer Service is 0171 918 4219... and good luck. Or you might try Amnesty International.

A better way to go between Heathrow and central London is the BAA Heathrow Express. The 100-mile-an-hour trains run every 15 minutes and take 15 minutes between Paddington and Heathrow Central Station – 30 metres below the airport (serving terminals 1, 2 and 3) and on to a separate station at terminal 4. The one-way fare is £10 (first class is £20, about half the cost of a cab). Touch-screen ticket machines take seven currencies. You can also buy your ticket on the train.

The trains have airline-style seating and service with BBC news on TV and plenty of luggage space, and you can infuriate your neighbours with your mobile throughout the ride, including the tunnel section.

Airline passengers can check in at Paddington up to two hours before departure (one hour if you only have hand baggage). The 27 check-in desks are served by American Airlines, Air Lanka, Air Liberté, Air New Zealand, British Airways, British Midland, Canadian Airlines, Finnair, LOT, Lufthansa, Qantas, SAS, Swissair, Thai International, United Airlines and Varig Brasil.

Being able to drop off your suitcase in the early morning, choose your seat and get your boarding card saves a lot of hassle if you have meetings in London during the day. Finish your business and head straight out to the airport.

Arriving at Paddington, you have three options: plunge into the Underground, take Hotel Express, a bus service that runs every 15 minutes between Paddington and eight West End hotels (fare £2), or find a taxi.

Heathrow Express has started a novel taxi-share scheme during peak hours. If the normal taxi line gets too long, two official 'taxi marshals' – cab drivers themselves – will ask for people willing to share, who are then matched with someone going in the same direction. A flat rate includes tip, and you'll generally pay less than you would for a taxi on your own. (The Heathrow Express Web site is at www.heathrowexpress.com)

The most civilized way to get to or from Heathrow (or Gatwick) is a free limo transfer that some airlines, including Air New Zealand, All Nippon Airways, Cathay Pacific, Continental, Emirates, Northwest, Royal Brunei and Virgin Atlantic, offer first- and business-class passengers – typically within a 30- to 50-mile radius of the airport.

Intrepid travelers in Upper Class (business class) with Virgin Atlantic can opt for the limo-bike instead of a limo.

'When you book a ticket, we ask how you want to get to the airport. We take about 100 passengers a week by Limobike – 40 per cent women – it's not a male thing; it's partly about speed, partly about exhilaration,' says Paul Moore, a spokesman for Virgin Atlantic. 'Central London to Heathrow at off-peak times takes 30 to 35 minutes. Even in gridlock traffic it'll probably take you 40 to 45 minutes at worst – without going hell-for-leather, you can safely pick your way through even traffic. Richard [Branson] is a massive fan. We picked him up from a traffic jam on the M25. He was sitting in a car, called up for a bike and he was at the airport in 30 minutes.'

The Limo-bike (a Honda ST1100 Pan European, since you asked) can carry a full-size suitcase widthways behind the pillion – upon which you can lean back reassuringly – and carry-on baggage in side-panniers. You get thermal overclothes – padded jacket, gloves, waterproof trousers if it's raining – and helmet, and an apron is available for women wearing skirts. (Riding side-saddle, it seems, is not an option.) The helmet has a microphone and headphones so you can tell the driver to slow down fah crissake and make and receive mobile phone calls.

TaxyBike (0171-387 5858) can whiz you to Heathrow in 35 to 40 minutes or to London City Airport in 15 to 20 minutes for a flat rate of £39.50 and £17.35, respectively. From an address in the City you can get to Waterloo (for Eurostar) in 10 minutes, cost £10. A bike should arrive to pick you up within 20 minutes of your call.

'The trickiest part of our business is convincing people that it's safe,' says Julian Baker at TaxyBike. 'It also depends on the client; some people don't want to rush, just get through the traffic. Ladies love it – it does grab attention. We have a lot of City and showbiz people, fashion models, in a hurry for Heathrow, or getting across London. There's plenty of room for carry-on luggage – a briefcase and a suit carrier – but a large suitcase defeats the purpose because you can't weave through the traffic.'

Taming the hostile airport

Six billion passengers worldwide by 2002? Yes, according to the pundits. Travelers suffering the misery of air travel – packed planes, congested airports, gridlock getting to the airport, unaccountable delays – may feel that Armageddon has arrived. Where on earth are all these people going? How can they afford it? And, more to the point, why do they all seem to be traveling with me?

I have a recurring nightmare of waiting behind two dozen people in the check-in line at a strange airport. Some of them have so much baggage that they seem to be moving house. My plane is leaving in 20 minutes and oddly the line is getting longer as I struggle to move forward. And now the woman at the desk has picked up the phone and the line is not moving at all.

A variation of this is arriving at JFK with two planeloads ahead of you for the refugee shuffle at Immigration. Or waiting in limbo at a distant departure gate for your delayed flight while the airline is drip-feeding you disingenuous information on how long you'll be stuck there and why. Goodbye budget meeting. You may not even be able to phone to tell them you won't make it. This is the kind of nightmare where you wake up and it is really happening. Welcome to life in the slow lane.

Of course, everyone blames everyone else for the terminal misery. Airlines blame airport authorities who blame air traffic congestion along with civil aviation policy and inflexible immigration and customs (not to mention security), not always symbiotic cohabitants in the wide world of the megahub.

Airlines would like us to buy their myth that where service is important is at 30,000 feet over the Atlantic rather than level three in the main concourse. But reality is on the ground. Frequent travelers are asking, 'What are you doing to mitigate the misery?'

'Whenever possible, I try to take a regional flight from small airports,' says Anthony Sampson, author of *Empires of the Skies*. 'Airport strain is what's exhausting. Sir William Hildred, the first head of IATA, said that in the early prewar days, the stress of flying was in the flying itself, the airports were wonderfully comfortable. Nowadays, it's the other way round. I endorse that completely.'

Most flights these days in whatever class you fly are reasonably enjoyable. Would that this were true for quality of life on the ground. Congested terminals, air traffic delays and the need to check in two hours early for security controls have made airports a nightmare. Many airports seem to be more concerned with duty-free areas and schlock boutiques that pay high rents than with providing public amenities such as telecom centres, day beds, showers and more civilized eating places.

Savvy travelers often choose an airport first and an airline second. One choice often determines the other. So choose your megahub – or international gateway – carefully; and decide where you want to change planes: at the start or the end of your journey.

Ways to beat the crowd

 Travel light: you're always at a disadvantage if you have to check in luggage. Look for a check-in desk for passengers with 'hand-baggage only'. If not, go to the first-class or airline 'club' desk, look at your watch anxiously, and say with a disarming smile that: 'I've only got hand luggage'.

 Try to check in and get your boarding card before you get to the airport. Some airlines have check-in desks at hotels or railway stations. Some airlines allow telephone check-in. You may be able to check in when you drop your car off at an airline-affiliated car rental office. Virgin Atlantic allows business-class passengers arriving at Heathrow or Gatwick in the complimentary limousine to check in with the driver and go straight to the airport lounge.

 You may qualify for the Fast Track lane through immigration and security at certain airports. (This is usually reserved for first- and business-class travelers or 'elite' members of the frequent-flier programme. But it's always worth asking.)

You get a special sticker at check-in that allows you access to a completely separate security and passport-control channel, along with 'dedicated' banking windows and duty-free shopping. Swissair is testing a Fast Track Card at Zurich Airport for passengers with only hand luggage 'that may eventually make both conventional check-in and the boarding pass a thing of the past'. The card contains a chip with your 'personal identification number' which automatically identifies you and checks you in when you pass through the 'passport control station'.

 One of the best ideas for smoothing out airport hassles is INSpass adopted by the US Immigration and Naturalization Service at airports such as JFK and Newark. The system uses a combination of a smart ID card and identification of your palm print.

Instead of waiting in line with the hoi polloi you go to a special channel, insert an INSpass card in a special reader and stick your hand on a hand-geometry scanner. You can then proceed straight to Customs.

The INSpass programme is open to US citizens plus nationals of 24 countries who travel frequently on business to the United States. The next step will be pre-clearance for 'INSiders' before boarding at certain airports. Marvellous what a simple handshake can achieve.

A few dollars more

The pain and paradox of travel are that value often has nothing to do with how much you pay. With car rentals, for example, there is usually less price differential between the cheapest and medium groups than between the medium and the most expensive. So you often get better value by trading up. At some airports a taxi direct to your hotel is far better than toting your bags to the airport bus and then looking for a taxi to take you the last 20 blocks. It may not cost much more – except of course at remote airports like Dallas, Narita and Gatwick.

Lounging around

Having the run of an airport lounge is one of the prime perks of flying first or business class or enjoying 'elite' status in the airline's frequent-flier programme. It takes some of the pain from flight delays, cancellations and long connecting times. You can relax with a drink or catch up with work, away from the madding crowd, safe in the knowledge that you will be just a few yards from the gate when your flight is finally called.

But some lounges are more equal than others. British Airways has an arcane hierarchy of lounges at Heathrow – Concorde, first class, executive club, business class (sometimes more of a zoo than the main concourse). Not all airlines have business-class lounges at all airports.

Returning from Berlin to Nice the other day with Lufthansa, my business-class ticket did not qualify for the Senator Club – the only Lufthansa lounge available at Tegel Airport. So during my connection in Frankfurt (nearly four hours with delays) I was looking forward to a Bloody Mary. Sorry, no vodka. Only soft drinks, wine and beer. The Senator Club next door had the full treatment for sure. Never mind: I was grateful for a port in a storm.

But with many business travelers downgrading to the back cabin (economy class accounts for 74 per cent of corporate air travel spend, according to American Express), more and more travelers are being denied access to the sanctum sanctorum.

'Travelers are increasingly being denied access to lounges, not only because of trading down to economy but because many corporations are negotiating special net fares with airlines,' says Don Osvog, managing director of Diners Club in the United Kingdom. 'These low fares often exclude lounge access even if they are for business class in the air.'

Diners Club International offers card holders (plus a guest) free use of 84 airport lounges around the world. They include four new lounges at Moscow Sheremetievo Airport (three in terminal 1 and one in terminal 2), plus others at Prague Ruzyne Airport, Rome Leonardo da Vinci Airport and Rio de Janeiro's Avenida Pricesa Isabel. In Britain, cardholders have the use of three lounges at London Heathrow, two at Manchester and one each at London Gatwick, London Stansted, Birmingham, Edinburgh and Glasgow. All lounges offer free snacks and beverages. Some have a business centre; others allow free local calls and some provide bar facilities.

The International Airline Passengers Association (IAPA) has a lounge programme called Priority Pass that allows you access to 200 airport lounges around the world, whatever your choice of airline or class of travel, offering free beverages and snacks, newspapers and magazines, business services and a quiet area to work, telephone and fax, with Internet access and meeting facilities. 'Standard' membership costs $99 a year plus $21 per visit; 'Inclusive' membership costs $199 a year with unlimited free entry to any participating lounge. Either plan allows you to bring a guest for $21 a visit. (IAPA members get a 25 per cent discount.)

Priority Pass
Tel: (44 181) 680 1338
Fax: (44 181) 688 6191
E-mail: info@prioritypass.co.uk

WEXAS International, an independent traveler's club based in London, offers members access to 55 airport lounges around the world from £6 to £14 a visit. Three lounges that joined the programme in 1999 are at Hong Kong, Kuala Lumpur and London Luton. Lounges in Oslo and Copenhagen will soon be available.

Wexas International
Tel: (44 171) 589 3315
Fax: (44 171) 581 1357
Web site: www.wexas.com

US airlines are obliged by law to offer club membership to everyone. American's Admiral's Club, Delta's Crown Room Club and United's Red Carpet Club cost around $250 to join with annual dues of $175.

Many lounges are run by airport authorities or ground-handling agents and are sometimes open to all-comers for a fee. So it's always worth asking. 'Subject to space limitations' may depend on dress and demeanour: like getting the nod from the doorman of a fashionable disco.

Such is the case with the new lounge at Luton, which is run by Reed Aviation. It is open to international passengers for £16 per visit and offers a complimentary bar, newspapers and snacks.

'We're working on a scale of charges depending on the length of your visit,' says Larry Nolan at Reed Aviation in Luton. 'Starting at £6 for half an hour.'

Just the ticket when checking in early for a no-frills flight.

'The dress code is smart casual,' Nolan adds. 'We definitely do not want the bucket-and-spade brigade.'

BAA, which operates Heathrow, Gatwick and Stansted airports in London, opened its first lounge at Stansted, 'The Lounge,' in May 1999. It was the first in Satellite 1. The charge is £15, which includes 'unlimited refreshments', armchair seating, office facilities including connection to the Internet and e-mail, newspapers, TV and music centre. Customers can also use the FastTrack security channel through the airport. BAA plans to have lounges at all terminals at Heathrow by the middle of 2000. The first Heathrow lounge in the landside arrival area of Terminal 3 is designed for arriving long-haul passengers. There will be showers, valet facilities (steam and press for suits and shirts, shoe cleaning), hot breakfast and business facilities (www.baa.co.uk).

BCP, an airport car parking service, offers executive lounges at 12 airports around Britain – Aberdeen, Birmingham, Bristol, East Midlands, Edinburgh, Glasgow, Leeds/Bradford, London Gatwick (North and South Terminals), London Heathrow (Terminals 1, 2 and 3), Manchester (Terminals 1 and 2), Newcastle and Stansted. The charge is £16 a visit (£16 at Heathrow). This includes bar service (except champagne). Telephone and fax machines are available at a modest charge (44 1293) 594 505.

Heading for gridlock in the skies

Europe faces terminal gridlock in the skies in the next five years unless the 37 member states of the European Civil Aviation Conference (ECAC) can agree on a radical new strategy – ATM 2000+ – to generate sufficient capacity at airports and in air-traffic control systems to meet the growth.

The challenge is daunting. The 27 members of the Association of European Airlines carried an estimated 177 million passengers on scheduled international flights in 1998 – an increase of 13 million on the previous year. The Association now forecasts growth of up to 9 per cent a year, which year-on-year means that the number of passengers will double about every eight years.

UK airports handled 160 million passengers in 1998, a record. According to the UK Department of Environment, Transport and the Regions, demand for air travel in the United Kingdom will double by 2015 to 310 million passengers.

In 1998, 22.5 per cent of the scheduled departures of planes affiliated with the Association of European Airlines were delayed by more than 15 minutes – a substantial deterioration over 1997. Seventy per cent of delays were attributed to airport or air-traffic control (ATC) congestion, or to planes missing their departure or landing slots.

'We've got to provide sufficient capacity to cope between now and 2015 with something like a 120 per cent increase in traffic – that's aircraft movements, not people,' says Phil Hogge, director, infrastructure Europe at IATA, the International Air Transport Association, in Brussels. 'Aircraft delays increased by 30 per cent between 1997 and 1998 within Europe. Our concern is that with traffic growing at the current rate, the system will soon clog up. We'll be right back to 1987–1988. You remember people camping at Gatwick? This will translate to horrendous delays of several hours, which will not be socially sustainable.

'What we're trying to do with this new strategy is to reinforce the co-ordination between states of the whole air-traffic system, which involves airports as well as airlines, to produce sufficient capacity to prevent delays. It involves integrating systems on the ground – terminals, aprons, runways, taxiing areas – with en route airspace so you get a co-operative network across Europe. Unfortunately, states are not always willing to pool what they regard as their sovereign air space to achieve the most efficient system for European air traffic as a whole. So the strategy could be compromised.'

The new strategy aims to increase capacity by up to 140 per cent by 2015 with existing infrastructures while reducing costs and improving safety. It is the result of 18 months' work between all parties to air transport – IATA and member airlines, airports, traffic-control providers, civil aviation authorities, the military, general aviation and Eurocontrol, a Brussels-based agency that manages air traffic for the 37 states of the civil aviation conference (ECAC).

The strategy depends on restructuring 'highways in the sky' with new satellite navigation systems that will replace the radio beacons on the ground, which makes life easier for air-traffic controllers and increases capacity.

'Think of it as a network of roads converging on a series of roundabouts which are radio beacons,' Hogge says. 'Now with direct navigation you don't need those convergences, you can go directly. Suddenly you find you have more capacity and more efficient routes.'

There are three main reasons for hold-ups: airline delays, through late-arriving passengers or technical glitches; congestion at airport immigration and security points; the bunching of traffic on runways, and more traffic in the air than the system can handle. Planes are also delayed for weather, and all of these problems may have a ripple effect.

When the pilot says, 'We've lost our slot', it means there's been some sort of delay, either caused by the airline or the airport, and he has to renegotiate another departure time, which might be 20 or 40 minutes later, without overloading the system. Then you might lose your arrival slot and be stuck in a holding pattern for half an hour.

Talk to Hans Krakauer, senior vice president and veteran consumer advocate at IAPA, the International Passenger Association, in Lisbon, about capacity and congestion at airports and he becomes irate. 'The congestion problem for planes is one thing,' he says. 'The congestion problem that interests me is the effect on passengers. Everybody talks about techniques and forgets about passengers. Nobody gives a damn.

Talk about capacity should include passengers, not just planes. There's a lot that can be done with present airport capability to increase capacity for handling passengers. The idea of slots has to do with parking a plane; it has no relationship with people. There is very little co-operation between airlines and airports. And what little there is, is in the interests of their efficiency, not the interests of passengers.

'What could be done? Co-ordinating arrivals, for example. You have two wide-bodied aircraft arriving at the same time and you can wait two and half hours at immigration. Airports and airlines not only need to agree on slots but how this fits with passenger handling capability at airports. Nobody looks at that. If things go wrong, everybody blames everybody else. Once airlines have dumped passengers off a plane, they say it's the airport's problem. But airports have no legal covenant with passengers.'

The lowdown on airline upgrades

Few things are more stressful to the frequent flier than waiting at the departure gate for the crucial nod: Shall I have the exquisite joy of an upgrade – from economy to business or business to first – or be sequestrated in the class that's printed on my ticket? Look around as the flight is called. Management styles are clashing: executive egos are on the line.

Airlines have themselves to blame by debasing the class system with a blizzard of promotions and deals, from free upgrades and half price 'companion fares' to 'two-for-one' offers. Social climbers know how to move up a class by redeeming frequent-flier miles or buying a consolidation ticket and saving 50 per cent on whatever it was they were supposed to have paid. Assuming anyone knows by this time.

And the stakes are high. With first class costing around twice the business-class fare, which in turn can be three times as much as the full economy fare, an upgrade to a better class of cabin is worth more than a 50 per cent discount – the maximum you're likely to get on a consolidation ticket. Plus you get the run of an executive lounge. (Competition for the hearts and minds of business travelers has led to all kinds of desperate measures. One might even envisage airlines offering cash bonuses to passengers who volunteer to stay in their original class.)

Airline promotions sometimes blow a fuse. 'A lot of our clients bought two tickets for an airline that was giving upgrades "subject to availability" – in economy and business class,' says a London travel agent. 'They'd present the economy ticket to see if they got upgraded; if not they'd scrap it for a refund or to use next time and present the business-class ticket; which created absolute chaos with the yield management of the airline. It's a game of bluff and counterbluff.'

There are two types of upgrade: those that are pre-ordained, as it were, in the computer, and those that arise for 'operational' reasons (overbooking) at check-in or the departure gate; requiring both a strategic and tactical approach. The first facilitates the second. Try to make sure that your PNR (Passenger Name Record) carries a 'pre-authorization to upgrade'. Failing this, aim for the designation SFU (Suitable for Upgrade) and the magic 'Do all possible to assist' in the DCS (Departure Control System) – the 'operational' side of the CRS (Computer Reservations System), and you'll be top of the list for an upgrade at check-in – unless your coding is trumped at the last minute by a mileage millionaire wielding a better class of plastic.

An (almost) sure-fire way to get an upgrade is to be a frequent flier with a platinum or gold card traveling on a full-fare ticket. It also helps to be a VIP or a CIP (commercially important person).

VIPs come in many guises – from an authentic celebrity with whom the airline is glad to be associated to simply somebody with some kind of business relationship.

'You could be a VIP for me in public relations, sales or marketing. VIP means an important contact with the airline,' says an American Airlines spokesman. 'Not only might I type in an upgrade request for you, but I'd do a message "Do all possible to assist" to "Special Services" to meet you at check-in and walk you through.' Would an FFP member with a consolidator or discounted ticket have priority over a full-fare passenger? 'Not necessarily. What it comes down to is the more you've paid for your fare the better chance of an upgrade, particularly at peak times.'

Tactically, it can pay to target flights that are likely to be overbooked in economy and benefit from a 'cabin roll' – the process of 'rolling' people to the next class if the flight is overbooked to avoid bumping people off the flight. Unless you have a confirmed upgrade, your priority will be determined by your computer coding, and possibly the way you are dressed and your demeanour at the gate.

In summer, for example, most flights across the Atlantic are full with a lot of leisure travelers. So if you've paid a good fare for your economy ticket you have a very good chance of being upgraded.

Some flights are more popular than others. Most flights to New York will be departing Heathrow around, say 10, 11, midday, 1 o'clock and they're likely to be more crowded than flights which leave later in the afternoon. The first flight in the morning is very popular: you've got a very good chance of getting an upgrade on that. But airlines are not going to upgrade for the sake of it. If there are 100 seats in economy and 80 people turn up, all 80 are going to sit in economy no matter what fare they've paid.

'We give priority to upgrading any full-fare passenger along with any member of JAL Mileage Bank,' says a spokesman for Japan Airlines in London. 'We have no specific dress code: but smart casual is expected for upgrades to business class and a jacket and tie are necessary for first.' According to an SAS spokeswoman in Stockholm, the pecking order for upgrades is: passengers holding EuroBonus award tickets; EuroBonus gold card holders; VIPs and CIPs.

'At its most basic, what the airline wants to do is fill more of its seats at the highest fare; so the guy who flies a lot of miles on full fare they like; and the guy who places a million of business with them they like,' says Richard Lovell, vice president European operations at Carlson Wagonlit in London. 'So airlines start by giving labels like, silver, gold, platinum, which give you some sort of upgrade potential.

'For example, the BA gold card is a space-available upgrade. There are lots of codes on those cards that you can't read; so it might be that the chairman of a company who does 5,000 paid miles is more likely to get an upgrade than a salesman who does 50,000 miles. My code shows up as CIP because we spend £120 million with BA. So I would get an upgrade, but not ahead of someone who does a large number of paid-for miles.

'A travel agent can help by putting through a message to an airline for a VIP classification. It's all relative, we can't forge a code; but if we really ask an airline to pull the stops out they do. We would call the Special Services manager and say, it's critically important, can you arrange an upgrade, have someone met, waft them to a lounge, motor transfers between terminals. But you don't cry wolf too often.'

Upgrades are one of the most sought-after benefits of frequent-flier programmes. Redeeming points for an upgrade is often better value than a free ticket. Once you achieve 'elite' level, or Very Frequent Flier status, you may qualify for automatic upgrades. But only top-of-the-heap elite members can confirm free upgrades when making reservations.

Upgrades could be one of the first casualties of airline alliances. The problem for elite FFP members is sharing scarce upgrade seats with travelers belonging to partner programmes. Some alliances prohibit 'cross-upgrades'. The Star Alliance, for example, does not allow elite members to use individual programme upgrades in partner airlines. Even when airlines allow cross-upgrades, partners' elites face more obstacles than 'home team' members.

'Your best contact for an upgrade is the airline station manager: he's there, he sees you, he's the guy who can fix it at the last minute,' says a former country general manager of British Airways. 'The best thing that can happen to you is to have a problem with the airline: that gives you an excuse to meet the station manager and build a relationship with him. He's much more important to you than the commercial managers. Call him on some pretext a couple of days before you fly; have a coffee together; write a flattering letter to the president mentioning him; say that you're giving the airline another chance...'.

Whatever the computer says, when it comes to the crunch it still comes down to management style.

Dos and don'ts

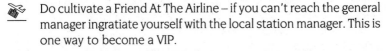 Do cultivate a Friend At The Airline – if you can't reach the general manager ingratiate yourself with the local station manager. This is one way to become a VIP.

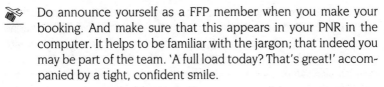 Do announce yourself as a FFP member when you make your booking. And make sure that this appears in your PNR in the computer. It helps to be familiar with the jargon; that indeed you may be part of the team. 'A full load today? That's great!' accompanied by a tight, confident smile.

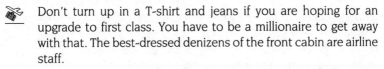 Don't turn up in a T-shirt and jeans if you are hoping for an upgrade to first class. You have to be a millionaire to get away with that. The best-dressed denizens of the front cabin are airline staff.

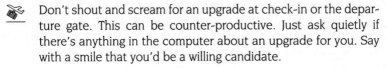 Don't shout and scream for an upgrade at check-in or the departure gate. This can be counter-productive. Just ask quietly if there's anything in the computer about an upgrade for you. Say with a smile that you'd be a willing candidate.

Avoiding the airline bump

You can expect it sooner or later. That gaggle at the departure gate waving tickets as people file past to board the plane is not a champagne reception. It means that the flight is overbooked and you as a late arrival are about to be bumped. The law of averages has finally caught up with you. Whether you make the flight (and your meeting in Hong Kong) and in which class you fly (you might be upgraded or downgraded) is likely to depend on how much you paid for your ticket, your pre-eminence in the frequent-flier hall of fame, and your management style. It's much the same as trying for an upgrade; except this time it's a matter of survival – getting a seat on the plane!

Bumping, or 'involuntary denied boarding' in airline jargon, is what happens when you are refused a seat on a flight for which you have a confirmed reservation. The reason passengers are bumped is because airlines oversell flights by up to 50 per cent to compensate, they claim, for no-shows – people who fail to turn up for a flight on which they are booked. This is the work of airlines' 'yield management' aimed at maximizing 'load factors', or the number of seats filled.

'No-shows' are most likely to be full-fare business travelers with flexible tickets who fail to cancel a booking, or make multiple back-up bookings on several flights or airlines. Bumping for them can mean bumping down a class (or bumping up a class if you're lucky): it is leisure (and business) travelers on restricted tickets in the back of the plane who are most likely to be left at the gate.

Ironically, you are least likely to be bumped off a low-cost no-frills carrier; you either show up or lose your ticket.

'We do not overbook because we don't have the problem with no-shows that afflicts our high-cost brethren,' says Tim Jeans, marketing director of Ryanair in Dublin, 'because the majority of our tickets are non-flexible and non-refundable; if people don't show up, they forfeit their fare.'

Airlines claim that bumping doesn't happen nearly as much these days because their yield-management systems are fine-tuned to forecast no-shows on a seasonal, daily and per-flight basis. 'We would never remove a must-fly premium passenger from a flight; normally we get more volunteers than we need,' says Philip Maddock, supervisor passenger services for American Airlines at Heathrow.

Industry insiders are sceptical. 'There are signs that airlines are increasing levels of overbooking to keep planes as full as possible,' says Mike Platt, director commercial affairs at Hogg Robinson Travel in London. 'This in turn is resulting in more travelers being turned away despite having a confirmed reservation.'

Sefik Yuksel, general manager trade affairs at the Association of European Airlines in Brussels, says: 'Competition between rival computer reservations systems, such as Sabre, WorldSpan, Amadeus and Galileo, in some markets encourages travel agents to make duplicate bookings – including fictitious names – to fulfil incentive targets. Airlines find it hard to manage unpredictable no-show rates; it really screws up their systems. So airlines compensate by overbooking more, which may mean that travelers are more likely to be bumped.'

'Airlines have tried to embarrass each other by dirty tricks such as by making fictitious booking reservations to try to upset them,' says an IATA source in Geneva. 'They feed names like Donald Duck and Mickey Mouse into the CRS; while the airlines are working out that they're spurious, they've got such a load on some flights that they cannot accept any more bookings; it throws confusion into the system.

'An airline is thoroughly embarrassed when it has to bump somebody, although the depth of embarrassment varies from airline to airline. Those in southern Europe, Africa, and the Indian subcontinent and the Middle East tend to be more cavalier in their attitudes.'

But not all horror stories in these parts are confined to Third World carriers. 'I was bumped off a KLM flight at Paramaribo in Surinam and stranded for four days,' says an aviation consultant in London. 'The Middle East is a complete nightmare before and after the holidays. Coming out of Lagos at peak times, everyone's overbooked. I would be a bit cautious even about British Airways. We have worked with non-European carriers who have displaced full-fare passengers for high-level airline staff or government employees.'

'I was bumped off a British Airways flight in Delhi returning to London,' says Jane (not her real name), PR manager for a major travel agency. 'I was connecting from an Air Nepal flight from Katmandu and checked in at Delhi four hours before the BA departure. I didn't get any compensation. They did offer us alternative flights on Lufthansa via Frankfurt, but we weren't told until half an hour beforehand and that was six hours later. I had actually reconfirmed my flight with BA; they had said, you don't need to do that with us!'

There are similar tales closer to home. Simon Evans at the Air Transport Users Council, a consumer watchdog, in London, was bumped off a BA flight on a day trip from Gatwick to Brussels.

'I was on my way for a job interview,' Evans says. 'I arrived at 7.15 to pick up a Eurobudget ticket – the next most expensive – for a 9 o'clock flight. "Oh, we can't check you in here, sir, you'll have to go to the gate." I went to the gate; even then they wouldn't answer directly that I was being bumped; quite outrageous. They finally got me on a Sabena flight 40 minutes later. I was 10 minutes late for my interview. Eight of us were bumped off that plane.'

Richard Lovell, vice president Europe for Carlson Wagonlit Travel, says: 'We don't have any hard figures, but we're getting more complaints about airline overbooking. Four years ago, you could usually get a seat on another flight within a short time; nowadays, if you're bumped, there's a pretty good chance there's nothing available for a long time because of higher loads.

'I commute to Paris and, coming back to London Friday evening, I know damned well that if I don't get my flight at 7.30 I will not be able to get the one at 8.30 and probably have little chance of getting on the one at 9.30. In which case I have to stay over or dash back to Paris and try the Eurostar.

'It's only happened to me once, but it's inevitable that as planes are fuller the impact of any bumping is greater because there's less capacity to be bumped into. This encourages business travelers on a full-fare ticket to make duplicate bookings. You don't know whether you can make it for 6 or 7.30 so you book on both, because if you wait until six, you probably won't get on the 7.30. The airlines allow for this by overbooking even more.

'It's unlikely if you turn up in good time with a full-fare ticket that you'll be refused boarding. But business travelers are used to sliding in to the airport in a four-wheel skid just before the aircraft doors shut; it's late-shows that get bumped on the assumption that they are no-shows. If you do get bumped then you are into the hierarchy of coloured plastic and so on and what it says on the screen about you.'

Melody Goodman, a director of Gray Dawes Internet Travel in London, says: 'You're always going to have an overbooking problem as long as airlines allow people to book a full-fare ticket without paying for it now and people don't cancel and there's no penalty if they don't turn up. When you have an agent you have a certain amount of control. But with more people booking through the Internet, airlines are more vulnerable to no-shows and one assumes that they'll be overbooking more.

'Premium fare travelers often get bumped at the moment. If you can't get a pre-assigned seat, you know there's going to be some sort of problem. If airlines won't pre-assign you a seat it means they haven't got one to give you. So you have to turn up early and hope it works out. A lot of the time it doesn't work out. You're unlikely to be left behind; but if you're expecting to travel in business class to the Far East, it's no prize to find yourself in economy – but they'll bump an economy passenger off the plane to give you a seat. If time allowed I could put you on to a couple of first-class travelers who could tell you their experiences. They gave one passenger I know three seats in economy; if he wanted to travel, it was the only thing they could offer him. Depending who you are, airlines may give you a full refund on the round trip, a voucher for future transportation, or frequent-flier miles as compensation.'

The Department of Transportation in the United States requires airlines to first ask for volunteers if a flight is overbooked. This may be conducted as a kind of auction at the gate, usually for cash or travel vouchers plus travel on another flight. If you are bumped involuntarily, airlines must pay you $200 if they can't get you to your destination in less than two hours on domestic flights and four hours on international flights. If the delay is longer, you are entitled to a maximum of $400 plus overnight expenses and a refund on your original ticket. The European Union has similar rules for airlines departing from airports in Europe.

'If we are overbooked, we automatically go into the auction process, offering compensation to volunteers to go on a later flight,' says Andy Plews, a spokesman for United Airlines. There are no set limits. For example, if you are traveling from Washington to London, you might be offered departure an hour later on our flight to Paris connecting to Heathrow with arrival two or three hours later, plus cash or vouchers of, say, $200. If there's no later flight, we'd pick up hotels, meals, telephone calls and so on; there are no set limits. We try to solve the problem right there at the gate.'

Fiona O'Farrell at American Airlines in London says: 'We wouldn't have an auction. Compensation would vary depending on the route, how many people you need to come off, and if we can offer another flight within an hour or have to wait till next day. Everybody on the flight would be offered the same thing; we decide an amount and that's it. It might be $500 or $1,000 on the same flight on different days in different circumstances. If we only need five people to get off, you can set compensation at a lower level. Sometimes people arrive very early, three hours beforehand. How about going earlier? That solves our problem.'

'We start looking for volunteers as people check in,' says Paul Moore, a spokesman for Virgin Atlantic in London. 'We might offer a free round trip or the equivalent in Freeway miles to any Virgin destination – which encourages people to fly with us more – plus accommodation and meals if we can't get them on a later flight. Ultimately, the last to check in would be the first to be bumped. But we don't want too many people looking upon the offer of compensation as an opportunity.'

Don Garvett, vice president of SH&E, an international air transport consultancy in New York, says: 'Most of the leading carriers do an excellent job of balancing the trade-off between no-shows and overbooking. The biggest problem is how they handle passengers at the airports and how do they preserve the integrity of their booking base. If you solve those two problems you've done a lot more good than improving the yield management systems.

'Some airlines will check for duplicate bookings only on the same flight; others will check on duplicate bookings on all flights between that city pair that day; others will look at the day before and the day after. Some airlines require passengers to reconfirm flights. Strange as it may sound, that actually decreases the reliability of the booking base because a lot of passengers simply do not hear or ignore the announcement. So airlines who don't enforce that requirement usually do better. Airlines who assume that a passenger who no-shows on the outbound flight is likely to no-show on the return flight have to be careful because, if it's a bad weather day, or bad traffic at the airport, you shouldn't cancel because the passenger may be going on adjacent flights.

'Again, how do you define who gets offloaded? On a first-come-first-served basis? Frequent-flier status? What fare they paid? If an airline doesn't get enough volunteers, do they raise the level of compensation? To all volunteers? Individually or in public? There are different ways of dealing with these issues. I've observed situations where an airline asks for more volunteers than it needs and the unhappy passengers were the ones who were not bumped.'

How to avoid being bumped (or vice versa!)

 Book directly with the airline.

 Reconfirm with the airline.

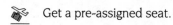 Get a pre-assigned seat.

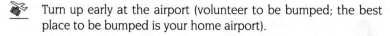 Turn up early at the airport (volunteer to be bumped; the best place to be bumped is your home airport).

Get your luggage on board; you become a harder target.

Join the frequent-flier programme (elite status may get you an upgrade).

Book on the last flight of the day.

Avoid (or choose) leisure-dominated flights at peak times.

Make friends with the local station manager.

Sizing up the rules for carry-ons

Traveling light can be heavy going these days as business travelers face up to stricter limits on the amount of baggage they can bring on board a plane. I say limits not rules because airlines have no consistent rules, leaving it up to check-in staff to arbitrate – whether or not your laptop or briefcase counts as an extra 'piece' or a 'miscellaneous' item such as a duty-free bag or video camera. It's a question of, how much can I get away with?

A notice may say, one piece of hand baggage only. Well, yes, but I only have this giant garment bag containing my sales presentation, an overnight bag-cum-briefcase with retracting handle and wheels and a duty-free bag containing my laptop. You hold it all up in one hand to show how light it is. And they let me on with all of it at Broken Springs, Colorado. Sorry, this is Zurich and the flight is fully booked: you'll have to check this one, which means you'll never make your connection in Frankfurt. If you're lucky (or unlucky), they may place your bag in a special frame or mould by the gate – a Procrustean device that brooks no argument. It's often down to the mood of the person at the gate – or your management style.

Airlines have discovered that rationing carry-ons by class is an excellent way to discriminate against business people who travel in the back of the plane. Anytime now we'll be invited to spend frequent-flier miles for more carry-ons: 50,000 miles, for example, might buy you an upgrade to two bags.

Most people agree that hand baggage has got out of hand. Apart from being a nuisance, excess cabin baggage is a safety hazard. Some people use bags as a battering ram to reach their seats. Sitting in the aisle of a crowded 737 you risk being thumped in the face by swinging shoulder bags or your ankles scythed by pull-along luggage of folk who've just been decanted off a 747. Expect to see the pull-along ones fitted with blades on the wheels – like Queen Boadicea's chariot.

An obvious solution is to provide more overhead baggage space like the Boeing 777, which United Airlines claims has the biggest bins in the sky. Or, perhaps, a compartment in the hold that can be reached from the cabin by trap-door.

More than 65 per cent of travelers say they want more space for carry-on luggage just when airlines are asking the US government to reduce the number of bags they can take on board, according to the Yesawich, Pepperdine & Brown/Yankelovich Partners National Business Travel Monitor, based on in-depth interviews with a nationally representative sample of 1,500 US households.

'It's hard for business travelers to imagine that the air travel experience could get any worse, but it appears the airlines have managed to make it happen. It compounds the horrible fear that travelers have about check-in luggage,' says Peter Yesawich, president and CEO of Yesawich, Pepperdine & Brown in Orlando, Florida. 'Clearly, what's driving this is that it's a seller's market. First the airlines downsized meals, then they jacked the fares – the typical business fare today is 20 per cent higher than a year ago – and now they say you can only take one bag on board.

'I don't think you'd have seen this happening a couple of years ago when loads weren't at 70 per cent but in the high 50s. Airlines know that checking in bags is burdensome at best. So they put another speed bump in our way. The FAA is taking a wait-and-see attitude – they are concerned strictly with safety. This is the ultimate caste system. They'll soon be rationing slots in the john.'

The Federal Aviation Administration in the United States requires all cabin baggage to be stowed safely in overhead bins or under the seats: all other bags must be checked. (The FAA is currently reviewing carry-on luggage rules.) IATA guidelines state that 'passengers should be encouraged to carry no more than one piece of cabin baggage' measuring 115 centimetres (45 inches) overall (length plus height plus width) plus miscellaneous items such as duty-free bags, sundry purses, cameras, a 'reasonable' amount of reading matter, coats, umbrellas, walking-sticks, crutches and folding wheelchairs.

The problem is that rules – and how they are interpreted – vary widely by carrier, class of travel and type of plane and how heavily a flight is booked, which adds to bewilderment, confusion and apoplexy at check-in. Some airlines go by weight, others go by a variety of dimensions; some allow two bags, others allow one bag and a garment bag; a laptop may or may not count as a bag. You may end up last on board with nowhere to stow your legitimate one bag.

Northwest Airlines has a 'one-plus' carry-on policy whereby economy passengers are restricted to 'one carry-on bag plus a briefcase, laptop or purse', plus coats and the usual paraphernalia. Previously, the one-plus rule applied only to flights with a 'booked load factor of more than 70 per cent or at the discretion of gate and cabin personnel'. First- and business-class passengers or members of International Gold Elite or WorldPerks Gold programmes are allowed an extra carry-on item.

Michael Levine, executive vice president marketing and international at Northwest Airlines, says: 'The last third of passengers on any given flight now are unable to stow their baggage in the cabin because the bin space is already taken. This frustrates passengers and too often creates delays as luggage is taken back out of the cabin, tagged and hand-carried for loading in the cargo holds.'

American Airlines changed its carry-on policy, allowing one bag on domestic and two bags on international routes 'if the flight is not full'. Carry-on bags must fit under the seat and not exceed 70 pounds. 'Approximate' dimensions for transatlantic flights are 23 by 13 by 9 inches. 'Delta and Northwest are trying to restrict to one bag,' says Lizann Peppard, a spokeswoman at American Airlines. 'We're waiting for the FAA to make a ruling for an industry standard. It would save a lot of confusion. In the meantime, we'll allow people to bring on two bags if the flight is not full, leaving some leeway for flight attendants...'.

United Airlines allows two pieces – including a laptop or garment bag – not exceeding 50 pounds (22.6 kilogrammes) and 45 inches (115 centimetres) overall for all passengers on domestic routes. On international flights, you're allowed two bags in first and business class but only one bag in economy.

'We're running an experiment in Des Moines allowing only one bag for people traveling on excursion fares,' says Andy Plews, a United spokesman in London. 'Complaints? Not many so far. This is driven by the fact that planes are much fuller these days: everyone is looking around for solutions. There's the question of safety, on-time departure and the sheer hassle factor. Airlines are getting tighter about carry-ons and enforcing the rules. It's a very live topic.'

Cathay Pacific restricts all passengers to one piece of cabin baggage not exceeding 56 by 36 by 23 centimetres: first- and business-class passengers may also carry on a garment bag (20 centimetres folded) and a laptop computer.

British Airways has recently down-sized its cabin-baggage allowances. In first or business class, you can take one bag or garment bag

(20 centimetres folded) plus a briefcase, with a total weight of 9 kilogrammes (20 pounds): in economy class, only one bag, weighing less than 6 kilogrammes, is allowed. KLM imposes a maximum of one piece of carry-on baggage weighing up to 10 kilogrammes and measuring no more than 55 by 35 by 25 centimetres, plus a laptop. In addition, business-class travelers are allowed a garment bag (maximum weight 8 kilogrammes and depth when folded of 20 centimetres) or a briefcase or other bag up to 8 kilogrammes. And, to end any arguments, KLM is providing special moulds to measure cabin luggage at the airports it serves. If the bag doesn't fit the mould, it's banished to the hold.

You can find a bag to fit by trawling the advertorials in the travel magazines. There are shoulder-bags, saddle-bags in leather, canvas or 'ultra-tough ballistic nylon' with exotic names like the Epsilon Equilibrium Transporter, the Spark Ultra Transporter, and a galaxy of Overnighters 'which take you from boardroom to hotel'. Some are like Russian dolls with one bag fitting inside another for all eventualities. But make sure that the outside dimensions do not exceed 115 centimetres (45 inches). And take a metric tape measure along. You may have to prove your case.

How to become a light traveler

If time is of the essence when you're on the road, then traveling with as little as possible is a necessity. Here are a few suggestions to lighten your load.

Avoid the misery of checked baggage – long delays at check-in lines where the people in front of you seem to be moving house – and are sure to have their bags go missing, broken or mislaid. Instead, travel light, really light – say, with a briefcase that hooks on to a carry-on suitcase, preferably one with wheels and a telescopic handle.

In the days of steamer trunks and porters, a *voyageur sans bagages* would have been viewed with ineffable disdain if not outright suspicion. 'Is this all your luggage, sir?' An equivalent scene today would have an intrepid business traveler trying to pay the bill with cash instead of plastic. Times have changed. Road warriors of the millennium travel light and travel mean with uncanny zeal. This is because business trips have become shorter and, consequently, more action-packed.

Light travelers want a hassle-free trip; they like to be independent, with nothing messing up their schedule and they like to move fast. So no self-respecting light traveler checks luggage. When it comes to carry-ons, every ounce counts.

It's a matter of priorities. The light traveler doesn't bother with pyjamas or thermal underwear, rarely venturing into the inclement outdoors except for the door-to-taxi dash. Jettison that rack of ties, the jacket you know you'll never need and the spare pair of shoes. Make room instead for the laptop computer or at least the pocket organizer or GSM mobile phone. Start by emptying the briefcase of everything left over from the last trip. This is known as zero-base packing. Be ruthless with paper. Mail or fax the stuff in advance and refuse to carry anything back with you.

Traveling for up to a week in the summer, I can get away with a light-weight linen jacket, a pair of trousers, three shirts, two of my less vulnerable ties and expensive black loafers that can pass for formal or informal. Shirts are important: a fresh dress shirt can redeem a jet-lagged jacket. My washing gear simply consists of an airline amenity pack, plus a couple of disposable razors, Alka Seltzer and heavy-duty antacid tablets. In winter I am compelled to take Mr Wong's 36-hour Hong Kong suit and perhaps an overcoat. But overcoats are a burden. I once left mine with Cathay Pacific in London on my way to Hong Kong. Taken a serious step further, I have friends who have stashes of formal and leisure clothes in strategic left-luggage lockers for use on 'business-extension' forays such as weekend 'wrap-ups' on the golf course or by the pool.

Women are expert light travelers. You may think that's a myth, but Novotel, in its annual survey of hotel guests found that men take twice as much luggage as women for a typical two-night stay. Change a blouse, a few accessories, and everybody wonders how on earth the female executive has managed to pack so many outfits in such a small case; everything from a pin-striped bikini for the rooftop pool bar to a long skirt and change of blouse with a pearl choker for the welcome cocktail in the Graf Zeppelin Salle.

However light you travel, there's no sure-fire way to avoid a hassle with carry-ons. You can usually get away with another bag in business class. One solution is to carry your papers in a giant duty-free bag and stuff with everything else into a folding garment bag-cum-suitcase-briefcase.

Holding on to your luggage

Overheard at the airport.

'Hi, I'm going to Paris, but I'd like this bag to go to Tokyo.'

'I'm sorry, sir. We can't do that.'

'What do you mean? You did it last week!'

It's every traveler's nightmare. The carousel stops, but your bags haven't appeared. All you have is your briefcase and the clothes you stand up in. Your sales presentation is in your luggage. Not the best way to start a five-week trip of the Asian markets.

But you're not alone. According to the 1999 Baggage Survey by IAPA (International Airline Passengers Association), of 150 frequent fliers, 61 per cent said that they had experienced some form of loss or delay in the last 12 months. Although half of them got their luggage back in less than 12 hours, many were not so lucky. A third had to wait up to 24 hours, 7 per cent had to wait until after they got home, and 8 per cent said goodbye to their bags for good. At least half of those who retrieved their bags said that someone, somewhere had rummaged through their possessions – often resulting in theft. Among baggage losers, only 35 per cent received compensation for delay, loss or damage and 40 per cent said that, as a result, they would never travel on the same carrier again. Despite the promise of better service, business-class passengers fared worse than those in economy class with 70 per cent and 60 per cent respectively receiving no compensation or recognition of their lost bags.

Lost, delayed and damaged baggage was the second most common complaint to the Air Transport Users Council – a consumer watchdog in London – in its 1999 report.

You must claim from the airline. Its liability is limited under the terms of the Warsaw Convention of 1929, which provides derisory compensation because it is based upon weight rather than the contents of the bags, so you'll get the same amount whether your wardrobe consists of Armani or Marks & Spencer. Currently, the fixed limit is $20 (£14.45) per kg for permanently lost baggage. So the maximum permissible claim for a standard baggage allowance of 20 kg would be £289.

But what price do you put on business documents? A contract lost? Your job! The only sure-fire way is to become a Light Traveler and schlep your essentials into the cabin. To check, or not to check? That is the question.

If you decide to check and the worst should happen, tell the airline (or its handling agent) at once. Make sure that you fill out a Property Irregularity Report (PIR), and keep a copy for yourself. The more accurately you can describe your bag and its contents, the more likely you are to get it back quickly. The airline should know where your bag has gone in a day or so, and deliver it to you. Make sure they know where to send it – such as a hotel along the way rather than back home.

Agree with the airline representative how much you can spend on essentials, such as underwear and toiletries, to tide you over. Don't be fobbed off with a business-class amenity kit.

Claiming on insurance

Your policy should give you at least $5,000/£2,500 worth of cover for lost, stolen or damaged luggage and personal effects, with a single item limit of $500. Make sure that valuable items, such as cameras, are covered with a separate policy. You should be able to claim essential expenses (up to $300) if your baggage is delayed for more than 12 hours.

Survival tips

 Take a direct flight whenever possible. Avoid tight connections at transit airports where you may catch the plane but your baggage won't.

 Clearly identify your baggage inside and out and lock them if possible.

Pack essential items, such as business materials, toiletries, medicines and a change of clothes in your carry-on luggage. Checked-in luggage may fail the security scans if it contains electrical equipment or aerosols.

 At check-in, check that your bag is correctly tagged before it disappears down the conveyor belt. Double-check your luggage receipts (which should be stapled to your ticket) to see if the flight number and destination are right. Show your frequent-flier card and ask if your bags can be upgraded to 'priority status' as you have a tight connection.

 Don't arrive too late at the departure gate. 'Baggage reconciliation' (which ensures that no unaccompanied baggage travels on board) usually begins about 10 minutes before departure. If you're not on board, your bag may be taken off.

 Take a copy of your insurance policy with you – in your hand baggage!

IAPA was established in 1960 to represent airline passengers around the world. It has more than 400,000 members in 200 countries who collectively make 6.4 million flights a year.

IAPA offers every member access to the services, savings and benefits normally reserved for large companies with substantial travel budgets who have the power to negotiate with airlines, hotels and car rental firms. IAPA also provides insurance, emergency assistance and business travel consulting.

Members also get Bag-Guard tags and stickers that carry the member's name, membership number and a special airline communication code – a SITA code – which allows IAPA to track missing baggage anywhere in the world.

Web site: www.iapa.com or call (44 171) 208 681 6555.

Mobile phones: the cost of keeping in touch

Mobile phones have become a way of life for road warriors of the millennium. The new generation of mobile phones that work on the global system for mobiles (GSM) digital network and allow for 'roaming' in more than 60 countries (except the United States and Japan) are great for keeping in touch (What budget meeting? Hal, my batteries are fading...'), staying out of touch (state-of-the-art means never having to say you're sorry), impressing fellow travelers or simply annoying everybody around you.

'Roaming' means that you are registered with your 'service provider' or telecom to use your GSM phone on a foreign cellular network. You keep your home number – encoded on your SIM (Subscriber Identity Module) card, or smart card, which slots in to any GSM handset – and the system 'finds' you to deliver calls to your handset wherever you are. You are billed on your home account. It sounds easy and it usually is.

Almost too easy. GSM phones should carry a health warning: 'Indiscriminate roaming can seriously damage your budget'. You not only have to consider the cost of making calls but the cost of receiving them! 'Don't call us, we'll call you' has taken on a new level of meaning.

Mobile phones can cost more than twice as much as fixed phones in the same country and maybe 10 times as much when you're traveling abroad. You are paying for convenience – round-the-clock ability to send and receive voice and data messages. Plug in your laptop or palmtop/handheld computer, otherwise known as the Personal Digital Assistant (PDA), for a galaxy of functions such as accessing your e-mail;

talking to the office PC; uploading and downloading files; and surfing the Internet.

Simon Rockman, editor of *What Mobile* magazine in London, says: 'If you want international roaming you pay a lot of money: you have to expect calls to cost you £1.50 a minute, that kind of money, because another network is taking a mark-up; whereas, if you're just calling within, say, Britain or France, it'll only cost you about 20 pence a minute. Getting a GSM phone to work across borders without paying a lot is very, very difficult.'

Let's say you've taken your GSM phone from Paris on a trip to Hong Kong. You want to use it to make local calls within Hong Kong as you move around between meetings and to call the office back home from your hotel room.

Local calls may cost you 35 per cent more than they would in Paris, but that's not going to break the bank. But if someone in Hong Kong wants to return your call, he or she has to make an international call to Paris, for which they will pay, and then your mobile is charged for you to receive the incoming call even though you might only be the other side of the harbour in Kowloon. Likewise, if Aunt Vera in Brighton calls, thinking you are in Paris, you will be charged two international legs between France and Hong Kong – at mobile rates. You may be able to dispatch Aunt Vera in a couple of minutes; but what if it's a customer who needs to talk? Conversely, if somebody gives you their mobile number, beware. Check where it is domiciled; you may find yourself paying a costly international leg between, say, Paris and Athens, to reach someone a few miles away in Versailles. The rule is wherever your SIM card is based, that is where all of your callers will call no matter whereabouts in the world you happen to be.

There are several strategic options. You can elect to bar incoming calls when you go roaming. You may be able to do this selectively – only accepting calls from predetermined numbers. Or you can divert all calls to a voice mail system back home (which you can retrieve later from wherever you are) or arrange for short text messages (make sure that your service has SMS – Short Message Service capability) of up to 25 characters delivered to your handset if it is switched on. Or else switch it off until you need to make a call.

If you travel a lot to certain countries, it may be worth while taking out a local GSM subscription. I know people who have several SIM cards that they slot in to their handsets depending on where they are. But, of course, you have a separate phone number for each, making it more difficult for people to get hold of you. Which may be part of your communications strategy anyway.

In some countries, such as Italy and France, you can buy prepaid SIM cards for your GSM phone that allow you to make and receive local calls. You pay slightly more. But there's no subscription and the phone number comes with the card.

France Telecom, for example, sells SIM format 'mobicarte' cards through retail outlets such as cafes, 'tabacs' and news-stands. The cards, costing 270 francs, are good for 30 minutes of domestic calls in France. You get a cellphone number for the card by inserting it into any GSM phone and dialling 222. Calls are then made by dialling 222 followed by any number in metropolitan France.

Once the credit has been used up, you can reload credit by buying a 'scratch' card costing 144 francs that gives you an additional 30 minutes of credit. The new credit is activated by dialling 222 and entering a 14-digit code found on the scratch card. The initial card costs 9 francs a minute; after that you pay about the same rate as a low-usage domestic subscriber on peak time – around 5 francs a minute.

Tips for roaming with mobile phones

 GSM handsets these days are sleek and handsome and cost from $40 to $1,000 or more. Compare what they do with what you need along with size or weight. The Ericcson GSM, for example, weighs in at 4.7 ounces; the Nokia 9000 Communicator – which doubles as a palmtop PDA – is a hefty 14 ounces (too bulky for our pocket); the Philips Spark mobile incorporates fancy features such as Voice-Dial. This is claimed to be the first mobile with 'voice recognition'. Or the last word in 'hands-off' management.

 Battery life. New 'lithium ion' batteries (unlike nickel cadmium) can be recharged any time you like before they are completely drained. Lithium ion batteries on the Philips Spark phone, for example, give you 10 hours of talk time and 350 hours standby time.

 Work out how many calls you are likely to make and where you are most likely to travel. Mobile phone contracts are usually based on a sliding scale from light occasional users who pay a low monthly charge and a relatively high cost per call to heavy business users who may pay a higher monthly charge and a lower cost per call. Check how easily you can switch from one type of contract to another. How much will roaming cost in Europe/the world?

Does the service provider have roaming agreements with network operators in the countries you plan to visit? Not all cellular networks have the same reciprocal agreements. You can check this out on www.gsmworld.com

 When roaming, can you bar some/all incoming calls? What about voice messaging? PS compatibility? E-mail, fax and Internet access? Make sure the phone has a PCM CIA link with your PDA.

Calling the shots with global calling cards

Business travelers know that the best way to avoid extortionate phone charges (mark-ups of 900 per cent or more) is to use a telephone charge card, or calling card, or a mobile phone. But making and receiving voice or data calls is a complex equation of cost, convenience and quality of the line depending on where you are and where you need to call.

Mobile phone calls can cost five times or more than calling-card calls, but are still far cheaper than hotel charges. Calling cards can save up to 70 per cent on hotel calls, but in turn can be as much as five times more than using cash or a local pre-paid phone card in a pay phone or from an office or residential phone.

Everyone is sold on calling cards. The question is which card is best for where you are and where you want to call. Charges between cards can vary by more than 50 per cent. For example, a five-minute call from Japan to the United Kingdom costs £9.99 ($16.70) with a BT Chargecard, £8.25 with a Cable & Wireless Calling Card, £6.99 with a World Telecom Global Calling Card and £4.53 with an AT&T Calling Card.

Calling cards all work in a similar way. You call a toll-free number from any telephone, either speak to an English-speaking operator or enter your account number and PIN in response to voice prompts and the call is then connected. You can either buy a certain amount of call time using your credit card and top it up as you go along, or settle an itemized bill every month, showing exactly who you called, from where and for how long. Many companies require that travelers will be reimbursed for phone calls only if they are made with a specified calling card.

Major telecoms such as AT&T, BT and Cable & Wireless (which owns Mercury in the United Kingdom) use their own networks to route card calls. If you make a call from Bangkok to London using an AT&T card, for example, you will be routed via the AT&T network rather than the local Thai system. Other card providers like World Telecom and Interglobe do not own their own phone lines but buy spare capacity at a discount rate from the major telecoms – sending calls along the cheapest and most reliable route.

Then there's the question of line quality, because some card companies reduce costs by 'compressing' calls to get up to five times more calls on a line. This is okay for voice, but not for data calls like faxes or trying to retrieve your e-mail.

'What we're finding from research is that travelers are taking incoming calls on their mobile phones and making outgoing calls with their calling card,' says a BT spokesman in London. 'The reason is you get better call quality using a fixed line and there's less risk of a call dropping out midway through. Business people use audio-conferencing more and more and calls tend to be fairly long. So a calling card is a good means of participating.'

Calling card companies compete for space in your wallet with a galaxy of 'added value' services, such as speed-dial 'short-codes' for frequently dialled numbers; 'follow-on' call facility (which can save money on hotel access charges); travel and business services; fax mail, which delivers all your fax messages to the number of your choice; message forwarding, which sends your messages to any telephone in any country for the time of your choice; and conference calling replete with an online interpreter. Some cards have a 'call-back' facility to avoid high local or hotel phone charges.

There is no overall cheapest calling card. AT&T has the lowest costs for calls from the United States and from the Far East and Middle East but tends to be more expensive than other major cards for calls within Europe. It has the advantage that it avoids value-added tax (VAT) on calls that originate outside Europe.

Here are some points to consider:

 Decide which type of calls – voice or data – you are most likely to make or receive and how flexible you need to be. You can meet most contingencies with a clutch of calling cards and a GSM (global system for mobiles) mobile phone along with your laptop.

 Have at least one major calling card programmed into your laptop for message calls.

 If you travel a lot to certain countries, it may be worth while taking out a local GSM subscription, which gives you a local number at local rates. This avoids exorbitant charges for having calls routed back through your home country. Rules vary. In the United States, the receiver pays for a mobile call from overseas: in Europe, the sender pays. In some countries you can buy prepaid SIM cards for your mobile that allow you to make and receive domestic calls. You pay slightly more than the local mobile rate. But there's no subscription and the phone number comes with the card. France Telecom, for example, sells a mobicarte costing 270 francs, which is good for 30 minutes of calls within France. Once the credit has been used up, you can reload it by buying a 'scratch-card' for 144 francs which gives you another 30 minutes.

 Deciding which calling card is cheapest and most convenient depends on which countries you are visiting and the countries you are calling. When calling back home, say to France or Germany, it's usually cheaper to get a card from France Telecom or Deutsch Telekom, especially if it is billed to your home or office account where you may be able to pick up discounts. But look out for exceptions. Using a BT Chargecard from Australia to the United Kingdom costs about twice as much as an AT&T Global Calling Card or a Global One Calling Card, according to a report in *Holiday Which?* magazine published by the Consumers' Association in the United Kingdom.

 When calling to third countries, or within a region such as Europe or South East Asia, you may find it cheapest to use a calling card issued by a telecom company in one of the countries. The cheapest way to phone within a foreign country is to use a local pre-paid phone card or cash at a pay phone.

 You can apply to use your American Express, Diners Club or Visa card as a telephone calling card. Charges can be competitive with the major calling cards.

 How important is line quality versus the cost of a call? Would you use 'added-value' services such as sequential dialling, ability to receive and send voice and fax messages, multilingual operators or conference calls? What are the charges for these services? Check which cards allow you to make data calls, or make two calls simultaneously. Or how many frequent-flier miles you can earn.

 Check which card offers freephone access numbers in the countries you visit regularly. Major calling cards claim 'global reach' but you don't want to be caught out.

Here's a list of the main cards:

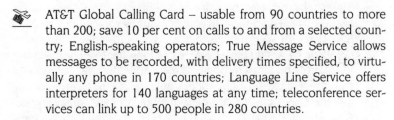

- AT&T Global Calling Card – usable from 90 countries to more than 200; save 10 per cent on calls to and from a selected country; English-speaking operators; True Message Service allows messages to be recorded, with delivery times specified, to virtually any phone in 170 countries; Language Line Service offers interpreters for 140 languages at any time; teleconference services can link up to 500 people in 280 countries.

- BT Chargecard – usable between more than 115 countries; fax and data calls and e-mail can be charged to the card from a laptop, plus remote access, Internet connection and file transfer facilities.

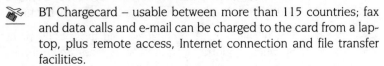

- Cable & Wireless Calling Card – usable in 60 countries; voice and fax mail; conference calls.

- Global One Global Calling Card (Deutsche Telekom/France Telecom/Sprint) – voice and data services between 150 countries; travel assistance; follow-on calls; partnerships with 18 airline FFPs.

- Interglobe Calling Card – operates in 52 countries; claims to be 35 per cent cheaper than BT on US/UK calls; multi-lingual operator assistance; SpeakEasy service offers discounts of up to 29 per cent on national and 55 per cent on international calls; claims 70 per cent savings on international calls against hotels and GSM mobile phones.

- World Telecom Global Calling Card – freephone access in 130 countries; claims savings of 50 per cent over major calling cards, 30 per cent on overseas GSM calls and 60 per cent on hotel phones; World Directory allows up to 50 short phone number codes for swift access; voice messages can be forwarded every half hour up to three hours until received; conference calls with online interpreter for up to eight people can be made on any touch-tone phone; access to news, stock prices and travel bookings; Call Me facility for countries without free access codes; call-back to avoid hotel charges; calls can be pre-booked to be made via the operator to a number abroad.

Smart cards getting smarter

It's 9.30 am in New York when you get a message confirming the meeting in Paris tomorrow morning. No problem. You've brought a bag to the office just in case, so you book a flight through the Internet or online to your travel agency. You then download the flight confirmation details, along with your seat assignment, hotel and car rental reservations to your 'multi-function smart card' (PCs, laptops, even palmtop computers now incorporate smart-card readers); show up at the airport, wave your card within a few inches of the airline 'kiosk' (automatic card-reader in travelspeak), which prints out your boarding pass (ah, yes, you've got an upgrade), and go straight to the gate. The kiosk is a two-way reader and has automatically updated your card with frequent-flier miles for the trip.

When you arrive the next morning at Charles de Gaulle, you go to an automatic teller machine and instead of getting cash, send a flow of electronic money to your smart card, which you then use as an 'electronic purse' for incidental purchases. At the car-rental kiosk your card confirms your identity through passport information and details of your driver's licence and releases your key with instructions on how to find your car. At the hotel you check in and check out in the same way. When you leave the hotel, your receipt, along with loyalty programme points, is downloaded to the card.

Back in the office, you transfer all of the expense data stored on the smart card and turn it into an expense account with a few key strokes on your PC. During the trip you will have checked your e-mail by inserting the card into a 'smart' telephone.

This scenario may only be a year or so away thanks to phenomenal advances in smart-card technology, which promise to bring 'seamless' travel a tad closer.

Smart cards, or 'chip' cards, are a space age away from the traditional magnetic-stripe card in that they carry a computer chip, or microprocessor, with a memory of 8,000 bytes of information and a potential for much higher storage through compacting techniques. The magnetic-stripe card is no more than a magnetic ID – a simple sequence of characters, with no intelligence or processing capability. It cannot interact with anything; it is only capable of being read.

Smart cards, on the other hand, are personal computers – except for a screen and keyboard, which you get when you stick the card into a PC or a terminal. Ultimately, the smart card in your wallet will be able to load software onto the equivalent of a disk drive.

Smart cards have been around for some time for single-function applications such as electronic ticketing by airlines and other travel operators, and pre-paid phone cards. They make electronic commerce over open systems secure and efficient. Smart cards are said to be the Internet's 'killer' application.

Gemplus, a French company and a pioneer of smart-card technology, and its arch-rival, Schlumberger, a 70-year-old oilfield and measurement systems conglomerate, account for 70 per cent of the $1 billion world market. Industry sources estimate that the world market for smart cards in 2001 will be 3 to 3.5 billion units. Banks around the world are running pilot programmes with the aim of replacing magnetic-stripe plastic with smart cards.

David Boyles, senior vice president and head of the 'Smart Card Center of Excellence' at American Express, says: 'We are developing a multi-application smart card which we call the "ultimate travel card". You tell us what you want and we'll put in a personal profile – not just a basic ID, but passport, driving licence, medical records, along with biometric information – a digital picture of your thumbprint or palmprint for "fast-track" immigration procedures. You'll be able to make more secure travel arrangements on the Internet, pick up electronic cash advances, and check-in at airports, hotels and car rental kiosks.

'You'll be able to put a whole lot of personal data on the card. Do you like an aisle or a window seat? First or business class? Which airline gives you most FFP miles for the trip? All this will be on the card and you won't have to keep repeating it.

'The neat thing too about smart cards is you can make a transaction any place any time – in a taxi, in a plane, at the North Pole, anywhere there's a device that can read that card. You don't have to be "online": through some telecom back to the host computer. You can upload or download information any time. Smart cards typically upload a bunch of transactions, say once a week, to the host computer. We can mirror the information on the card, so should you lose it, we can provide a replacement card anywhere in the world through one of our local offices. You can also load your own applications on to the card. This is not futuristic stuff: we're doing it in the lab today.'

American Express began a pilot programme in December 1996 of a multifunctional card with electronic ticketing at 21 airports in the United States, in concert with IBM and American Airlines. But the smart card simply identifies the traveler at an 'enhanced gate reader'. It does not carry the actual reservation, nor does it transfer FFP miles to the card.

A test announced in May 1997 by Amex with IBM and Hilton Hotels Corporation has added more functionality. Travelers check in at a kiosk in the lobby that displays their reservation, selects a room based on their preferences, and issues a key. At the end of the stay, the traveler checks out by swiping the card in the kiosk to review and confirm the bill and get a printed receipt.

'We're not yet downloading reservations information on to the chip,' says Melissa Abernathy, a spokesperson for American Express in New York. 'But the chip can transfer data. For example, if you get to the kiosk and want to change your address or other information on your Hilton Honors account, you can do that: you can reprogramme the chip; add other FFPs or change your preferences. But it's not the full picture yet.'

The full picture may emerge when industry standards have been agreed upon and when there is enough demand for smart-card applications to achieve critical mass.

'This will happen when the banks really start to issue smart cards,' says David Dingly, a consultant with IBM in London. 'For example, leading banks in South Africa are going to issue a million chip cards this year. Banksys, a company owned by 60 Belgian banks, is running a test with American Express. Once people like Amex and Hilton start to do their stuff with volume presence, then demand will begin to happen.'

Pierre Briant, manager of ticketing, at IATA in Geneva, says: 'We're working with airlines to develop common standards for smart cards, especially between interline partners, similar to that for paper tickets, so that you can travel the first sector with, say, United, and transfer to BA, and so on. So when you check in at the airport, your electronic file is ready for you, and allows you to endorse tickets between airlines if you wish to change your reservation.

'Where it gets complex is how to provide "keys" to separate common information from proprietary information stored on the card. You only have so much space, or "real estate". And while you need systems to be compatible, you have to avoid companies having reciprocal access to information without the cardholder's permission. Airlines want to make sure that the information on the card is the same as that on their mainframe. Which is why most airlines prefer not to download reservations information to the card as if it were a ticket, but simply to use the card as a passenger ID.'

Then there is the issue of 'contact' cards (which you swipe, or 'dip', in the kiosk) versus 'contactless' cards (which you simply wave in front of the kiosk). The latter depends on radio frequency (RF) technology, which can read a smart card several metres away – even in someone's pocket, which raises civil liberties and privacy issues. You have to know when you're being read.

Delta Air Lines is currently using contactless smart cards on its Air Shuttle between New York and Boston and Washington. The card acts as a ticket and boarding authorization. There is no need to stop at the ticket counter.

Lufthansa has issued 130,000 ChipCards – a multifunctional smart card – to its frequent fliers and Senator Card members for use on German domestic flights and to London and Paris. The card acts as a ticket and boarding pass and serves as a German phone card, a Miles & More frequent-flier card, and for access to airport lounges.

Money management on the move

It is late when you arrive at Brussels airport and you join an impatient line of travelers in front of the bureau de change. All you really need are enough Belgian francs to get you to the hotel and for tips. Should have bought them in London, but you'd run out of sterling and didn't want to be ripped off going from dollars to francs. Still, you've got a 100 Swiss franc note plus dollar travelers cheques. And you're going to need deutschmarks tomorrow. Save the Swiss francs for that. So let's cash a $50 cheque. What's the rate? What the hell! It's a zero-sum game. Sort it out when you get home.

I'm sure you are better organized. But not everyone thinks of the cost of money itself as a manageable item in a travel budget. Most of us take a bunch of cards, some traveler's cheques, a bit of cash and hope for the best. Yet you can lose quite a lot of money just by changing it in the wrong places and in the wrong form. The art of managing money on the move is to have the right mix of payment for every kind of trip, taking into account security, cost and convenience.

These days you can pay for most things with plastic. (In the United States, you can't get by without it.) Using a card can put off the evil day of repayment. But you're exposed to currency changes from the time you use them to the time the voucher is processed by the system. This can vary from a couple of hours to a couple of weeks.

The only snag is that the exchange rate used by your bank is that of the day it records the transaction, not when you incurred the charge. It's a question of roundabouts and swings. You may make a killing or be in for a shock depending on whether your home currency has strengthened or weakened against the other. It may also be worth acquiring a dollar-based card.

What counts with cards is that you can get cash wherever you are in local currency from growing networks of ATMs (automated teller machines). There are daily limits on how much you can draw (typically $300 a day), depending on the colour of your plastic. Electronic cash can cost you up to 3 per cent 'handling' charge, and according to some insiders, the exchange rate isn't as good as you can get over the counter for cash.

Cash, it is said, is the poor man's credit card. But there's no sign of it going out of style. Cash, of course, is also the most vulnerable to loss and theft – and to the cupidity of money changers.

Banks make their money from the 'spread' between the 'buy' and 'sell' rate. This can be confusing. The buy rate is the rate at which the bank will buy your dollars, say, in London and sell you pounds. The sell rate is for buying dollars. The narrower the spread, the better the deal. And then you'll pay a commission of around 1.5 per cent. The easiest way to figure it all out is to ask how much they'll give you for $100 after all deductions.

If you need several currencies, make sure they don't charge separate commissions on each, instead of treating them as a single transaction. Another rip-off is charging you for two transactions when you change money into a third currency. Let's say you go into a bank in London and ask to change Swiss francs into dollars. Yes, they can do that, you'll be told. But first they have to be changed into pounds and then into dollars, meaning a double commission for the banks. Countries with soft currencies and vertiginous inflation rates often have stringent controls on imports and exports of their own currency and foreign money. Keep receipts of all transactions. And do not expect to be able to change back local currency into hard currency when you leave.

Should you change money at home or abroad? Generally speaking, you get a better rate when you buy the foreign currency in your own country. But it's always worth checking.

You may get a slightly better rate for cheques than cash, especially when cashing large sums. But the commission rate is sometimes higher. Normally you pay a commission of 1–2 per cent on cheques when you buy them and when you return unused foreign currency cheques to your bank. But a good business travel agent should be able to waive the commission.

Dos and don'ts

 Do take a sensible mix of cash, credit cards and traveler's cheques.

Do ask your travel agent whether it is better to change money before you leave or at your destination. Remember, you might have to order some currencies in advance.

Do consider prepaying as many expenses as you can: air tickets, hotels and car rental. Or get guaranteed rates in your own currency.

Do watch for spending limits on credit cards, and place your accounts in the black to avoid interest charges.

Don't keep traveler's cheques, cash and cards in the same place. Keep a list of cheque numbers and phone numbers to call in the event of theft or loss.

Do check for restrictions on importing or exporting cash in some countries.

Off and running with the euro

Travelers are learning to love the euro – the new single European currency that came into being on 1 January 1999. You will no longer have to figure out how many zillion lire to the dollar or pesetas to the French franc or Belgian francs to the guilder – plus you'll save a fortune not having to change money back and forth.

With euro notes and coins not due to enter circulation for another three years, the euro may seem unreal: an invisible currency that can only be used in non-cash transactions, such as charge-card payments, traveler's cheques and direct debits.

On 1 January 2002, euro notes and coins will be introduced and all prices will be posted in euros. National currencies will be gradually withdrawn and will cease to be legal tender by 30 June 2002, at the latest. The four European Union members that are not in the European Monetary Union (EMU) – the United Kingdom, Sweden, Denmark and Greece – may join the second wave around 2002.

Consolidating expenses in euros means that you just have one foreign exchange cost – between the euro and your own currency, such as dollars, yen or the UK pound. And with a euro–dollar exchange of one-to-one for practical purposes (the euro was almost at parity with the dollar by mid-July 1999, having lost 15 per cent of its value in the first six months) it's easy to see what you're spending and compare euro prices – and therefore the value of goods and services in various countries.

Even in the United Kingdom – perhaps especially in the United Kingdom – where sterling still reigns, major retailers are already accepting euros and major businesses are starting to denominate contracts in euros, forcing suppliers to do the same.

Price transparency in the 11 countries of the euro-zone – Austria, Belgium, Finland, France, Germany, Ireland, Italy, Luxembourg, The Netherlands, Portugal and Spain – will make it much easier to shop for the best cross-border air fares, hotel rates and other travel services in different countries once all prices are posted in euros. This ability to compare prices should lead to more competition and bring prices more in line across borders.

It's worth stating the obvious: that during the three-year transition, national currencies still exist alongside the euro. The 11 euro-zone currencies are locked in a fixed exchange rate with the euro. Thus there are 6.55957 French francs; 40.3399 Belgium-Luxembourg francs and 1.95583 deutschmarks to the euro. So there are no more fluctuations between the euro currencies and, therefore, no exchange costs because they are all expressions of the same money – the euro.

However, don't expect merchants or banks to round all those decimal places up or down in your favour. And some banks in euro-zone countries are charging 'handling fees' – officially frowned upon in Brussels – to replace the foreign exchange 'spread' between the buy and sell rates for currencies that you see posted in banks and bureaux de change.

Single-currency rules apply also to the four countries outside the euro zone – the United Kingdom, Sweden, Greece and Denmark, so that if you want to change, say, French francs to deutschmarks in London, you should be able to save money through the fixed-rate system. But many banks still charge for two foreign-exchange spreads by taking you through sterling. Banks normally make 1 to 3 per cent on each transaction, So you could end up paying 6 per cent.

Travelers are seeing prices posted in euros alongside national currencies. But you are not obliged to pay in euros – nor are merchants obliged to accept euros – during the three-year transition.

But it makes sense to start thinking euros, and make as many transactions as possible in euros with euro-denominated traveler's cheques or on your charge card.

'Travelers are able to pay for tickets in euros or local currency,' says Anita Macleod, head of a euro task force at the International Air Transport Association in Geneva. 'We have common ticket stock available that accepts the euro or local currency – but we're not forcing airlines to deal in euros.'

Most major airlines already accept the new currency. Travelers, for example, on Air France or British Airways flights from euro-zone countries can choose to pay in euros or local currency. Major hotel chains are 'euro compliant'.

American Express, Thomas Cook and Visa International issue euro traveler's cheques in denominations of 50, 100, 200 and 500 euros, and banks are starting to issue euro-denominated credit and debit cards for corporate and individual travelers.

Keith Meyrick, director of worldwide-acceptance traveler's cheques at American Express, says: 'We've been selling about $100,000 a day in euro cheques since 1 January 1999. Apart from Europe, the majority of sales are in long-haul markets into Europe – like Japan, the United States, Australia and Korea. People are saying, "I'm visiting two or three countries, so instead of taking dollars, francs or deutschmarks, I'll just take euros, which is a distinct advantage traveling across borders." You don't have to bother about getting small amounts of local currency and worrying about exchange rates every time.'

Paying by card is likely to be more straightforward. You don't need a euro-designated card to deal in euros – your normal card works the same as for any foreign currency. If the merchant accepts payment in euros and you pay in euros, euros will show up on your statement, converted into your own currency. There is no financial gain. But it enables you to compare prices in euros, avoids you having to check half-a-dozen exchange rates and makes it easier to fill out expense reports.

Frequent travelers to Europe should consider opening a euro account along with a euro-denominated card. Thus, whatever the transaction currency, your statement will be expressed in euros. This depends on your bank's capability. Citibank has launched a euro current account and debit card – where payments are taken directly out of your account – while some banks, such as NatWest in the United Kingdom, are planning to launch corporate euro cards. Lloyds says it can open a euro account in London with a euro debit card.

'You don't need to have an account in euros to be able to have a euro-designated credit card,' says Hasan Alemdar, head of the single currency unit at Visa International. 'You get your statement at the end of the month and make your payment in the normal way from whatever bank you hold your money. Several banks in the euro-zone are offering currency accounts that can be debited in euros or national currencies. A euro account enables you to choose the right time to transfer money into it depending on the exchange rate between, say, the dollar and the euro.

'Judging from cross-border euro transactions going through our system, acceptance of the euro is quite wide and will increase. A significant proportion of traffic is from Belgian, French, Spanish and Portuguese card-holders.'

Whatever card you carry, be aware that there are several types of terminal where your card is swiped at the point of sale: mono-currency terminals which work either in euros or national currencies – which may display the euro equivalent for information only; and dual currency terminals, where you decide which currency you wish to sign for.

Make sure you sign for the same currency that you agreed for the transaction. It's easy to be misled or confused when you see euros and local currency on the cardholder's receipt. There's quite a difference between 500 francs and 500 euros.

The art of keeping out of touch

Do I sincerely want to take the office with me when I travel? This is the question that business travelers need to ask themselves in the face of growing pressure to spend as little time as possible getting where they're going, while being as productive as possible on the way. In-flight phones and faxes, notebook computers that pack the punch of desktop PCs, e-mail, voice mail, and the new generation of digital mobiles, enable you to catch up with office work and keep in touch with anyone anywhere in the world at any time. And, more ominously, for anyone to keep in touch with you.

But if you're going to do all your business on the phone and fax, there doesn't seem much point in traveling. Business travel is about face-to-face relationships. What we need is a strategy for keeping out of touch – or rather, keeping in touch on our own terms.

In the late 1960s, life on the road was fairly simple: 'Is there a number where we can reach you?' Or 'Please call when you arrive' my boss would say when I was leaving for the airport. Those were the days before direct dialling, when you sometimes had to book an international call. The worst that could happen when you got to the hotel was a garbled telex, which you then decided whether or not you had received. You could go missing for days on the strength of a fugitive telex back home.

In-flight options were simple too. There was the in-flight movie and elevator music on the sound channels and earphones with those little plugs that used to bore their way into your brain. So as a back-of-the-envelope man, I would wine and dine and lip-read the movie while drafting the long-range plan. Which ensured me a good night's sleep.

Nowadays you have to make the agonizing management decision whether to watch the seat-back video or chat with the corporate Kremlin by telephone, fax or online with your laptop (although I've never actually seen anyone doing this except in airline ads). You lift the handset from beneath the armrest or the seat-back in front and insert your credit card to be in touch anywhere in the world either via terrestrial cellular systems or satellite. You are now expected to stay completely wired at all times, providing you with several more hours in which to work, drain laptop batteries and forget to call your loved ones.

Seat-back telephones have long been a familiar sight. The latest digital systems offer fax transmission and reception (via a keypad and seat-back screen) along with news, weather, and real-time stock market reports.

There is now the promise (or threat) of ground-to-air telephone calls. Fortunately, you are able to reject an incoming call when the caller's number appears on the screen. If you're not at your seat when the phone rings, the incoming number will be stored as a message. So you may want to ask to change seats.

But wait for the new generation of featherweight digital personal communications network (PCN) mobiles, allowing people to call you wherever you are. They can even be patched through by the office switchboard. Soon there'll be no place left to hide.

The secret of Management by Absence is to convince people that it's their fault that they cannot get hold of you. And that you'd get hold of them if only you could. But it's important to keep the initiative. There's nothing like firing off electronic messages from a moving target to keep people on their toes. This allows you to pre-empt calls to you. Exploit time zones by leaving voice-mail messages when there's nobody in the office. Never do business in the country you are visiting, but always contrive to be on the phone to somewhere else. Experts leave a trail of unrequited requests to call back. ('Ah, he's just left for the airport. You may be able to catch him in Sidi Barrani.')

It's hard to go convincingly missing these days although I have been known to check out of my hotel with the bedside message light still blinking.

A major problem (and opportunity) with faxes is never knowing if they've arrived. (Some people connect the fax to the paper-shredder, on the principle we applied to top-secret documents in the army: 'Destroy before reading.') The question 'Did you get my fax?' is far from rhetorical. It usually elicits a pause followed by the doom-laden words: 'Look, I'm going to give you another number.' So it's always safe to say later that you never got a fax.

The best approach if you really want to get through is to scatter your faxes to several numbers in the hope that at least one will get through. Or use the scrambler. The latest fax machines have a special control which randomly squeezes lines to unreadability or else expands them into a sort of supermarket bar code. State-of-the-art is never having to say you're sorry.

How to beat Murphy's Law

Robert Louis Stevenson got it wrong: 'To travel less hopefully is better than to arrive'. After all, an optimist is simply a pessimist who is badly informed. The only way to beat Murphy's Law is rigorous planning and attention to detail.

That, in turn, comes down to preparing worst-case scenarios and contingency plans for every eventuality. The pain and paradox of travel are that small things make a big difference.

You've thought of the predictable nightmares – like forgetting your malaria tablets (carry a prescription); or taking off with the car keys, leaving your wife stranded at the airport (tape a spare set of keys under the seat); or risking the death penalty in Singapore by smuggling chewing gum.

You've stowed a folding umbrella to ensure that it doesn't rain, or a heavy coat if you're hoping for warm weather; plus your *feng shui* talisman to placate angry dragons.

But the savvy traveler is always tuned to expect the unexpected, a paradigm of business itself. Planning for things to go wrong is the best way to make sure things go right.

When it comes to serious paranoia, it is airports, not airlines, that are the slowest common denominator of air travel.

One of the worst things that can happen is missing a connecting flight on a multi-sector itinerary just when you thought you had hours to kill checking out expensive bargains at the duty-free boutiques, resulting in a cascade of broken appointments and concomitant recriminations.

Check points for fated travelers

 Never trust official 'minimum connecting times' at airports. Even the best travel agents can lead you astray. The OAG *Pocket Flight Guide* gives minimum connecting times between carriers (inter-line) and between the same carrier (online) at more than 500 airports around the world. If your connection is crucial, allow twice as much time for changing planes, especially to another carrier.

 Book a non-stop flight whenever possible. Next best is a 'direct' flight when you stop somewhere but don't change planes. Watch out for 'code share' flights where a single flight number conceals a change of plane or carrier. This may not always show up on computer screens. Check that the airline will respect your seating (or dietary) requirements, especially if you have to change to a smaller plane.

 If you cannot avoid changing planes, try to stick with the same airline or code-share partner. Such connecting flights are often in the same part of the airport. And airlines are more likely to hold a connecting flights for late-arriving passengers. A curse unless it's you who arrives late.

 Build a file of airport information – plans, diagrams, phone numbers for airline reservations, limos and taxi firms, and airport services. Keep crucial phone numbers in your top pocket to allow for when the chap meeting you doesn't turn up.

 Carry enough local change to get to the office or hotel. Otherwise, you'll find the bureau de change is closed.

 Should it become clear during the flight that you're likely to miss your connection, check with the cabin staff for an alternative flight. Ask them to reseat you near an exit door for a faster getaway. Ask for the gate numbers so you can plan your safari across the terminal. It helps to have packed all you need for 24 hours in your hand baggage.

 Avoid booking the last flight of the day that connects you to your final destination. You may be stuck at the hub overnight. If this is unavoidable, try to persuade the airline to put you up at an airport hotel. You have more clout with a full-fare ticket or an elite-level frequent-flier card.

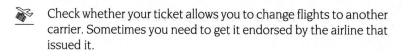 Check whether your ticket allows you to change flights to another carrier. Sometimes you need to get it endorsed by the airline that issued it.

Check that your travel insurance covers what you need and is there when you need it. Insist on direct settlement of hospital bills, not reimbursement. Medical cover must include emergency repatriation. Make sure you have adequate personal liability cover when renting a car in the United States.

Never hit the car rental desk without a reservation. Otherwise, the 'only car available' at 10 pm in Frankfurt is sure to be a top model Mercedes.

Above all, pace yourself. Don't try to accomplish too much. Leave a day here and there for R&R – and to allow for things to go wrong.

Fighting for survival in cattle class

There is no vaccine, no miracle cure. But recognizing certain symptoms and doing something about them can help to minimize the misery.

Premium cabins, of course, allow you space to stretch out and suffer in comfort. But whether you turn left or right at the top of the steps, well-being in the air depends a lot on the quality of air in the cabin (at least 50 per cent of which is re-circulated). And this can depend on the efficiency of catalytic air filters, which remove harmful ozone (a short, hard cough is typical of ozone – along with eye discomfort, nose and throat irritation, and headache) – and high levels of carbon dioxide. Oxygen shortage can lead to euphoria, behavioural changes, memory impairment, and lack of judgement and physical co-ordination. (Tell the flight attendant, *sotto voce*, that 'the air's a bit thick in here. Could you please ask the captain to tweak up the AC unit?')

There are two facets to discomfort in the air. First is the way you feel during the journey and immediately on arrival. Second is jet lag. The two are completely different. If you took a 10-hour car journey back home, you'd feel much the same – having been up all night in cramped conditions, all of the environmental things. Jet lag steps in subsequently when your body tries to do things at all the wrong times.

A lot of the discomfort you feel in the cabin is not due to dehydration through the atmosphere, but because you are stuck in your seat. Dry air is a factor in making your eyes, nasal passages and throat uncomfortable – but only a minor factor in fluid loss. What happens when you're sitting upright in an incredibly uncomfortable position is squashing the central blood vessels, which makes it more difficult for blood to get back to the heart. The effect of that is to shift fluid out of the bloodstream into the tissues where it's not available to the circulation. So your feet and legs swell. By the end of the flight you may have about four pounds of fluid that is sequestered in the tissues. Unless you drink water, you are dehydrated by that amount.

A minor consequence of swollen feet is that you can't get your shoes back on at the end of the flight. Much more alarming is the risk of a blood clot or thrombosis forming in the veins of your legs. This can be life-threatening if a clot detaches and goes to the heart. A British woman had to have her leg amputated the day after traveling for 10 hours in a cramped plane. Research carried out in the United States confirmed what doctors have long suspected – that 50 per cent of patients suffering blood clots (or DVT, deep vein thrombosis) had recently been in the air for four hours or more. Don't ignore pains in the calf muscles or chest when you arrive. Seek medical advice.

Researchers at the Johnson Space Center in Texas say that prolonged immobility in flight causes the body to lose large amounts of potassium – which is vital to optimum physical condition.

The prescription is to stretch your legs as often as you can, and take a minute every so often to contract and relax your calf muscles during the flight to pump blood up through your veins. Turn your feet in circles from the ankles, first in one direction, then in the other. Stretch your feet with your toes pointing upwards. Hold for a minute, then breathe out and relax. Drink plenty of water – at least a pint every three hours – but avoid alcohol, coffee, chocolate and tea, which promote dehydration, and eat sparingly. Some doctors advise taking low-dose aspirin to thin the blood.

Airline food is very dry – it's low in water and low in fibre. Best to bring a picnic with crusty bread and fresh fruit. Get rid of the meal tray fast so it doesn't keep you pinned in your seat.

Little things can make a big difference. Bring a neck-support pillow or wedge a pillow behind your neck, take a nasal saline spray and a moisturizer or a water atomizer to refresh the skin and wear loose-fitting clothes. Doctors advise against wearing contact lenses for any flight longer than four hours.

But the strategic advice is to find a plane where you have space to stretch out. There are only two kinds of plane – an empty plane and a full plane. You can put up with even the worst cattle-class seating if you find an empty seat next to you. The ideal position to travel is horizontal. Nothing beats stretching out across four seats in economy – better than business class, where you can't put the armrests up. (Even first class doesn't always allow you to get the feet higher than your head.) Failing that, try to sit behind an empty seat, push the seat-back forward and stretch your legs over it. Or at night, lie on the floor.

On a wide-body plane, you can increase the odds of having an empty seat next to you by asking for an aisle seat in the centre section. At least you can stretch your legs in the aisle from time to time. And join the queue for the lavatory. Jogging on the spot is fine, but avoid shadow boxing – it can send the wrong message. Avoid the middle seat at all costs. Most wide-bodies and some narrow-bodies have exit doors in the middle of the cabin. The seat rows right behind those doors have extra legroom. In narrow-bodies, seats next to the emergency exits over the wings usually have more legroom.

When it comes to medical emergencies, such as cardiac arrest, you cannot rely – as airlines do – on a doctor being on board – or at least the right sort of doctor. I think I'd sooner succumb with a 'Singapore Girl' soothing my fevered brow than have a tracheotomy performed by a $100-an-hour shrink from Manhattan.

You might be lucky. On an Aer Lingus flight from Frankfurt to Dublin, a passenger had a heart attack and the call went out for a doctor. Thirty-five hands shot up – cardiologists on their way to a conference with all their equipment! But only a handful of carriers – including Virgin Atlantic, American Airlines, and Qantas – carry automatic defibrillators that can safely be used by trained cabin staff. This may be your only hope of survival on a plane far from land.

Travelers with circulatory, pulmonary or cardiac conditions should be aware that low humidity and pressurization can seriously alter the effects of medication. Consult your physician. And check which airlines carry the drugs you need.

Better still, carry your own drugs in hand luggage. Asthmatic patients will take their own inhalers and salbutamol with them. But in the case of a severe attack, you may need steroids. Diabetics traveling through several time zones may need to carry injectable glycogen or dextrose. Low concentration of blood sugar can be a real emergency.

Setting your biological clock

One of the most daunting management decisions I ever made was not to self-destruct on vintage champagne and a premature lunch when I flew Concorde from London to New York for a job interview. I compromised with a glass or three of Moët et Chandon, a sandwich and a cup of coffee. I finally lunched with my inquisitors at around 5.30 pm my time and flew back economy (this was before the days of business class, but still!) at 7 pm, which was midnight for me. I landed in London at 8 am (3 am in New York) in quite good shape. I unwittingly beat jet lag by staying on my home time. (I got the job by the way.)

Jet lag, of course, is what happens when the biological clock gets out of sync with the chronological clock of a new time zone. Your body is geared for sleep at a time you are expected to be awake, and vice versa. Most people say they get more jet lag flying east than west. They find it easier to cope with a longer day than a shorter night. The reason is that the circadian rhythm has a natural tendency to run at a sleep–wake cycle of 25.2 hours. So if you fly west you're gaining on yourself the whole time and the clock has to run a bit faster whereas coming the other way it has to run slower, which it seems is harder for it to do. Westward flights produce premature awakenings plus sleepiness in the evening. Eastward flights result in difficulties staying asleep and morning sleepiness.

Light is the main trigger, or synchronizer, of the clock, although social cues, like mealtimes, also affect circadian rhythm. Most people adjust at the rate of one time zone per day. This means you would need a week to properly adjust to a flight from, say, Europe to the Far East.

Ask a dozen frequent travelers how to cope with jet lag and you're likely to get a dozen different answers – from elaborate diets, in-flight aerobics, and aromatherapy, to seeking nirvana through meditation (or medication).

Conventional wisdom says you should adjust as fast as you can to local time by resetting your watch and thinking in the destination time the moment you get on the plane. Expose yourself to bright light – especially sunlight – depending on which direction you are traveling. From London, for example, traveling to Tokyo, try to get out in the sunlight later in the day when you arrive. Going west to Los Angeles, try to get a good dose of sunlight as soon as you arrive. The idea is that light suppresses melatonin – a sleep-inducing hormone secreted in the late evening, and thought to be the master synchronizer of circadian rhythm.

However, recent studies suggest that the best strategy for trips of up to 48 hours is not to adjust but stay on your home time. This is the advice that many airlines are giving to their air crew members.

If you are staying less than 48 hours and have to work when you come back, it is important to stay with your home rhythm and try to eat sparingly. Wear sunglasses at times when it's dark at home, get artificial light to simulate sunlight when it's supposed to be daytime there and don't sleep when you shouldn't. Going west, go to bed as soon as you can and get what doctors call 'anchor sleep' for, say, five hours. You can still go out for late dinner. It's important to get plenty of sleep before you leave home. Napping can help.

But you have to compromise between what is going on where you're going and at home: you'll find there's an overlap of some four hours. If you're going for longer than 48 hours, adjust to local time. It's a strategic decision.

The real challenge is traveling to the Far East with a 7- to 9-hour time shift.

Says one old Asian hand: 'I've tried leaving Europe in the morning and getting to Hong Kong first thing in their morning; and I've tried leaving Europe in the evening and arriving Hong Kong at 3 or 4 the next afternoon – by far the best. There is nothing worse than arriving at 7 in the morning, when you've been up all night and you're confronted with a full day ahead of you. You can't even check into your hotel for another five or six hours. Whereas if you arrive at about 3pm local time, then you can either have a quick nap or even better hold off until 9 pm local time and then go to bed.

'It's best to stay on your home schedule. Your day starts later and finishes later – so plan your business meetings for the afternoon and evening. The worst part is not so much the time change, but how much sleep can you really get on that long, 12-to-14-hour eastward flight.

Beyond that, even if you try to adjust immediately to the local time it catches up with you about the third day.

'Therefore, in a perfect world, if I am flying out east for more than 48 hours, I would fly on Wednesday so that on the third day, when the loss of sleep hits you, you are on a weekend to recover without losing any business.'

The moral is that next time you face a midnight lunch appointment, make sure you get a proper day's sleep.

Dos and don'ts

 Do try staying on your home time for a trip less than 48 hours. But adapt as quickly as possible to local time if your stay is longer.

 Do try when traveling east to schedule your arrival for late afternoon. Have a meeting, go to bed late, and start late local time next morning. Traveling west, try to have meetings from early morning through early afternoon. Then sleep on your home time.

 Don't expose yourself to sunlight when it is supposed to be your normal night.

 Don't skip meals but make them smaller than you'd like, especially during your normal night. Avoid alcohol, tea and coffee on the plane. Cut out fatty foods. And consider ordering a vegetarian meal.

Tokyo's Hotel Okura has a novel 'Jet Lag Plan' to help arriving business guests reset their body clocks. The plan includes a health club workout, with a spell in the 'body sonic massage chair'; a 'light box' to help you adjust to the new time zone; 'relaxation videos' for when you're tired but cannot sleep; bespoke pillows (kept for your next visit), and special menus – a high-protein breakfast and carbohydrate-loaded dinners. 'Teriyaki Beef with Yuba and Tofu' at the crack of dawn is said to sort out the most recalcitrant circadian desynchronism.

The full jet lag treatment costs 10,000 yen, or about $120, plus meals. But the treatment comes free for members of Okura Club International, which you can join for free when you arrive.

A friendly voice on the road

Road warriors of the millennium are slaves to progress. In-flight phones and faxes, laptop computers that pack the punch of desktop PCs, e-mail, voice mail and the new generation of digital mobiles enable (and compel) you to catch up with office work and keep in touch with anyone anywhere in the world at any time. And, more ominously, for anyone to keep in touch with you. There's no excuse these days for not being totally wired.

Stunning advances in speech-recognition technology now allow travelers to dictate documents such as faxes and e-mail into a laptop computer at twice the speed of the average professional typist and to have e-mail and fax messages read back to them. All you need is a microphone/speaker and some inexpensive software. Should you find yourself – heaven forbid! – without your laptop or a friendly neighbour-hood computer, you can do much the same thing from any touch-tone phone. Just call a personal 800 number from anywhere in the world and have your e-mail, faxes or travel information, such as airline schedules, read to you. You can respond to, say, a fax, with an e-mail or voice-mail message, or edit and redistribute faxes and voice messages as e-mail. Marshall McLuhan is vindicated: the medium is the message and the message is the medium.

Talking to a computer, either direct or on the phone, is the ultimate user-friendly interface with your personal cybernetic secretary. No need to type or click with a mouse, just speak naturally to your PC to open files and e-mail, format text or surf the Net.

Premiere Technologies, Inc. in Atlanta, Georgia, has a product called Orchestrate that allows you to receive and redirect messages from one medium to another either with a laptop PC via the Internet or by telephone. You sign up for an e-mail address – your own home page – with a 10-digit access number and 4-digit PIN on the Orchestrate Web site at www.orchestrate.net, plus an 800 number that you can call from anywhere in the world to do much the same thing via voice prompts.

Steve Walden, vice president Internet strategy at Premiere Technologies, Inc., says: 'Your personal 800 number virtually makes the telephone and the computer interchangeable; so as long as you have access to the Internet, you can go to your personal Web page and check your voice mail, your e-mail and faxes either through a screen or by voice through the telephone. The basic premise is: that you can reach – or be reached – by anyone, no matter where you are, through whatever medium you choose. Let's say I get a fax at 11 pm at the hotel that I want my staff to read, I can click on an icon, either on my laptop or the hotel PC, and it will send the message to them by their preferred method of delivery – Joe prefers it by e-mail, Sally by fax, John prefers a phone message.

'But let's say I just have a phone – I'm changing planes in London. You dial into your personal 800 number and a voice says, "Good afternoon, Roger. Would you like to hear your messages?" It will play your voice-mail, read your e-mail or faxes and then it will give you options through a series of voice prompts, to which you respond by hitting numbers on the key-pad, such as, Do you want to forward this? Do you want to respond to this? It will take you down a decision-tree: you have six e-mails, two voice messages, six faxes, which would you like to listen to? You can decide what messages you want to listen to, store for later, or delete. You can also direct a fax or e-mail to a local fax machine if you want it on paper. And on the Internet version, you can attach a voice message to an e-mail message.

'There are two levels of voices. A pre-recorded voice with the 25 to 30 prompts that are needed to take you through the menu; and a digitized voice that recognizes texts and translates that into speech. The next stage will be actual voice recognition where you won't need to give a password.'

David Dingley, a travel and transportation specialist at IBM in London, says: 'You have to make a distinction between a machine understanding your dictation and turning your words into text and a machine understanding the meaning of anything you say and replying to you – an open-ended conversation. That is a huge challenge and I'm not aware of anyone having got near that yet. What we do have is software that will understand and act on relatively simple commands in what you might call a bounded context, such as travel or emergency medicine.'

IBM's most advanced speech recognition software – ViaVoice Gold – allows you to speak naturally, without pausing between words, to your PC. It will respond to any voice with a high degree of accuracy and check for spelling mistakes. But you can train it to your personal voice and vocabulary (it has a 260,000-word dictionary) and key words, which automatically trigger commonly used phrases, paragraphs or salutations.

PureVoice, offered by Qualcomm Inc. in San Diego, California, a company that develops wireless communications systems and Internet messaging products, provides enhanced voice quality on the Web.

'PureVoice produces a very clear reproduction of your voice in a digital format with high compression, which means a smaller file and a faster transmission time,' says Arnold Gum, product manager for PureVoice in San Diego. 'That format is something that you could e-mail or use in a program over the Internet. PureVoice enables you to add voice attachments to your e-mail. A lot of people like to hear a message in a natural voice; it's more personal and it allows you to communicate more information faster than a typed text. People say we love sending e-mail, but we don't type. So you add a PureVoice message to your e-mail message. It's great. It's as easy to use as a tape player on your PC.'

'The next step towards voice recognition is, will this thing understand what my words mean and interpret a relatively complex command?' Dingley says. 'We gave a demonstration of a flight enquiry system to IATA recently, "Show me flights from London to New York", in the way a normal person would phrase the question. And the system read back the flight times. We had all sorts of people asking it about flights, any way they chose; and it was giving the right answer most of the time. You could do that over the phone.

'I can see other devices that you can talk to and they'll do things for you. For example, if you ring up our lab in Hawthorne, you can say, "Connect me to Sally", and it does. It's like the flight enquiries thing, a bounded context. Another approach is when I speak to this thing, can it identify me as Dave Dingley through my voice-print with enough accuracy for it to be a secure device. In other words, whenever I speak to it, whether I've got a cold or a hangover or I'm talking down the phone, it will know it's me. There are rumours that some military establishments are capable of doing that. But we're talking serious computer power.

'One use for voice recognition is in customer service. Right now we're running an exercise with a major airline. Imagine a situation at check-in where reps moving around without a keyboard need to interact with the computer and the customer. They could be wearing one of these tiny microphones so that when they say, "Good morning, Mr Dingley", to the customer, they would get a voice whispering back in their ear from the computer, which had looked up Dingley, saying something like "Dingley, flight 123, difficult customer, look after him".'

Some of my best friends are strangers

Slot me into an airline seat next to an interesting-looking neighbour, with a gin and tonic and a back-up copy of *War and Peace*, and I'll surrender to serendipity. After all these years, and goodness knows how many expense-account miles, my think-bubble still fills with anticipatory asterisks and exclamation marks at the prospect of meeting someone new. I remain an unreconstructed Walter Mitty who has not accepted that the most interesting person on the plane is sure to be sitting two rows in front of me. Human contact – however inhuman – is probably the last adventure left in air travel.

Not that Fate has always given me an even hand. Sartre knew what he was talking about when he said: 'Hell is other people.' There was the man who spent six excruciating hours trying to sell me a corporate jet; the woman I spent six delightful hours trying to seduce, only to have the cool dry handshake after touchdown. 'No, I'm OK, thanks, my husband's meeting me.' And the long-distance life story: 'You're a writer! My life has been so interesting. I'll tell you my story, you write it up and we'll split the proceeds.'

(Even worse was boasting about being a writer, only to meet a real novelist on a promotion tour for his new book – the kind where the author's name is three times as big as the title.)

But why do people have this urge to tell you their life story? And why are instant friendships forgotten as soon as the wheels touch down? The truth is that nobody wants to remember. As Groucho said: 'I never forget a face; but in your case I'll make an exception.'

My theory is that the relationship between passengers sitting next to one another in a plane has a confessional element to it. Relaxed by food and drink and the prospect of never meeting your captive companion again, you can unburden your soul without trepidation.

In the old days, before seats were assigned, you had to target a seat mate in the departure lounge, follow him or her up the steps into the plane, and fling your briefcase on to the adjacent seat with a disingenuous smile.

Nowadays, you're left to the mercy of the check-in clerk. On long flights I ask for an aisle seat so that I can escape from my seat mate or adopt a custodial stance as circumstances demand. 'Shall we share a central table?' or perhaps a more risqué, 'Your armrest or mine?' are useful gambits when the drinks come round.

People who complain about getting shanghaied by in-flight bores often have themselves to blame. Simple stratagems like putting on the headset, fiddling with your laptop or pretending to read (or write) A *Brief History of Time* should do the trick. The ultimate conversation killer is to answer 'What do you do?' with: 'I'm in deep-sea sewage'.

One way to attract attention is to delve into a crowded briefcase (people can't resist squinting at someone else's belongings). You can lubricate the gambit with a conversation piece, like bundles of $100 bills or a stuffed boa constrictor.

But don't make the same mistake as a former colleague of mine on a flight home from India. He showed a necklace he had bought for his wife (this is a true story) to the woman he'd been chatting up – which she graciously accepted.

One idea might be to allow us to change seats half-way through a flight so everybody gets the chance to meet. After all, on a long-haul flight you may be in the air for up to 16 hours. That's almost long enough to get married, start a family and get divorced, although not necessarily in that order. (No, I have not, is the answer to your question.) The next generation of 600-seat jumbos promised/threatened by Boeing and Airbus will be like airborne villages with infinite scope for social congress, should we so desire.

Meanwhile, I think airlines should offer more latitude (not to mention longitude) in choosing in-flight companions. One idea might be to use the reservations computer for a spot of computer dating. They would simply punch in your high-altitude likes and dislikes and match you with a suitable seat mate.

We might even see appeals like the following in the personal column of the *New York Review of Books*.

Sales executive, 35 (can pass for 34), attractive management style, into white-water canoeing, Indian artefacts, client lunches, seeks upwardly nubile flight companion for meaningful business-class relationship, view sharing seat-back videos, tall stories. Sincere replies only, please.

But if you find, as I do, that most fruitful in-flight encounters take place in the mind, beware of the 'snore syndrome' – floating off into a Mittyesque trance, and waking up to dusty looks from your neighbours.

Dos and don'ts

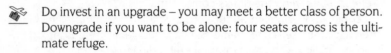 Do invest in an upgrade – you may meet a better class of person. Downgrade if you want to be alone: four seats across is the ultimate refuge.

Do avoid the middle seat at all costs. Yes, you have a choice of two neighbours but it's hard to escape. The aisle seat offers strategic flexibility.

Do avoid children (they're usually up front of every cabin) – unless you want advice on the latest computer software.

Do take plenty of reading material for emergencies. If you don't have *War and Peace*, pretend you're writing it.

Don't go overboard eating and drinking everything in sight; you never know who may be sitting beside you. Wrap-around magenta shades and mineral water with a musical score or screenplay invite more scrupulous attention.

Don't say to a celebrity: 'I've seen your face before. Give me a second...'.

Don't boast or make indiscreet remarks until you've positively identified your neighbour. He or she may know your boss/client/auditor/husband/wife.

Don't hand out someone else's business card – unless that is the statement you really want to make.

Have expenses, will travel

You may not have heard the story of the salesman who is summoned by his boss to explain an egregious item in his expense account. 'Now see here, Joe. I know you've had a tough month chasing the Fingelstein order up in Niagara Falls. But $500 for an overcoat! You know there's no way I can approve that. You'd better go away and re-work these expenses.'

The next day Joe's boss is apoplectic. 'Joe, these expenses come to the same as before. What about that overcoat?'

Joe is unchastened. 'Ah, yes, Mel, I know it's the same total. But now you find the overcoat!'

Had Joe's company given him a fixed daily travel allowance for meals and incidental expenses, he could perhaps have bought the overcoat with a clear conscience by skipping a few lunches or dinners – or by making a pre-emptive call to his boss. 'Mel, I've landed the Fingelstein business! He's invited me up to Yellowknife for the weekend... Mel, listen, I'm going to have to buy an overcoat.'

The moral: Travel expenses – however outrageous – should be transparent. The best place to hide something is out in the open; you can get away with (almost) anything if you can show that you are: 1) saving the company money and 2) getting results beyond the call of duty. Always make the most of your moral mileage – not to be confused with frequent-flier mileage.

'Travel Management' in most organizations is mainly about accounting control of travel and entertainment – who is allowed to travel first or business class; or stay in a certain category of hotel; and how many signatures are needed to sign off on expenses. Nobody takes much notice whether a trip is necessary as long as the procedures are followed. Look after the expenses and the trip will look after itself.

The converse of travel management is Management by Expenses, which can range from creative exploitation of the rules (enshrined in the corporate travel policy and procedures) to grand larceny. It's rather like the legal difference between 'tax avoidance' and 'tax evasion' – between being smart and being dishonest.

Expense account aficionados swear by corporate plastic. A corporate charge card helps no end with personal cash-flow. But it can lead to hassles with the bean counters when you're trying to sort out who owes whom at the end of a trip. This is fairly clear-cut when you're 'extending' a business trip to Hong Kong to include a long weekend in Bangkok with your loved one by getting the travel agency to 'pro rata' the difference to your account. Trying to get a hotel cashier to let you pay for personal items on the bill with cash or your own plastic can be a nightmare. Checking out is bad enough at the best of times.

In my corporate days, I preferred my own plastic in felicitous conjunction with a cash travel advance (better you owing them than them owing you) and then ostentatiously deducting personal expenses, like private telephone calls, drinks in the disco, or the cost of a friend joining me for breakfast. There's no point in being virtuous unless you are seen to be virtuous.

Make the most of full-fare business tickets by exploiting two-for-one promotions or half-price companion fares. Some airlines offer a free 24-hour stopover package as an incentive to fly through their home hub. Or combine a money-saving point-to-point fare on the way out with a fare that allows stopovers on the way back. And, of course, traveling full fare allows you to earn more expense-account miles to buy yourself or your partner upgrades or free tickets.

'Planning business trips can be more daunting than doing business when you arrive – assuming you still know what you're supposed to do and where,' says Stanley Zilch, director of Blue Skies Travel Research Institute in Broken Springs, Colorado. 'We've developed a kind of "yield management" system for the expense account traveler called Expenses Monitor, which flips the whole expenses reporting system upside down.

'Let's say your boss wants you to visit customers in Hong Kong, Bangkok and Tokyo. But you could also visit customers in Sydney, Chicago and New York. And yes, it would be nice to spend a weekend in Bermuda. Expenses Monitor allows you to "model" these factors along with how you can earn maximum frequent-flier miles consistent with company travel policy and come up with the optimum itinerary – such as a first-class round-the-world ticket. You might even get your boss to believe that it's his idea.'

Then you can say you have arrived – expenses-wise.

Visa survey

A Visa International survey of 1,253 frequent travelers from six European countries (the United Kingdom, Belgium, France, Germany, Italy and Spain) published recently shows that preparing travel expense claims can take as much time as two round-trips to New York. UK travelers spend nearly two hours every month filling out their expenses – three working days a year. The average time taken across Europe is 98 minutes a month. Italians take the most time (122 minutes); followed by the Germans (94 minutes); Spanish (93 minutes); French (90 minutes) and Belgians (83 minutes) – the most, or least, creative depending on your point of view. All executives were found to be out-of-pocket by nearly $40 a month through failing to claim expenses and losing receipts. Of the 50 per cent of executives not using a corporate card, 42 per cent say they are not given cash advances and have to fund trips out of their own pockets and wait to be reimbursed.

Claims that companies query most are in-room videos (three-quarters of respondents say they would never be reimbursed); 'personal entertainment' (Germans and French are least likely to be refunded for extra-curricular activities – at 86 and 82 per cent, respectively – while the British are more relaxed – only 74 per cent being refused); 56 per cent are not reimbursed for mini-bar rip-offs; 79 per cent of British, but only 56 per cent of Germans are likely to be reimbursed for laundry; and French and Belgian companies are most likely to refund personal phone calls, with UK companies a close third. Bar drinks are always queried – 47 per cent in Germany, 31 per cent in Italy, 27 per cent in Spain and 18 per cent in Belgium.

PART 3

Arriving

The airport city as a destination

Who needs to go to Stockholm when you have SkyCity 24 miles away at Arlanda Airport? Depends where you've come from and where you're going. I find more and more business travelers saying, 'Let's all meet at the airport' – the question being, 'Your airport or mine?'

SkyCity has brought the city to the airport with a beguiling complex of hotels, restaurants, supermarkets, boutiques, bars, conference and exhibition facilities, and a galaxy of business services, banking and telecommunications, as well as a fitness centre, doctors, pharmacies, travel agencies, dry cleaners and a non-denominational church, all located in a vast semi-circular building of glass, Swedish pine, Canadian cherry wood, marble and stainless steel between Terminals 5 and 4. Why suffer the hassle of a two-hour trek downtown and back when you are already there? There may come a time when people don't travel to cities any more, but to airports.

Airports like Chicago-O'Hare – the world's busiest – with 70 million passengers a year, London-Heathrow with 52 million, Tokyo-Haneda with 45 million, Frankfurt with 36 million and Paris-Charles de Gaulle with 30 million, have a larger daily population than many major cities. In 1998 the top 50 airports around the world handled 1.3 billion passengers. Scheduled air traffic is expected to rise to 1.6 billion in 1999.

SkyCity is a paradigm of the airport of the future – the megahub not as a means to an end but an end in itself, a destination in its own right. Airports have come a long way since they moved from the city centre to the next county, and beyond, and became supermarkets. Many new airports are so remote that they no longer serve cities but 'catchment areas' of far-flung towns and conurbations. We're talking about a world-wide network of alternative cities – what you might call the

241

terrestrial equivalent of space stations – with their own business communities and civic amenities plus their own high-speed rail links to other megahubs.

Airports such as Amsterdam-Schiphol, Zurich, Geneva, Brussels and Frankfurt already have their own railway stations. Frankfurt plans to open a second airport station to accommodate high-speed InterCity trains. The station is expected to open in 2000, and is already being dubbed Terminal 3. (Frankfurt Airport is the transport centre of Germany and one of the major crossroads of Europe next to the Frankfurter Kreuz – the most important junction in the European–German highway networks.) From the TGV station at Paris-Roissy Charles de Gaulle Airport you can travel to Nantes, Lilles, Brussels, and beyond.

A Sheraton hotel at Paris Charles-de-Gaulle means that you can avoid Paris (if you must) by staying at the airport – right above the new TGV railway station in the heart of Terminal 2 – with Eurostar links to Lille, Brussels, Amsterdam, London, and points south. It is two minutes from check-in. And has all that you'd expect from a good business hotel – fast- and slow-food restaurants, four-hour laundry service; fitness centre; plus a 'Daybreak' service that supplies a dayroom and a 'Transit Survival Kit' of essential toiletries.

The airport city competes for travelers with other megahubs in its region. Amsterdam–Schiphol was famously marketed as London's third airport. (Stansted, London's third airport 30 miles north-east of London, competes with Birmingham, East Midlands, and even Manchester); SkyCity competes with Copenhagen, Copenhagen with Frankfurt, Singapore–Changi with Hong Kong and Bangkok.

The challenge for airport authorities – whether they operate private or public monopolies – is how to reconcile the pursuit of profits with civic responsibility in providing public services for the traveler. Typically, only 20 per cent of airport revenues are derived from aviation, the rest coming from non-travel sources like restaurants and shops. Catching a plane at Heathrow, for example, means running the gauntlet of schlock boutiques and high-rent concessions: it's hard to find the gate, let alone a phone.

SkyCity is a mini-metropolis with 12,000 working inhabitants and 15 million travelers and visitors a year. There are 10,000 square metres of office space, 75 meeting rooms, an exhibition hall for 1,000 people, an auditorium for 350, and 25 shops. An elevator takes you from the heated two-level underground garage to SkyCity Plaza and the terminals.

'SkyCity is the meeting centre of Sweden – typically, two executives coming in from Stockholm and two or three flying in from the provinces,' says Lars Sj'lander, area vice president Sweden and Finland for

Radisson SAS, which controls the hotel and catering concessions. 'This is the only place in Sweden where you can do banking business on New Year's Eve. We have around 100 weddings a year at the SkyCity chapel. People may meet here, fall in love, come back to get married, and then take off on their honeymoon. Next to the airport is what we call the City of Arlanda – a huge shopping centre open 24 hours a day, where you can buy anything from flowers to furniture.'

'People are forced to spend more time at airports: congestion and delays, but at least you can use the time you're here,' says Bjorn Boldt-Christmas, senior vice president information systems at SAS in Stockholm. 'SkyCity has a hotel right in the middle of the airport. Sometimes, when I have an early morning flight, I sleep at the airport – 300 metres from passport control. There are good restaurants, even night life. What I do is check in for my flight the night before.

'Business people often don't bother to go downtown any more. SAS has board meetings at the Sheraton or the Conference Centre at Frankfurt Airport, which is the most convenient venue for people coming in from all over the place. They charge us outrageously, but you can have everyone in by 11.30 in the morning and out by 5 o'clock.'

Driving a better bargain

At a strange airport at night renting a car can be a daunting experience. First you have to find the car in the parking lot, figure out by trial and error how the lights work, and crack the code of the airport maze to get out.

Faced with a forest of signs at the Frankfurt *Autobahnkreuz*, you have two seconds to scan the scribbled directions on the back of an envelope clamped to the wheel with your right hand. You flick the indicator to turn right and turn on the windshield wipers by mistake. With cars coming at you from all sides no decision is the only decision and you head irrevocably in the direction of Cologne or Darmstadt instead of downtown. Turn back. But how? As the man said: You can't get there from here!

If only you'd grabbed a cab to the hotel and rented a car from the firm's city office the next day. Even better, had it delivered to your hotel and collected at the end of your stay for about $40 extra – well worth it if you're renting for several days.

Renting a car at the airport can cost 15 to 30 per cent more than renting from an office in the city. For example, collecting a Peugeot 206 from Hertz at Paris Charles-de-Gaulle Airport for three days (with unlimited mileage, collision-damage waiver and taxes) will cost you around 965 French francs. The same car picked up at Porte Maillot near the centre of Paris, would cost around 100 francs less. To have the car delivered and collected from your hotel would cost 140 francs each way.

But do you need to rent a car in the first place? If most of your meetings are in the centre of a city like Paris, Frankfurt or Milan, probably not. You'll have a frantic time finding your way around and parking. In which case, consider chauffeur drive. Major firms such as Hertz (1 800)

654 3001, Avis, (1 800) 331 1084, Budget (1 800) 472 3325 or Europcar (44 113) 242 2233 offer a chauffeur service – cheaper and more comfortable than a taxi, especially if you have meetings in the suburbs where taxis charge a higher rate and may not know their way around.

'Chauffeur drive is not as staggeringly expensive as you might think,' says Roeland Moens, vice president sales and marketing at Budget Rent a Car in London. 'You can hire a car by the hour or the day. For example, between Heathrow and the City, a black cab costs £35 to £45, and a chauffeur transfer £40 to £45 in a comfortable car – about £200 for a full day driving around London. This compares with £40 to £45 a day for renting a car and driving yourself. Going to Oxford from London, a black-cab or mini-cab would cost £80 to £100 just to get there, whereas you could have chauffeur drive for a full day for about £220.

'Chauffeur drive is most popular in countries where people are less likely to want to drive themselves – like Russia, the Middle East and Africa, where labour costs less,' says Gareth Wynn at Hertz in London. 'It becomes less of a luxury and more a practical option. In Dubai, for example, you'd pay £46 a day for an intermediate car plus £27 a day for a chauffeur.' In Moscow, Budget quotes $34 to $38 an hour for a chauffeured Lincoln town car and $30 an hour for a Ford Mondeo.

One-way car rental – where you pick up a car in one place and drop it off in another – is worth considering if you're traveling between major cities and need to make visits along the way; something you couldn't easily do by other means.

The best way to travel between Paris and Brussels is by train. But if you have meetings in Lille or Ghent, it makes sense to rent a car. Similarly from Toulouse across to Spain along the coast; from Germany into Austria, or Austria into Hungary.

But look out for drop-off charges. Most firms allow for one-way rental at no extra charge between major cities in the same country. But you might have to pay $100 or more if you want to leave the car in another country. It depends on demand for cars between city-pairs. Paris–Brussels is no problem; but Madrid–Copenhagen would be more expensive than Amsterdam–Frankfurt. (However, you might get a special deal if you were to bring a car back from, say, Madrid to Paris.)

Hertz has one-way rental between mainland Europe and the United Kingdom called Le Swap which enables travelers to swap their rental car for a left-hand drive equivalent at Calais (and vice versa). Europcar offers one-way rental without penalties between main cities in Europe under its Business Drive programme. Budget offers a similar deal in Europe plus One Way USA between about 100 airport locations across the country – with no drop-off charges.

One-way rental is a great way to bridge the gap between cities with an 'open-jaw' ticket (fly to one gateway, return from another). For example, fly to Paris, drive to Milan and fly back from there. Or combine car rental with high-speed trains, such as the TGV in France or ICE (Inter-City-Express) in Germany.

A EurailDrive Pass allows you to combine first-class rail travel with car rental in 17 countries. The pass – which costs $439 for a compact car – allows any four days unlimited train travel within two months plus two days Avis or Hertz car rental with unlimited mileage and tax and free drop-off at selected locations. You can add as many car days as you like for $80 a day.

You can buy a national rail-drive pass in many countries. A France Rail'N'Drive Pass, for example, for $345 for first-class with a compact car allows you any three days' unlimited first-class rail travel for one month, two days' Avis car rental with unlimited mileage and free drop-off at 520 Avis rental locations in France.

It always pays to book and pre-pay your car before you leave home for rental abroad. This can save you up to 60 per cent on the standard 'walk-up' or rack-rate (sometimes called the national tariff), often with conditions far less onerous than with excursion air tickets. (Look for cheap weekend rates – collect after midday Friday, return before 9 am Monday – in business cities.) You may stand a better chance of getting the car you want, or an upgrade, if it's not available. Business travelers who need a car for several days, including a Saturday night, can save as much as 30 per cent on regular prices by shopping for a leisure programme.

'Satellite navigation systems overcome one of the biggest objections to car rental by people who are afraid of getting lost and find it hard to follow a map,' Moens says. 'They are becoming standard options on executive cars, and will gradually be fitted to all cars. You key in the destination and the system navigates you from wherever you are to where you want to go. You have various options like highways, scenic routes and getting around in a city.'

A screen on the dashboard displays an ever-changing map with an arrow showing where to go – and a voice saying, 'Take the third exit to the left at the next roundabout'. If you go wrong, the system recalculates where you are and guides you from that point. Unlike a human navigator, the voice never loses its cybernetic cool.

Getting lost is now state-of-the-art.

Dos and don'ts

 Do check fly/drive deals when you buy an airline ticket.

 Do compare like with like. Car groups vary between firms and countries. Look for the SIPP (Standard Interline Passenger Procedures Code), which helps you reserve exactly what you want. These four-letter car codes have largely replaced the old ABCDE codes. For example, a Ford Fiesta is known as ECMN (economy, three-five door, manual, non-air-conditioned). But you won't find a Fiesta in France. Instead, you'll get a Renault Meganne under the code CCMN (compact, five-door, manual, non-air-conditioned).

 Don't be misled by 'come-on' ads that quote a daily rate way out of line with the final cost when you add the extras. Find out whether breakdown cover is included; is theft included in CDW (Collision Damage Waiver) or is it an extra? Check whether there is an 'excess' on CDW.

 Do decide the best deal before you hit the rental desk. This can depend on how long you want the car and how flexible you need to be. Save up to 50 per cent by booking in one country for rental in another.

 Do check whether you'll earn frequent-flier miles in your favourite awards programme.

 Don't sign the rental agreement before you've read it carefully. When charging the rental, see that your discount code is entered in the little box. Insist on having the charges worked out when you return the car.

 Don't sign a blank imprint of your credit card either before or at the end of the rental.

 Do keep copies of the rental agreement plus any paperwork to prove your case in the event of a dispute – such as being charged for a 'free' upgrade.

 Do compare the airport, 'off-airport' (where you phone to be picked up rather than going to a desk) and downtown rates. These may vary by up to 50 per cent. And remember, no car rental company has the best deal in every location. Check drop-off charges for one-way rental, and whether drop-off is allowed across borders or limited to one country.

Do compare a discountable rate with an undiscountable promotional (or leisure) rate. The latter may work out cheaper.

 Do make sure you buy 'top-up' liability insurance when renting in the United States.

 Do watch out for 'check-lists' on car rental agreements that say you have agreed the car is in safe working order. You shouldn't be required to spot anything more than superficial damage. Check for bumps and scratches when you pick up the car and get them noted on the rental agreement.

 Don't drive away without checking the car for damage – preferably in the presence of rental staff.

Planning your trip with Michelin online

Next time you plan a car journey to Europe, it's worth checking out the Michelin Web site – www.michelin-travel.com – for the best way to get there. Driving will still be fraught with dangers, you'll still scream at your navigator for holding the map upside down and the place you're trying to get to will still be on the fold. But now you have high-tech to blame.

Michelin allows you to create your own itinerary with your route traced on detailed maps with point-to-point driving directions, restaurant and hotel recommendations anywhere in 21 European countries. You just print your itinerary from the screen and off you go.

Avis offers renters who book and pre-pay for a car in the United States to build and download one customized itinerary on the Michelin Web site plus a 20 per cent discount on Michelin maps and guides. What you get is your route drawn across a high-resolution road map showing distances between any two points and elapsed mileage and traveling time on highways, with toll prices plus recommendations from the relevant Michelin Red Guide. Road information is updated three times a week.

You enter your departure and destinations and the date of your trip, and select one of four routes: the shortest route; the quickest; a route without tolls; or the route recommended by Michelin (the best compromise between time and distance).

Michelin's route-planning service on the Internet, begun in March 1997, evolved from 10 years of online experience with Minitel, the French vidiotex system. Ten million itineraries were plotted in 1997 and 1.5 million faxes sent to Minitel subscribers. The Web site covers 21 countries, 1.1 million kilometres of roads and 60,000 hotels and restaurants from the Red Guides. A full 'consultation' costs about $3.

'Once you get onto the home page, you have two possibilities,' says Christophe Vystrecil, online manager at Michelin in Paris. 'If you're not a subscriber, you can have a free demonstration or ask for an itinerary and pay with one of four credit cards; if you're a subscriber, you enter your user password and use up your subscription little by little. You can go back in later and change the itinerary you have chosen from, say, a scenic route to the fastest journey.

'The scale of the map depends on the length of your journey. If you travel from Nice to Avignon, you have a scale of one million (1 centimetre for 10 kilometres); Nice to Gibraltar will give you a scale of 3 million. We'll soon be able to offer a bigger scale of 200,000 or 400,000 for a journey such as Nice to San Remo. We also plan to introduce more material from our Green Guides.'

What travelers want from hotels

Business travelers' needs and priorities have changed over the last five years, and will change even more in the future, when it comes to choosing a business hotel. They require much more these days than a quiet, spacious room with high safety standards and service. They see the room more as a high-tech 'command centre' from which they can manage their business and communicate with clients and the office. Recognition will still be important but it is reward that will increasingly motivate travelers in future. The top three loyalty programme perks are free upgrades to better rooms; free weekend leisure stays for two; and the opportunity to earn airline miles.

Mike Stajdel, senior vice president, sales and marketing, Inter-Continental Hotels and Resorts, says: 'More and more, travelers want control over their journey, air travel as well as the hotel experience. They want to be able to do business in their room at the time they choose, and having food – and a wider choice of dining – when they want to have it. They want flexibility, being able to check in and check out when it suits them, and to choose the kind of reward that is appropriate for this particular trip.

'What we're picking up is that no two trips are necessarily the same: there can be one trip where I need full support facilities in the hotel for meeting clients or entertaining; another where I need to be in touch back and forth with my office, so I prefer to do that by e-mail out of my room. One trip may be a quick overnight, so I just want to be able to get in and out fast; or I might have a longer stay, some associates I'd like to invite up for a drink, therefore I need more space, perhaps a suite.

'What surprised us is that in-room business communications facilities have become top priority in choosing a hotel. We didn't realize the

extent that this was happening. Travelers in the past used business centres, now they want to do the work themselves, especially e-mail. When
all things are equal, loyalty programmes may influence choice of hotel.
It is not the main criterion: location and ability of the hotel to satisfy my
needs are always coming up first.'

Hotels that dare to be different

London has always been well endowed with small, luxury hotels, what some people call town-house hotels, boutique hotels, or baby grands; ranging from country house to contemporary; often deliciously eccentric. These are the 'hidden gems' – upholders of bygone grace and tradition – that aficionados love to discover. Typically, they are privately owned, independently run and quite as expensive as the Savoy, Ritz, Connaught or Claridge's. But the best of them often redeem the clichés of the glossy ads and the PR splurge – 'the personal touch' and 'the sense that you are a guest in someone's home' – often achieving that elusive amalgam of comfort, friendliness and efficiency that I call hospitality.

Now a new wave of 'design' hotels has joined the genre – hip home-from-homes that are 'concepts' where everything behind the Victorian and Edwardian façades, from the visual choreography of the lobby and chairs you are likely to sit in the wrong way to the bedside reading light and toothbrush holder, is a tribute to the interior designer's genius. What they have in common is that they are all different. Design hotels are supposed to reflect who you are – or who you aspire to be. The idea is to choose your lifestyle before choosing where to stay.

'They are called 'design' hotels because they are designed to meet the needs of mainly young, affluent, image-conscious travelers who want to feel that their lifestyle is reflected by where they stay,' says Nigel Massey, a London consultant. 'They break all the ground rules of classic hotels: they are sensationally different, simple in design, elegant and very fashionable. They attract people from the four "Ms" – the music, modelling and fashion, movie, and media industries – creative people and executives who love these kind of hotels. They are hip, cool, at the cutting-edge of design in what they do, the cars they drive, what they wear: and hotels are merely an extension of that. In the case of the classic town-house hotels, the following is very clearly institutional – banking, law, finance and mainstream corporate.

'People started talking about design hotels around the time the Halkin opened in 1991, followed by the Metropolitan last year. They've both taken London by storm. Then you have the Malmaison hotels where they've taken landmark buildings like churches and warehouses, Behind the original classic facades is stylish, slick, modern design. Their appeal is that they are priced around £85 a night, which has made them an instant success.'

The Halkin and its sister hotel the Metropolitan are the brainchild of fashion guru Christina Ong who lives in Singapore. The Halkin, just behind Hyde Park Corner on a quiet Belgravia street, offers chic Milanese design and Italian food and a wealth of high tech. In the lobby a marble mosaic floor and arched windows complement the clean lines of square blue-leather chairs and ochre sofas. A couple of busts on plinths, bay trees and white drapes give the general idea. Guestroom corridors curve at a gentle angle and the ceilings arch downwards to meet the walls. All 41 rooms have dual-line telephones, a fax machine for which you get a personal direct number, a VCR with a central video library, satellite and cable television, and wall safe. A teletype centre gives instant access to market and news reports and there are private rooms for business meetings.

The Metropolitan off Park Lane, larger with 154 rooms, has similar clean lines, with light hardwoods and marble and natural fabrics. Bedrooms are crisp and comfortable with three ISDN phone lines for global data transmission, US and UK modem points, voicemail and desks you can spread your work all over. There's a high-tech gym with awesome stepping and rowing machines, a cafe/lounge-cum-bar, one of the hottest places to hang out, and Nobu, a Michelin-starred restaurant and sushi bar serving 'new style' Japanese cuisine.

Nicholas Rettie, general manager of the Halkin and Metropolitan, says: 'Travelers in the late 1980s who looked out for small boutique hotels had had enough chintz fabrics, fluffy curtains and four-poster beds. They were looking for the kind of modern design they have in their homes and offices. The idea is when you travel you go for an experience. Design is important, but it has to be style that you feel comfortable with.

'The Halkin design is contemporary Italian, whereas the Metro is more British contemporary. The Metro is younger, more overt, less sophisticated and more fun, more exciting, more energy, more buzz.

The place gives people energy, a hit, because of the sort of visitors they meet with; because hotels tell people a lot about you as well.

'The Metro has a narrower, more sharply defined focus: younger creative types 25 to 40 – musicians, recording artists, advertising executives, fashion designers; whereas the Halkin has broader appeal, and older people, 35 to 65, lawyers, property people and people wearing suits, a rarity at the Metro. There are similar hotels around the world – the Claris in Barcelona, the Pflaum Post Hotel in Bayreuth, the Delano and the Tides in Miami Beach, the Mondrian in Los Angeles which has 200 rooms, eye-catching design, lively, young clientele, hip and cool. Light years away from the branded chains.'

myhotel, a four-star property in Bloomsbury just off Tottenham Court Road (ideal for media people – two minutes from CNN), which opened in mid-1999, is a welcome addition to the genre. Owner Andy Thrasyvoulou, architect by profession and hotelier by vocation, seems to have found the right balance between technology and comfort and east meets west in terms of culture and design; juxtaposing the best out of each rather than a compromise. The idea is that the hotel works at your own pace.

'The solution is know as much about the guest as possible before they arrive,' Andy says. 'Maybe you want to check in the bar area with a coffee or drink, talk about London with one of our guest service people; or, if you're in a hurry and we know about that, you can sign off when you arrive.

'One of my frustrations was that if you wanted something done, you'd have this endless directory of numbers. You ring one up and they say, sorry, it's not us, it's the concierge, or housekeeping. I'm lucky that I haven't trained as a hotelier.

'Creating the new building is not the difficult part: breaking down the internal barriers needs a lot of effort. In the United Kingdom, there's a certain mind-set in the hotel industry towards attitude and service. We don't want to have all these departments. If I want a photocopy right now in the restaurant, why should I have to go to the business centre. I want it now: charge it to my room; I don't care. So what we've done is, you ring one number that goes to the guest service pool and there they'll have the computer and all the information. Even if they cannot help you immediately, they'll go and talk to housekeeping or whoever and come back to you. And we do not encourage tipping.'

Light years away from any design you could ever imagine is the Portobello, near Portobello Road market in the heart of Notting Hill, the oldest, most eccentric, design hotel in London, which has been a haven for movie stars, fashion celebrities, music and media folk for nearly 26 years. It is funky and fun with just 20 bedrooms decked out with a hotchpotch of antiques and military paraphernalia and a mixture of four-posters, a ship's bunk and even a round bed specially made for Alice Cooper. Four bedrooms contain enormous Victorian bathing machines complete with yards of brass pipe work, curved glass screens and eight different shower settings.

'We started back in the 1970s so a lot of our style is dictated by that era – antiques, palms, lots of colour,' says Johnny Ekperigin, owner of the Portobello. 'I don't think you can actually put a label on what we are; boutique doesn't do it, town house doesn't do it, design hotel doesn't do it; we are all individual hotels with our own individual style. Successful people don't like to stay in boxes, they want to feel comfortable like they're still at home. We have the sort of people who want to feel very relaxed, not disturbed, and blend into the hotel. We have all the business facilities like modems because that's what the world wants. But that's not important. We put the onus on our type of service, like a 24-hour bar and restaurant, which attracts our kind of people. If you've been working in a studio all night and get in at five, you want to be able to sit around and relax. If Dan Morrison, who's staying with me now, wants to be in all the papers, he wouldn't stay with me, he'd stay at the Dorchester. He stays with me because he doesn't want anyone to know what he's doing.'

The family-run Red Carnation group consists of four hotels in outstanding locations – The Chesterfield, off Berkeley Square, Mayfair; The Rubens, opposite Buckingham Palace Mews; The Montague in Bloomsbury, next to the British Museum (all four-star); and the five-star jewel of the collection, The Milestone opposite Kensington Palace – all of which can truly be called 'baby grands.' Carefully restored to reflect their individual architecture and decor, they share a family feel, epitomized by Bea Tollman's personal care and attention to detail. It is the closest I know to staying in a private home. To describe The Milestone as a miniature Connaught is to do it less than justice. It is one of the great hotels of the world.

David Naylor-Leyland, owner of Dukes, The Egerton and The Franklin, a handsome stable of town-house hotels in the best classical English style, aims to offer 'more comfortable rooms and top of the range services at a good 30 per cent less' than most of the grand hotels in central London.

Dukes, a 62-room bijou hotel tucked away in a gas-lit courtyard off Piccadilly, is a haven of good taste, comfort and relaxed charm. Rooms and suites are individually decorated and furnished with period furniture, *objets d'art*, fine paintings and porcelain, along with marble bathrooms. Barman Gilberto Preti is said to mix the meanest martini in town.

The Egerton and Franklin are smaller versions with 30 and 47 rooms, respectively. They share a terrace of Victorian town houses overlooking a lovely tree-lined Knightsbridge square. The feeling that you are staying in a private home is enhanced by the elegant drawing-rooms, antique furniture, bowls of flowers and a row of cut-glass decanters on the honesty bar.

'We attract people who don't need the security blanket of a big name, but want to feel they're staying in someone's luxurious house,' Naylor-Leyland says. 'For example, the chairman of one of the biggest banks always stays at the Egerton and a lot of people who run their own businesses. We don't market ourselves to music, media or movie people. Music industry executives stay here rather than the stars themselves. Stars do stay when they're not on a publicity thing, when they're closer to the leading ladies than they should be.'

One Aldwych, which opened in July 1998, is a palace of low-key luxury. The hotel offers 105 rooms and suites – two of which have private gyms. There are two restaurants, two bars and a cappuccino bar, an 8,000 square-foot health club with an 18-metre pool and a private cinema with an adjoining dining-room for 30 people. Rooms have the usual amenities – three phones, modem plugs (US, UK, European and ISDN), multi-channel satellite and cable TV, a CD player, and even a TV in the bathroom.

'We believe we've created a template for the luxury hotel of the late 1990s and beyond, what you might call contemporary classic, but not a hint of corporate about it,' says owner Gordon Campbell Gray. 'I wanted to avoid the predictable international deluxe style – like a club class lounge at Heathrow – but I didn't want it to be a trendy, over-designed hotel that doesn't always provide great service. We're not aiming to attract a very groovy clientele; we're more serious than that. But somewhere where you can check in the chairman of the board.'

The hotel is the first building on the left as you come into the curve of Aldwych. It was designed in 1907 for *The Morning Post* newspaper – long since subsumed in the *Daily Telegraph* – by architects Mewes & Davis, an Anglo-French partnership responsible for the Ritz hotels in London, Paris and Madrid. 'Being built for a newspaper, we were free to strip out the interior and design from scratch behind the facade,' Campbell Gray says.

Ken McCullough, Scottish hotelier and founder of Malmaison Hotels, says: 'I think "design" is a dangerous term; I wouldn't like to put a label on what we're doing. We started in 1994 with the idea of creating hotels that were high on style – classic contemporary design but not gimmicky – and good value for money, less than £100 [about $160] a night. We have an art deco French brasserie with real food, not acrobatic food, painting pictures on plates. But things like roasted cod, steak-frites, our own wines... food is the heart and soul of the business. Then we have our own toiletries, with natural ingredients, real soap, made specially for us on the Isle of Arran. We talk about hotels that dare to be different. People love it.'

Malmaison was the original home of Napoleon and Josephine and exists today as a museum, near Versailles, on the outskirts of Paris. McCulloch took distinctive buildings – the Glasgow hotel was a church, Edinburgh a seamen's mission, Newcastle a quayside warehouse – and created stunning interior designs that work: not formula design, but design that makes the most of the original architecture and setting. Amanda Rosa, now McCulloch's wife, who has designed all Malmaison hotels, describes the hotels as sisters, not twins; there's a common thread, a common identity, but each hotel is distinctively different.

The designs are striking, making use of strong primary colours and rich fabrics with amazing attention to detail. Bedrooms are large, comfortable and packed with amenities – two direct phone lines, your personal message centre, 10-channel satellite TV, a mini hi-fi system with a CD player (you can borrow CDs from reception), trouser press, hairdryer and tea/coffee-making facilities. Each hotel has a state-of-the-art gym and a dedicated business service called Meetings at the Mal with a choice of meeting rooms and stylish break-out areas.

'We attract a cross-section of guests; corporate marketing guys and a lot of media and music people,' McCullough says. 'Whitney Houston was in Manchester with a party of six and stayed for four nights; she'd booked out of another hotel to go to the Mal.'

Brown's Hotel – a Raffles International property – is the epitome of traditional English elegance and style. Opened in 1837, Brown's is London's oldest operating five-star hotel. Located in the heart of Mayfair, with a superb restaurant, it is a perfect venue for business or leisure – classic hospitality with state-of-the-art communications technology.

Brown's Hotel
118 bedrooms and suites
Albemarle Street
London W1X 4BP
Tel: (0171) 493 6020
Fax: (0171) 493 9381
E-mail: brownshotel@brownshotel.com
Web site: www.raffles-intl.com. Singles from £260

The Chesterfield
111 rooms and suites
35 Charles Street

London WIX 8LX
Tel: (0171) 491 2622
Fax: (0171) 491 4793
E-mail: reservations@chesterfield.redcarnationhotels.com. Singles from
£129.

Dukes Hotel
84 bedrooms and suites
St James' Place
London SW1A 1NY
Tel: (0171) 491 4840
Fax: (0171) 493 1264
E-mail: dukeshotel@compuserve.com. Singles from £165.

Egerton House Hotel
30 rooms
Egerton Terrace
Knightsbridge
London SW3 2BX
Tel: (0171) 589 2412
Fax: (0171) 584 6540. Singles from £130.

Franklin Hotel
47 rooms
28 Egerton Gardens
London SW3 2DB
Tel: (0171) 584 5533
Fax: (0171) 584 5449. Singles from £140.

The Halkin
41 rooms and suites
5 Halkin Street
Belgravia
London SW1X 7DJ
Tel: (0171) 333 1000
Fax: (0171) 333 1100
E-mail: res@halkin.co.uk. Singles from £285.

Malmaison Hotels in Glasgow, Edinburgh, Leeds, Manchester, Newcastle,
Tel: (0141) 221 1052
Fax: (0141) 221 1053
Web site: www.malmaison.com. Doubles/twins from $95.

The Metropolitan
18 suites and 137 rooms
Old Park Lane
London W1Y 4LB
Tel: (0171) 447 1000
Fax: (0171) 447 1100. Singles from £195.

The Milestone
57 rooms and suites
1 Kensington Court
London W1 5DL
Tel: (0171) 917 1000
Fax: (0171) 917 1010
Web site: www.themilestone.com

The Montague
193 rooms and 11 suites
5 Montague Street
Bloomsbury
London WC1B 5BJ
Tel: (0171) 637 1001
Fax: (0171) 637 2516. Singles from £110.

myhotel
76 rooms and suites
11–13 Bayley Street
Bedford Square
London WC1B3HD
Tel: (0171) 667 6000
Fax: (0171) 667 6001
E-mail: guest_services@myhotels.co.uk www.myhotels.co.uk £155–£355.

One Aldwych
105 rooms and suites
1 Aldwych
London WC2B 4BZ
Tel: (0171) 300 0500.
Fax: (0171) 300 0501
E-mail: sales@onealdwych.co.uk

The Portobello
22 rooms and suites

22 Stanley Gardens
London W11 2NG
Tel: (0171) 727 2777
Fax: (0171) 792 9641. Singles from £100 with continental breakfast.

Red Carnation Hotels
Web site: www.redcarnationhotels.com

The Rubens
174 rooms and suites
39 Buckingham Palace Road
London

The European Connection

The European Connection 2000 is a collection of 50 privately owned luxury hotels that the book's authors Nigel Massey and Diane Coyne like. A mix of sophisticated designer hotels and traditional town house hotels, 'they all offer outstanding service, great value and a unique style that makes them stand out from the bland, impersonal chain hotels found in most of Europe's cities'.

For a copy, write to The Massey Partnership Ltd, Suite 3, 31–32 Savile Row, London W1X 1AG; tel: (44 207) 434 3233; fax: (44 207) 434 3663 or at www.massey.co.uk

Design hotels international

A consortium directory of 29 design hotels in Europe, Asia-Pacific and the Americas. It includes The Halkin, The Metropolitan, myhotel and One Aldwych in London. www.designhotels.com and www.lifestyletravel.com

High-tech hotels of the future

Back in my corporate days (and I go back a long way) you could expect a quiet spacious room and a comfortable bed with a telephone on the night table (taking a call meant leaping across the bed, sending your open attaché case crashing to the floor – it still happens, it still happens), a radio with local news ('It's raining in South Bend'), maybe a coffee-table, an armchair, decent bathroom lighting, a shower that worked, and a wardrobe with nice wooden coat hangars that you were tempted to walk away with.

High tech meant a telex in reception (remember the telex?) and a gizmo I recall called 'Magic Fingers' or 'Massage Boy'. Put a quarter in the slot and the bed would gently vibrate, save you counting sheep. You had to go through the operator for long-distance calls ('There's a two-hour delay for Madrid'), so the office was safely out of touch and you'd be left to worry in peace.

Slow dissolve (via multi-channel satellite television, mini-bars, hair dryers, ironing boards, back-lit mirrors and in-room coffee/tea-making facilities) to the millennium. Road warriors today are driven by communications technology – the need to be totally wired at all times – which both facilitates and requires higher productivity. This means doing the job back in the office as well as on the road. The hotel room has become a high tech 'command centre' from which you can manage business with clients and the office as though you were in the office. Travelers want to be independent, be in control, not to be dependent on hotel services but to do it all in their room around the clock.

Hotels have responded. Hyatt came up in 1997 with its Business Plan at 90 hotels in the United States and Canada. For an extra $20 a day on any room-rate, guests get a raft of benefits including a large desk, fax

261

machine, desk telephone with computer hook-up and enhanced lighting, free local calls and no access charges on toll-free and credit card phone-calls.

'We've found that almost two-thirds of business travelers in America use laptops on the road,' says Norm Canfield, vice president rooms at Hyatt Hotels Corporation in Chicago. 'So someone can print out what they're doing in the room rather than going to the business centre. People are looking for instant convenience, lack of hassles and the ability to be productive when they want to be productive.

'We already have two-line phones with data-ports. But the biggest thing is the Internet and where does that go? We're testing systems for getting people connected – especially with high-speed data links. There's an interactive cable vehicle through the television set, which has a lot of potential because the bandwidth is huge, but the industry hasn't yet evolved to the point where you can exploit this – it's like having a 50-lane highway and a half-lane exit ramp; then there's a "Category 5" or hard-wire phone system but with a different jack that can connect laptops; and wireless systems. We're still trying to figure out the right mix of systems – the best delivery.'

Alistair Forbes, business development director of Quadriga, a provider of interactive hotel guest-room technology, in London, says: 'The television is the centre of the communications highway for the hotel guest. You don't need a laptop to access the Internet or deal with your e-mail but do it through a remote control key-pad. The technology is in the hotel basement using co-axial cabling for the signalling. But it all goes through the TV. The typical road warrior – the middle-manager in the four-star hotel – will probably still bring his laptop. The senior executive is going to see it as an opportunity to not take his laptop: providing he can access all his messages and respond to them, he can sleep at night. If you ask people what services would encourage choice of hotel, Internet access comes out at 20 per cent. If you asked that question two year's ago, it wouldn't have registered. Incredible. Internet usage is doubling every 100 days worldwide. But people can't conceive of accessing the Internet without a PC in the room.'

Hilton Hotels Corporation has launched Business Anywhere, 'unattended business centre kiosks' at 50 hotels in the United States. The centres provide a Pentium multimedia computer with a Zip drive, e-mail access and Web browsing through the Internet, a laser printer, a laptop print port, a copier, a plain paper fax machine, a laptop modem port and a 24-hour, toll-free hotline. They come with multi-lingual touch-screen. You pay by credit card.

Hilton is testing an in-room PC system called PCC Powerdesk at three London properties – the Hilton Heathrow, the Langham Hilton and the Hilton Park Lane. Powerdesk, developed by a UK company, is a high-tech PC built into a stylish wooden desk in the room. It comes with fax/e-mail/Internet access, a slimline flat screen, cordless mouse, a laser printer (stashed in the bottom drawer), scanner, and CD sound system.

Access to the Powerdesk is through a smart card, which you buy at reception, costing £15 for an hour and £30 for up to four hours' use. You can use the card at other hotels with Powerdesks. You can bring your own floppy disks or buy disks at the hotel. You also have access to Microsoft Office, the Internet, games and shopping, CDs from the hotel library and, via PCC Mall, market information, entertainment and sport.

You can find PCC Powerdesks at more than 30 Comfort, Clarion and Quality hotels in Norway and 15 in Sweden, The Stanhope in Brussels, the Grand Hotel Duomo in Milan, the Halcyon, The Howard and the Ritz in London. The Institute of Directors has 11 Powerdesks at its Pall Mall headquarters for use by members. There are plans to install Powerdesks in airport lounges and airline clubs.

'Most frequent users are people with laptops who find it more comfortable working with a full-size keyboard, plus the use of a scanner, printer and fax,' says Nina Christiansen, director of business development at Powerdesk Connect Card in Oxford. 'Normal laptop users want to check their e-mail either through their mobile or the hotel system, which is expensive. With our system there are no extra charges, you're connected right away through the local number. We find a lot people who have tried Powerdesk leave their laptop at home on their second visit.'

Nigel Massey, a hotel consultant in London, baulks at all this stuff. 'There's a blind assumption in the hotel industry that everybody is into high tech,' he says, 'so they stick all this kit in and what you actually do is alienate your guest, make him feel stupid because he can't figure out how to use the stuff and is too embarrassed to phone down and ask.

'We did quite an amusing lifestyle survey at the Halkin in London among 150 male and female guests from Europe and the USA. Men see rooms as an extension of their office and use all the available facilities – 62 per cent use e-mail, 74 per cent fax, 81 per cent voice mail and so on; but women see their rooms as places of relaxation rather than communication. Only 8 per cent use the technology compared with 39 per cent of men. Women like to relax in the bath or in front of the telly with a drink. Men are like boys let loose in a toy shop trying everything out.

'I believe hotels are in danger of introducing so much high tech at the expense of the human service element. I'm fed up speaking to voice mail; I want to speak to a person. Does anybody speak English? Does anybody speak?'

Getting connected on the road

So you've got the latest all-singing-all-dancing Banana 5 laptop computer and state-of-the-art GSM mobile phone to keep in touch via a fax/modem when you're on the road. But with more than 40 different types of telephone and power sockets worldwide, your chances of getting connected may be remote. 'Murphy's Law will ensure that crucial e-mail messages are stranded in cyberspace – unless you can get help at the desk.'

American Airlines, United and Delta Air Lines are among a growing number of carriers that enable business-class passengers to plug their laptops into power points at their seats. According to a recent American Express survey, 4 out of 10 travelers use a laptop during a flight, and 9 out of 10 use it in the hotel room.

Inter-Continental was one of the first hotel chains to provide such help in the form of a 'cyber-concierge' at many of its properties in Asia-Pacific. A cyber-relations manager meets you at check-in and offers to set up your computer and get you connected.

The Ritz-Carlton group has now come along with a 24-hour 'technology butler' trained to fix the most abstruse computer problems free of charge. Common questions: How can I get on to the Internet? How can I download a file from my office? How can I hook up my laptop to the business centre printer? Can someone reformat my hard drive? How do I dial out on a laptop from my room? How do I unfreeze my computer? How do I print off a disk? Where is the plug for my modem? Where do I get a 220-volt adapter for a European appliance?

Getting the right local adapter isn't always the solution, especially if the phone is hard-wired into the wall in that luxury hideaway hotel. Telephone systems work in different ways, and modems that work at home won't always work abroad without reconfiguration. Digital switch-boards, common in larger hotel chains and modern offices, can damage modems, sometimes fatally.

TeleAdapt Ltd, a company with offices in London, San Jose, California and Sydney, may have the solution with a range of packs containing all the adapters, plugs and sockets necessary for travelers to get connected virtually anywhere.

But getting connected does not depend on hardware alone: TeleAdapt provides a 24-hour telephone hotline to talk travelers through software problems.

'At least 70 per cent of business travelers carry a laptop and the vast majority – 95 per cent – use it for communications, to collect e-mail and faxes,' says Gordon Brown, managing director of TeleAdapt in London. 'Many road warriors hit problems. People call us from a hostile environment, from a hotel, wherever, "I can't get this thing to work". It's not just the hardware, it's the software behind it. We grieve if we cannot get a person connected.

'Let's say you've got a laptop, a telecom calling card, software from Microsoft or Lotus Notes or something, who is going to take responsibility? Everybody blames everyone else. Is it a hardware or a software problem and whose? "That's not our problem, sir, that's your calling card won't work with our software, it's a calling card problem." We stepped in the middle to make sure it all works together. That's the mission of the company. Some people only need a bit of help; others need the full Monty.'

Sarah Osman at TeleAdapt says: 'Let's say you're going to Spain. When you arrive at the hotel, you go to plug in your modem and it looks scary, not like BT. Call us and we'll courier a power and a phone adapter to you. You connect up and you keep getting "no carrier", "no carrier". You give us a call. What's happened is that your modem is not recognizing the dial tone. So we'd talk you through how to change it, how to ignore the dial tone. Then you may get connected, but every five minutes it'll be dropping the line again. We have a filter for that. So we'd get a filter to you as well.

'It's best, of course, to tell us where you're going, what laptop, modem and data software you have, and pick up the kit before you leave. We can tell you how to set up your software over the phone, tell you what to type in. So whenever you're in that country again you can go into that setting. Just click on.'

TeleAdapt publishes a 120-page *Mobile Connectivity Guide* containing crucial tips to stay connected on the road – from how to set your modem to ignore foreign dial tones and how to manually dial with calling cards, to connecting from airport and public pay phones and troubleshooting PC card modem problems.

Adapters cost from £29.99 ($49) plus VAT, while a WorldPak containing adapters for use in more than 200 countries costs £299.99 plus VAT.

United Kingdom
Tel: (44 181) 233 3000
United States
Tel:(1 048) 965 1400
Australia
Tel: (61 2) 9433 8363
Web site: www.teleadapt.com

Targus @ www.targus.com offers a range of laptop accessories for travelers, such as power adaptors, security drives and carrying cases.

Trading down to three-star luxury

Be honest. Do you sincerely need an enormous marble bathroom with a walk-in power shower and a galaxy of designer toiletries, a king-size bed or a club lounge with complimentary cocktails? Would it be a great hardship to forgo having your bed turned down and a good-night chocolate on the pillow? How often do you use the hotel pool, fitness centre or 24-hour butler service?

A growing number of business travelers, faced with the prospect of steep increases in hotel prices, fuelled by strong demand as the global economy improves, are discovering that they can enjoy as much comfort as they need (or almost as much as they aspire to) by trading down from a five-star deluxe hotel to four stars or even three stars.

You might call it trading across rather than trading down. The term 'mid-market' or budget hotel no longer means cheap and cheerful in the pejorative sense. Lower prices are typically reflected in smaller rooms, fewer bars and restaurants, and fewer staff to smile and open doors and forget your name. But you can expect a decent room and bed (hold the nylon sheets!), a direct-dial phone and desk, satellite TV, a modem for your laptop, and tea and coffee-making facilities. Business travelers these days want to be self-contained in their room, independent, quick off the mark. They want to be able to press their trousers or iron a blouse without calling room service and grab a coffee and a croissant in the lobby on the way out.

The expectation in five-star hotels is that guests need to be waited on hand and foot and order everything they need. Unless you need a good address to impress, there may even be times when you feel more comfortable staying with fewer stars. Especially when it comes to settling the bill. In London, for example, the published rate for a five-star deluxe hotel is more than £200 a night, compared with around £120 for a premium four-star, £85 for a good three- to four-star, and £50 for a 'budget' property.

Borge Ellgaard, vice president hotel relations group Europe at American Express, says: 'A good four-star hotel meets 95 per cent of business travelers' needs. The difference between a three-star and a four-star in my opinion is a slightly smaller room and 24-hour room service. What you're paying for in the five-star category is service and space, and then, of course frills – power showers versus ordinary showers, for example.'

'Three-star hotels are increasingly attractive to business travelers,' says Melody Goodman, of Gray Dawes Internet Travel in London. 'Many now offer business services and many of the facilities business travelers need – even small things like making sure the restaurant or coffee shop is open for longer hours. I think they're filling a definite niche in the market and are offering a good-value alternative to four- and five-star properties.'

Hotel chains are developing well-defined brands that vary from country to country but deliver our expectations. The Accor group has Sofitel, Novotel, Ibis and Formule 1, a no-frills brand at around $30 a night; Marriott has Courtyard by Marriott, a three-star brand; Sheraton has its five-star Luxury Collection, four-star properties and three-star Sheraton Inns; Forte with its five-star Meridien and three-/four-star Post Houses and budget Travelodges in the United Kingdom; Holiday Inn's three-star Garden Court and five-star Crown Plaza; and Shangri-La's Traders – three- to four-star properties in Asia – with almost all of the facilities of the five-star product for 25 to 45 per cent less.

Raffles International has, besides its luxury Raffles and Raffles Resort brands, the four and a half–star Merchant Court brand in key gateway cities – Singapore, Sydney, Bangkok, Berlin, Shanghai and London.

Staying at home on the road

What makes an ideal hotel? It depends on the purpose of your trip. Are you buying or selling? Are you on your own for two nights with wall-to-wall appointments or traveling with colleagues on a site visit or sales trip? Are you hoping to combine business with pleasure? Do you need high-tech business facilities, or a health club, or a suite for a power breakfast? Do you want 'a home away from home', or to paraphrase Le Corbusier, simply a machine for staying in?

Deciding where to stay is a complex equation of cost, convenience and comfort. But next time you need a hotel – especially for two or three nights or more – consider the apartment alternative: a studio or one-bedroom flat in a custom-built property with twice the space for up to half the cost of a standard double room in a hotel of the same quality. The stand-off: don't expect a fancy lobby, restaurants, concierge, a host of bellboys, round-the-clock room service, and other trappings of a traditional hotel, which you always pay for but may seldom use.

Apartments are a fast-growing sector of the lodging industry, says Charles McCrow, managing director of The Apartment Service, a marketing and reservations company in London. 'But there's a lot of confusion,' he says. 'We call the category serviced apartments, "apart-hotels" or apartment suites; in the United States, where the concept began, they're called all-suite hotels or extended-stay hotels. But their idea is not our idea because 90 per cent have kitchenettes: the Conrad Chelsea Harbour in London is an all-suite hotel but doesn't have cooking facilities. In the States, they reckon that the all-suite market will grow to about 30 per cent of hotel space. It's good value for travelers and more profitable for operators.

'But travelers should be wary about hotels with apartments attached, which quite often charge the same prices as regular suites, because they're going to be paying for the hotel services as well. Serviced apartments should be less expensive than a hotel room, not twice the price.

'The great thing with an apartment is that you get more space and privacy – a lounge and a kitchen. Even if you're staying just a few days, it helps cut down on room service charges: you can spend a third of the nightly room-rate on breakfast and all the rest of the jazz. And it's more of a home from home, somewhere to live rather than just to sleep.'

Extra space begins to matter when you're constantly on the road or constantly in one place. Two executives who share a twin-bedroom apartment can save 40 per cent over the cost of two hotel rooms. And women travelers can do business with associates without the awkwardness of bringing them into a hotel bedroom.

Apartments range from studios – one room serving as bedroom and lounge – to one- to three-bedroom apartments with a separate lounge and en suite bathrooms; equipped with direct line phone and fax, and cable and satellite TV. The kitchen will normally contain a cooker-microwave, refrigerator and freezer, and perhaps a dishwasher, so that you can bring in your own food and drink. No more $40 club sandwiches from room service and rip-off prices with mini-bars. Maid service is usually once a week: you pay extra for daily cleaning. Most apartments have a 24-hour reception. And you may get a free grocery shopping service.

'There are two main factors driving this market: more people are spending more time on the road, especially what you might call knowledge workers – IT specialists, lawyers, consultants, auditors, migrant academics like myself, who spend a week, sometimes longer, at a location and then move on, and the higher profit margins companies earn on serviced apartments by cutting down on labour costs,' says Michael Olsen, Director of Research at the International Hotel & Restaurant Association in Paris. 'A key element is quality of accommodations and the need to be independent. People tell you how sick and tired they are of having to deal with incompetent staff in these hotels; if they don't really know or understand how they can help, why do you need them? They only get in the way and create more problems than they solve. Hotels have gone out of their way to keep prices high; people are cranking up the time they spend away and so serviced apartments become a better deal.'

Extended-stay hotels are enjoying a boom in the United States, with around 20 brands in the sector. *Hotels* magazine says that as many as 25 per cent of guests staying in conventional hotels would be willing to stay in an extended stay hotel if they could find one. (According to Coopers & Lybrand, 29.6 per cent of hotel rooms in the United States under construction were of the extended-stay variety in 1997.) Extended Stay America, with more than 200 properties, is a lower-priced, fewer-frills alternative to Residence Inn by Marriott, which pioneered the sector in the early 1990s. Homestead Village plans to build between 40 and 50 properties a year for the next three years. And Villager Lodge, a budget brand with weekly rates from $175 to $225, aims to have 150 Villager properties by the end of 1999.

Staybridge Suites by Holiday Inn, which opened its first extended-stay hotel in Alpharetta, Georgia, in autumn 1998, expects to have 250 properties worldwide by 2003, with around 50 in Europe, the Middle East and Africa.

'We're looking at five main types of traveler: executives relocating, who need somewhere to stay for a couple of months while they sort out a house; consultants and auditors; people on training courses and company assignments; families on holiday; and very frequent business travelers, who are tired of normal hotel offerings, and independent business travelers, who are well traveled and don't want the pampering,' says Martin Quinn, director of Staybridge Suites by Holiday Inn for Europe, Middle East and Africa, in Brussels. 'We're a kind of hybrid between a hotel and an apartment; not an apart-hotel. People will have more room space, their own kitchenette and reasonable phone charges. But we'll have a club room – rather like an airport club lounge in a hotel context – where you can relax, meet people, have a coffee, have breakfast, which will be included in the price. It's a good option for business travelers. Some people want to be pampered; others want to do things for themselves. There'll be a place where you can work in your room without it feeling like an office, with a proper desk and links for computers; a fitness area; full front-desk service; a convenience store; and a launderette.'

Staybridge Suites offer studios and one-bedroom and two-bedroom /two-bath suites. Prices depend on how long you stay – from one to four nights, 5 to 14 nights, 15 to 30 nights, and 30 nights or more.

The two major apartment chains in Europe are French companies, Orion (18 three-star properties in Paris, London, Lisbon, Brussels, Geneva, Lyons, and Nice) and Citadines Aparthotels (34 three- and four-star properties in France, Barcelona, Brussels, Geneva, and London) recently acquired by Westmont Hospitality, a hotel management group in Houston, Texas.

'We're a mid-market product, like Novotel or Holiday Inn, and very flexible – you can stay for one night or one month. We're roughly the same price but with twice the space as a twin hotel room,' says Jan Dijksstra, development manager for Westmont in London. 'People who stay with us tend to be younger business travelers who know the city fairly well, know the good restaurants, and like to be flexible and organize themselves. The atmosphere here is a lot looser than a hotel. You have 24-hour reception; you can have breakfast, but you don't have to; we can get your groceries if you want, but you can get your own; and there are selected restaurants which will deliver meals off the menu.'

You also have your own phone line with voice mail plus fax and other business facilities, like a conference room. Prices range from 480 French francs ($80) a night for a studio at Paris Maine Montparnasse (432 francs a night for seven days) to 955 francs a night at the new Citadines property in Gloucester Road, London.

The best sources for serviced apartments are tourist authorities and travel agents. But a useful guide is the *Worldwide Guide to Serviced Apartments* 1999/2000, published by The Apartment Service; tel: (44 181) 944 1444.

Here you will find listed apartments such as a studio for two at Apartementos Gran Via 65 in Madrid, near the Royal Palace, for 16,000–20,000 pesetas ($105 to $131) a night, and 91,000 to 105,000 microwave, satellite TV and daily maid; or Art Hotels Hamamatsucho in the heart of Tokyo with 120 studios from 14,800 yen ($102) a night, with breakfast.

The Shangri-La Singapore offers 127 one- to three-bedroom serviced apartments within the hotel complex. You have the run of the hotel facilities (including the health club and business centre) plus a fully-equipped kitchen, daily maid service, and food and beverage delivery. The minimum stay is one month, but shorter stays are negotiable. The monthly rate for a 'deluxe' one-bedroom apartment of 7,500 Singapore dollars ($4,300) compares with 10,900 dollars for the cheapest 'deluxe' single room and 42,000 dollars for a one-bedroom suite for the same period.

There are more than 30 blocks of serviced apartments in Singapore, including Orchard Parksuites, The Ascott, Le Grove, Darby Park, Great World, Fraser Place, Park Avenue Suites and Palm Court.

According to property consultants Richard Ellis, Singapore's supply of serviced apartments is expected to double in the next two-and-a-half years.

Citadines Aparthotels
Tel: (33 1) 41 05 79 79
Fax: (33 1) 47 59 04 70
Web site: www.citadines.com

Orion
Tel: (33 1) 41 05 79 01
Fax: (33 1) 41 05 78 80

Room Service Deliveries London
Tel: (44 171) 431 5555
Fax: (44 171) 433 3300
Web site: www.roomservice.co.uk

Shangri-La Singapore
Tel: (65) 737 3644
Fax: (65) 737 3257

Staybridge Suites by Holiday Inn
Web site: www.staybridge.com

Villager Lodge – Extended Stay Living
Tel: (1 973) 428 9700
Reservations: 1 800 328 7829
Web site: www.villager.com

The Worldwide Guide to Serviced Apartments 1999/2000: free from The Apartment Service
Tel: (44 81) 944 1444
Fax: (44 81) 944 6744
Web site: www.apartmentservice.com

Dos and don'ts

 Do decide what facilities you need and how long you want to stay. Room rates are normally pegged to stay; the longer the stay, the lower the daily rate.

 Do get a specialist agent to help find exactly what you need, and to negotiate the best price, especially for stays of a week or more. For long stays, get the agent to show you several alternatives.

 Don't forget to ask about advance payment, deposits and cancellation penalties; there is normally no charge if you give four weeks' notice on a long let.

Do check what the rates include – tax; maid-service (daily or weekly); laundry; free grocery shopping service; and so on.

 Do check on telephone and fax charges. Don't assume that they are cheaper than normal rip-off hotel rates. You should expect free access to phone-card calls.

 Don't arrive late without advising the agent, unless there is 24-hour reception/security.

 Don't forget to bring/order provisions when you first move in. Some properties provide a 'welcome pack' of basic supplies to tide you over.

 Do check how many bathrooms (en suite) there are in larger apartments – important if you are a mixed group of colleagues.

Go native in London homes

When staying in London, temporarily vacant private homes are a reasonably priced and comfortable alternative to hotels and serviced apartments. Go Native offers more than 100 homes in central London: a warehouse apartment overlooking the Thames; lofts and studios in Clerkenwell, Soho and Bloomsbury; apartments and town houses in Chelsea, Little Venice, and Knightsbridge; even a houseboat on the river or a cottage in the former stable block of Kensington Palace. Prices range from £350 a week for a studio apartment five minutes' walk from Sloane Square to £2,000 a week for a five-bedroom town house in Chelsea. Most homes are one- to two-bedroom apartments in the £500–£1,000 range. Home owners include barristers, diplomats, bankers and landscape gardeners. Many are resident abroad or in the country but do not want to let their homes on a long-term basis.

Homes are serviced and come equipped with an operating manual and a local guide, prepared by the owner, to the best (and worst) of the local amenities – restaurants, bars, theatres, markets, etc.

Go Native London Accommodation
26 Westbourne Grove
London W2 5RH
Tel: (44 171) 286 1088
Fax: (44 171) 286 8595
E-mail: enquiries@gonative.co.uk
Web site: www.gonative.co.uk

'Dining in' in London

If you don't feel like using the fully-equipped kitchen that comes with your rented home or serviced apartment, if you're chained to the desk waiting for Tokyo or Hong Kong to open, if you're planning a power lunch, a crucial *tête-à-tête* dinner, or a chaste picnic in the park, call Room Service Deliveries, which will deliver meals from more than 125 of the best restaurants in town, ranging from American and Italian to Indian and Lebanese, to addresses in North West and Central London and the City. You pay restaurant prices plus a small delivery charge. Room Service's mobile bars offer a wine list at reasonable prices – cheaper than a restaurant, but more expensive than a supermarket. You can ask the delivery person to pick up supplies at an off-licence (liquor store) en route.

Meals should arrive within an hour from the time you order. But we're not talking fast food or take-aways. Food is delivered piping hot in green 'butler bags' by a fleet of bow-tied drivers, who will stay and serve the meal if you desire.

Room Service Deliveries
Tel: (44 171) 431 5555
Fax: (44 171) 433 3300
Web site: www.roomservice.co.uk

I miss you too

As every road warrior knows, rule number one for business travel is never to do business in the country you visit, but always contrive to be on the phone to somewhere else. You need to call the office incessantly to make sure you're still at the centre of the universe, and to keep other third-country nationals on their toes. The expert leaves a trail of unrequited requests to call back. ('Ah, he's just left for the airport. You may be able to catch him in Sidi Barani.')

Rule number two is always to ring home at least once a day. There are two main reasons: first to check that your loved one still loves you; second, to reassure your loved one that you are having a ghastly time struggling to bring home the bacon against all odds. But this is harder to pull off as the executive lifestyle becomes more transparent. ('I expect you're having a cosy dinner with that PR woman.' 'Sweetheart, this is my job!')

And there's competition between working couples. ('Darling, I had to go and be nice to Fingelstein, he knows my boss.' 'Helen, is that the television I can hear?' 'What do you mean, I wasn't in? We'd just gone out for a pizza. You're not the only one...'.) Hypocrisy rules OK.

I spend a lot of time on the phone chatting up all sorts of people I shall (fortunately) never meet. So I was intrigued at the chance to natter (on the phone, naturally) with Dr Guy Fielding, a psychologist, on a subject close to my heart: how to build a healthy 'tele-relationship'. It seems that people who master this 'find a better understanding of each other by the intimacy and focus of having to rely exclusively on the telephone'.

'If your relationship is central to you,' Fielding says, 'it will provide a number of needs, like intimacy, comfort, nurturing or challenge. You can put a relationship "on hold" for one or two days – but if you don't work at it, it will die; it has to be fed and watered. For some people their relationship will be threatened by telephoning when they are upset; for others, that may be the way in which they keep the relationship not only going, but actually progressing.'

This is all down to the exceedingly intimate nature of the phone. You acquire more information in listening to what people are saying and how they're saying it than you do from watching for visual clues. Intimacy is honesty. This means it is easier to tell if someone's lying to you on the phone than face-to-face. But if you really mean what you say, you're going to sound more convincing.

'In a sense, the telephone is as confessional as a psychiatrist's couch, because it allows you to talk to someone without distractions. You are focused entirely on them,' Fielding says. 'People often find it easier to deal with intimate or difficult topics. One of the things that the telephone does for you is to choose the right moment of contact, and to treat each moment as a peak experience. You then get samples of the person at their best, rather than as they are in general relationships at home.

'A lot of people we talked to think that separations have brought them benefits. There are several ways in which that is important. First, the fact that we have to set priorities, which means choosing to telephone them rather than someone else; that's an explicit affirmation of the importance of the relationship.

'Second, people did more talking on the phone than they would have done face-to-face, because when the call came it was very focused, and it meant that they did not allow themselves to do something else at the same time or be interrupted.

'The third thing was that the phone forced them actually to listen to what the other was saying: their tone of voice and whether they were sounding upset and the particular words they were using.

'Then the final thing is that when people are apart and talk on the phone, they actually have to make some things explicit which face-to-face they can let go by. That they miss each other, for example, which may never be said otherwise. What the phone does is allow people to get things sorted out and to build up, if you will, a set of explicit, shared understandings, which they may never have talked about together at home.'

People who are successful with a 'tele-relationship' say they don't expect to 'move the earth' with expressions of affection; it's more the act of calling that is important, talking about things that would perhaps not in themselves justify a phone call.

Women seem to be happier about it than men, both on the road and at home. This is because they are more conscious of the basic need to communicate – and less concerned about what is actually said.

'An international opera singer told us: "We don't go in for these grand declarations of love, we're too old for that. But it's very important for us to make it clear how we feel about each other",' Fielding says. 'There is this delicate balance between not being overly dramatic and yet being prepared to express things on the telephone that reassures the other person.'

Couples can help prevent resentment from the partner stuck at home by sharing the responsibility for keeping in touch, rather than putting the onus on the one that travels.

Making business trips less taxing

Growing numbers of business travelers are saving as much as 20 per cent on their travel expenses in Europe by reclaiming value added tax (VAT) on hotel and restaurant bills, telecom charges, car rental and other services.

But thousands more are losing serious money because they are not reclaiming VAT, says Ian Bryant, managing director of Quipsound European VAT Recovery in London. 'The main reason why people are not reclaiming VAT is that they can't be bothered; they write it off in their accounts and forget about it,' he says. 'Whereas if they took a little bit of time and trouble to pull out the invoices, they could save vast amounts of money. There are millions of dollars out there not being recovered by companies, not giving VAT recovery the priority it deserves.'

You don't have to live in Europe to reclaim VAT. Travelers from North America and Asia can reclaim VAT on many business expenses.

VAT is a consumer tax imposed on goods and services by all 15 member states of the European Union plus Switzerland, Iceland, Norway and Hungary. Japan, Korea and Canada also have forms of VAT. Unlike a straightforward sales tax, such as city and state taxes in the United States, VAT is a 'cascade' tax (the tax man taking his bite on the 'added value' of sales for every transaction), which is passed on to the next customer. The next customers (provided they are registered for VAT, which means they invoice VAT to their customers) can reclaim VAT on goods and services they have purchased.

VAT sounds complicated – and it is. It was invented by the French (who else?) and has been adopted throughout the EU.

Travelers based in the EU – as long as they are registered for VAT – recover the tax on travel expenses within their own country from their local tax authorities in the normal accounting process.

Reclaiming VAT for cross-border travel is a good deal more onerous. A business traveler – whether or not from another EU country – must submit the VAT claim from each national tax authority according to local procedures and in the local language. The redeeming rule is that all foreign travelers get the same VAT treatment as those in the country they visit. No matter if your company has a subsidiary in the country, provided it is a legal entity, not a branch office.

The legal basis for reclaiming VAT when traveling to another EU country is the 8th EU VAT Directive of 1980. The 13th VAT Directive of 1987 extended this right to business travelers from countries outside the EU. Japan, Korea, Switzerland, Canada, Hungary and Norway have followed the EU's lead and now refund VAT to foreign visitors.

The VAT year is normally January to December, with six months until the following June 30 to submit claims. (The exception is for non-EU companies claiming VAT refunds in the United Kingdom, where the claim period is July 1 to June 30 and the deadline for claims is December 31.) You can make up to four claims a year.

The European Union, which has launched the single currency, the euro, and has harmonized standards on pretty well everything from the curvature of cucumbers to beer and sausages and flushing criteria for the Euro-lavatory, is not about to harmonize VAT any time soon. It is up to each country to determine its VAT rates and conditions and procedures for reclaiming VAT within its own borders.

The result is a complicated matrix of what you can and cannot reclaim. You can reclaim all VAT in the United Kingdom (17.5 per cent) on hotels and restaurant bills (except for 'business entertaining'), car rental, telecoms, exhibition costs and training seminars; Germany (16 per cent) is much the same except that you can claim for entertainment; Austria (20 per cent) allows hotel bills but not restaurants and car rental; Belgium (21 per cent) but not hotels or restaurants and only half is allowed on car rental; France (20.6 per cent) does not allow for hotels and restaurants; Switzerland (6.5 per cent) only allows half the tax back on hotels, restaurants and car rental; Finland (22 per cent) allows most expenses except restaurants and telecoms; Italy (20 per cent), Ireland (21 per cent), Greece (18 per cent) and Portugal (17 per cent) only allow VAT reclaims on telecoms, conferences and exhibitions; Spain (16 per cent) allows hotels and business entertaining; and Sweden (25 per cent) allows hotels and restaurants but only half on car rental. Allow six months for refunds – two to four months in Britain, Germany and France, one to two years in Italy, Spain and Portugal, and for Greece three years or more. Fortunately, you get more money back faster from countries like the United Kingdom, Germany and France, which boast more business travelers, than the more lethargic Mediterranean countries where VAT refunds are more meagre anyway.

Unless you have your own corporate expert to do the work for you, the best way to claw back VAT is to use a tax reclaim agent. Agents typically charge 20 per cent of the VAT recovered on a contingency basis – no charge if the claim is refused.

Meridian VAT Reclaim, one of the largest agents with offices in 23 countries, charges 40 per cent for a full audit service whereby they will comb through a company's files for travel and entertainment vouchers and submit a claim to the tax people, or 20 per cent if you dig out the invoices yourself.

Quipsound charges 15 per cent for EU-based travelers and 20 per cent for those in other countries – 'Simply because it's easier to get correct documents from companies who know their way around the VAT system,' Bryant says. 'We're mostly talking about medium-size companies who don't have a local subsidiary to pick up visitors' expenses.'

Flexco Tax Reclaim in the United Kingdom, which specializes in small to medium-size companies, charges 20 per cent for VAT up to £2,000; 18.5 per cent up to £5,000 and 17 per cent in excess of that. The minimum fee is £75.

Karen Frain, reclaim manager at Flexco in London, stresses that you must keep original invoices and make sure they are made out properly, in the company name as well as your own; till receipts or charge-card vouchers are not acceptable to VAT authorities. 'We can claim VAT refunds even for an individual as long as the expenses are business related,' she says. 'A lot of people have their own name as business name: that's fine, but we have to have a tax certificate or a tax ID, such as IRS form 6166 [Certificate of Filing and Tax Return Confirmation] on your behalf. If you come from a country like the United States, where there is no VAT, you have to prove you are a corporate body elsewhere in another way. If you are from an EU country you just have to show that you are registered for VAT back home.'

Meridian VAT Reclaim has launched a prepayment scheme whereby clients get their refunds right away without having to wait for their claim to be paid by the tax authorities – for an extra charge.

'Once we've got your invoices in our system and submit the claim to the VAT people, we will pay you,' says John Ellis, strategic development director at Meridian in London. 'We started this for companies reclaiming VAT in the UK, Germany, France and The Netherlands. The idea is to help companies with their cash-flow.'

Visa International, for one, is developing an electronic VAT reclaim scheme for its corporate card-holders.

'The British and German tax people have accepted that an itemized electronic expense record is as good as getting a piece of paper from a hotel,' says John Chaplin, senior vice president commercial products at Visa International in London. 'There are three legs to this: getting the data from the supplier, churning out the expense report you need, and getting agreement from the tax authorities so that they can electronically audit a VAT reclaim instead of having to plough through mountains of paper – just call it up on a screen. We're running our first pilot with Steigenberger Hotels in Germany. I think during 1999 we should be seeing some major pilot programmes. This will change the VAT reclaim game. Our goal is that no more than 10 per cent of the amount of VAT reclaimed gets eaten up in anybody's fees.'

You can get useful advice on VAT reclaim from:

CB Cash Back
Tel: (41 41) 740 30 80
Fax: (41 41) 740 31 81

Fexco Tax Reclaim
Tel: (44 181) 563 7171
Fax: (44 181) 563 6690

Hogg Robinson BTI Travel
Tel: (44 118) 952 8100
Fax: (44 118) 958 9949

Meridian VAT Reclaim USA
Tel: (1 212) 554 6700
Fax: (1 212) 974 0673
UK Tel: (44 171) 435 5677
Fax: (44 435) 6541
Web site: www.meridian-vat.ie

Quipsound European VAT Recovery
Tel: (44 1959) 563 228
Fax: (44 1959) 564 740

Management by
Absence

There was a time when I used to dread holidays. The very thought of taking off for a glorious fortnight (or heaven forbid three weeks) to the sun-drenched Caribbean, the flesh-pots of the Côte d'Azur or one of those idyllic get-away-from-it-all islands in the Greek archipelago, would be enough to send me into a catatonic tail-spin.

Ah, yes, I can hear you murmur; one of those born-again workaholics. Not so, I'm as intrinsically idle as the next man. And as a professional wheel-spinner, I've always been able to rationalize any amount of time spent away from the office.

No, I was a victim of what management theologians recognize as 'holiday stress', a major factor in executive morbidity. Remove the day-to-day pressures of the office and a new kind of anxiety takes over. More insidious, more debilitating: a kind of free-flowing angst about your job and career that can make you a candidate for Paranoids Anonymous.

Holiday stress is endemic among business travelers and reaches an acute stage when the holiday is about to expire. This is known as the 're-entry syndrome'.

They say it takes the first week of a holiday to unwind, the second week to relax and the third week to worry about what you might find (or not find) when you get back to the office. Have they reviewed the budget figures without you? Can they do that? You bet they can!

Suddenly you see the dark significance of the chairman's parting words. Karl, your assistant, might be in the chairman's office right now mortgaging your department for the next three years. Maybe you are the chairman. But where was Mikhail Gorbachov during his management revolution? Why, unwinding at a Black Sea resort with the World Service of course.

You may fancy yourself as a latter-day Genghis Khan. But what are you going to do about the threat of a palace revolution if you're cruising on your yacht off the Turkish coast? To paraphrase Clausewitz: Holidays are simply the continuation of politics by other means.

So much for the aetiology of holiday stress; what can be done about it? A prescription of sorts was revealed to me in one of those rare Archimidean moments at the poolside of the Tel Aviv Hilton during a business trip last summer. I was exercising my management style with a toothsome bimbo at the bar, when I ran into my old friend Sammy Kalbfleisch (a half-generation American who had wisely refrained from anglicizing his name to Vealsteak). Shrugging off his entourage of American divorcees, he sat down to discuss the problem. Had I read Stanley Zilch's new book, *Zen and the Art of Holiday Management*?

It transpired that Zilch, director of Blue Skies Research Institute in Broken Springs, Colorado, had come up with a powerful management tool for salvaging the sanity of holiday exiles called Management by Absence (MBA). Since that fateful encounter, I've never looked back – except for an occasional glance over my shoulder when I go on holiday.

Sedulous practitioners of Management by Absence know how to stifle signs of incipient holiday stress by observing the following rules:

Make sure you are at the centre of the universe. Take the principal movers and shakers with you to limit the downside risk; send them on holiday themselves; or organise an incentive conference, say on a Caribbean cruise, during your absence. Or else hand them gruelling assignments that will occupy them fruitlessly while you're away. One way to do this is to get your secretary to release time bombs in the form of urgent memos every few days. Professional MBAs are adept at the Planned Crisis. The idea is to create a diversion from any thought of insurrection by creating a problem that has to await your return for a miraculous resolution.

While you're away, keep in touch. This doesn't mean phoning the office every day, but through your laptop. 'Don't call us, we'll call you' is an old cliché but a powerful one. There's no danger as long as you keep the initiative. Make ominous hints at a major reorganization when you get back to the office. Assign people spurious tasks to give credence to this eventuality.

Relax. After all, this is the object of the exercise. The best ideas are said to come in breaks between bursts of intellectual effort. Explore the siesta as a means of dredging the subconscious for new ideas.

Make sure you're missed. Nature abhors a vacuum. The planned chaos and confusion you have sown should make everyone clamour for your return. This should always be unexpected – say, the Friday before rather than the Monday morning.

With a bit of luck you may be hailed as a *deus ex machina*. In which case you might decide to take more holiday next year. It's a great way to run a business.

It's not what you say... it's how you say it

Ralph Waldo Emerson's counsel 150 years ago that 'No man should travel until he has learned the language of the country he visits' is reflected in the boom in language learning for business travelers. The key to success, we are told, is to do business in the other person's language.

But unless you can really cope in that language, it's usually best to save it for social chat. A little learning is a dangerous thing (although a few gracious phrases in, say, Chinese, Arabic and Russian, are always appreciated). English, of course, is now accepted as the *lingua franca* for business travelers in most parts of the world. But forcing people to speak it when they're not completely fluent can lead to serious misunderstanding.

There was the case of a former German chancellor who was presented to the Queen during a visit to London. He had brushed up his English for the occasion. But when he was introduced to her he said, 'Who are you?' instead of, 'How are you?' She replied, 'I am the queen of England.' That's supposed to be a true story.

A good compromise is for both parties to speak their own language, which may bring a dialectical, if not an entirely cultural, meeting of minds (although it may be worth remembering the old German adage that you should sell in the other language and buy in your own). A variation, perhaps, of the maxim 'Dress British, think Yiddish'. For most people this means speaking through interpreters. But the ability to work well with one is a technique, a skill in itself. You have to make sure that your message is received in a cultural as well as a linguistic sense.

You have to be very careful about using humour on formal occasions. If you make an after-dinner speech in the United Kingdom, you're heavily criticized if you don't make a joke; in France you'll be criticized if you do. They'll say, he's a clown, he's a lightweight. The British self-mocking humour is not understood.

It can be quite disconcerting with simultaneous interpretation. You make a witty remark and those people listening in English laugh; then the French and Italians laugh; then there's a pause because the Dutch and Germans are waiting for the verb at the end of the sentence before they get it. Meanwhile, you're saying, 'Yes, but to be serious I must make an important point.' At which point the Germans and Dutch burst out laughing.

The Japanese seem to have found a face-saving solution to this contingency. The story goes of the Japanese interpreter who said: 'The British gentleman has now started telling a joke. When he stops speaking, please laugh and clap loudly – or I'll be in trouble.'

Another solution when faced with strange English from a non-native speaker is to tune in to the French translation or hit the music button on your Walkman.

Alas, this is not possible in face-to-face meetings. Everything depends on the skill of the interpreter. Confusion generated by faulty translation is less hilarious. Experts recommend that both parties in a negotiation bring their own people to interpret for important discussions. It's convenient, but dangerous, to rely on the home side's interpreter, who may unconsciously represent the interest of his or her employer.

Keep sentences short and simple but avoid oversimplifying – which may give an impression that you're condescending – and pause frequently. Avoid vague and imprecise expressions; use visual aids when you can; and look at the person with whom you're dealing – not the interpreter; look for signs of confusion; keep eye contact when culturally appropriate (in the Far East it's sometimes interpreted as aggressive or challenging behaviour – only the occasional glance at another person's face is considered polite).

When it comes to the Far East, it's not so much 'read my lips' as 'read my mind'. The silences between utterances are just as meaningful as what is spoken. The Japanese method of listening comprises a repertoire of smiles, nods, and polite noises. The idea is to keep you talking, usually misinterpreted by Westerners as agreement.

If the Japanese have a reputation for inscrutability, it is because they have developed ambiguity of expression to an art form. They have delicate ways of voicing personal opinions. The British may have invented circumlocution (not to mention elocution) but the Japanese have made it an art form. It's not that they're hypocritical. But they manifest quintessential politeness, which can mean they say 'yes' when they really mean 'no'.

The Japanese are concerned with saving face and have developed a set of rules to prevent things going wrong. So try to avoid saying no or asking questions when he answer might be no. If you do hear a no in Japan, it is likely to be expressed as a sucking of breath through the teeth. The closest anyone will get to articulating the word no is, 'It is very difficult,' or 'We will need to give this further study.' The real message is likely to be, 'Let's forget the whole business'.

Closer to home, there are defective cognates between languages like English and French. The *entente cordiale* was in jeopardy when the French head office of its recently acquired subsidiary in the United Kingdom faxed: 'We demand your latest profit figures…'. *Demander* in French means to ask, not to demand.

Much more important than language, the psychologists, say, is your 'non-verbal behaviour', your awareness of different 'business modes' and 'non-verbal behaviour' or body language. This must take into account different notions of politeness, manners and social rituals. Actions speak louder than words. Saying the wrong things – eye contact, hand gestures, touching, bowing, using first names, how to eat and drink – can be a minefield for the unwary. The snappily-dressed young Chinese in Hong Kong with the portable phone may seem to talk the same business language, but if you unintentionally offend him, you may lose his trust – and his business.

You first need to know whether you are dealing with people from so-called 'low context' cultures (North America, the United Kingdom, Sweden, Switzerland, Germany), who spell things out verbally, or 'high context' cultures (France, Japan, Spain, Greece, Saudi Arabia, China and Korea) who communicate more by nuance and implication and are less dependent on the spoken word.

For example, the Swiss and the Germans like to lay their cards on the table. Talking to a Frenchman or a Spaniard, what is unsaid is often most important. Low context folk need to attune their listening skills; high context folk should try to be more explicit. 'Your context or mine?' is the dialectical ideal. The handshake is probably the most common form of greeting in the world (except in Japan). But even this simple gesture is fraught with complications. The British handshake is firm but used sparingly; in Italy and France – where handshaking is something of a national pastime (the French are said to spend 30 minutes a day shaking and re-shaking hands) – a gentler, kinder grip may stand you in good stead. In Germany and Denmark, you nod your head when you shake hands as a gesture of respect. Somebody who does not know this may interpret it as aggression (which it may well be). People in Mediterranean countries sometimes tilt the head back when they shake hands. Northerners may interpret this for arrogance (which it may well be). Anglo-Saxons learn to look people in the eye. This is sometimes interpreted as aggressive or challenging behavior, especially by Orientals, for whom only an occasional glance at the other person's face is considered polite.

Unless you really know what you're doing, close bodily greetings are best avoided. Kissing has many pitfalls – unless you are fortunate enough to have been coached by a French general. You need to know which cheek to start with. The British start with the right cheek. In Belgium you start with the left cheek; left, right, left. The French generally kiss twice; left, right. In some Middle East countries they kiss three or even four times – men kiss men, women kiss women. (In Saudi Arabia, greetings are particularly elaborate: after shaking hands a Saudi is likely to kiss you on both cheeks then take your hand in his as a gesture of kinship.)

Should you ever summon the nerve to kiss a lady's hand (a French aristocrat says it takes three generations to learn how to do it properly), your lips must never actually make contact. In Spain, men who are close friends often give a bear-hug, or *abrazo*. The story goes that a UK businessman so shocked the Americans he was with when he greeted a Spaniard with a hug, that he almost lost the contract he was negotiating. Look out now for the Slavonic bear-hug.

One area where handshakes, kissing and (heaven forbid) bear-hugs have not become established is Japan where such bodily contact is considered impolite. On the other hand, the Japanese custom of bowing can be daunting to a Western businessperson. (Let your hand slide down towards your knees, back and neck stiff with eyes averted.) The act has crucial social implications, depending on title. It is essential for Japanese to know the ranking order within any group because rank is applied to all circumstances – whether business or social.

The way other cultures like to put people at their ease can be confusing. The American use of first names as an instant form of friendship does not go down well in countries like Germany, even England. (Germans like to be addressed by their last name with full academic titles, like Professor Dr Schmidt, rather than Willy or Ilse. In Austria, you have to contend with Dr Dr Schmidt. In Italy, address anybody over 40 wearing a suit as Dottore.)

The British and Americans share at least one thing: they like to break the ice with a joke, which means sometimes being thought flippant. We in turn may think the Japanese are amused if they giggle: but they may sometimes do this when they are perplexed. In Japan, Korea and China, laughter is often a sign of embarrassment. In the Philippines it can mean, 'Take note! I'm about to say something important!' And Thais laugh at tragic news to cheer you up.

The Anglo-Saxon 'time is money' approach to negotiations is unlikely to go down well in Asian societies, which are based on personal relationships and building reciprocal trust before agreeing to clinch a deal. The cold call often brings the cold response.

The Japanese in particular set great store by long-term relationships and values. They need to know the sort of person they are dealing with. An evening's karaoke or a day's golf isn't enough. One must submit to an exhausting spiritual inquisition. 'What are your first impressions of Japan?' Four pairs of liquid black eyes are hanging on my reply. I venture something about the felicitous co-existence of tradition and the modern industrial state. 'What impresses me,' I hear myself say, 'is that traditional values seem to be an integral part of the business and social fabric. And that tradition is more than ever relevant in these protean times…'.

I seem to have passed the test. My host smiles. 'It is important for the Japanese to explore the heart of the person he does business with.' And refills my cup from his own sake flask, a gesture of friendship. Consequently, the Japanese take much longer than business people in the West to make a decision. They are more committed to group consensus. But once everyone is on board, implementation can be swift. The getting-to-know-you process often takes weeks or months instead of hours or days. Reaching an agreement takes five times longer than it does in the West. But it's usually time well invested. If you're late for a meeting or dinner in the Philippines nobody cares. But elsewhere in Asia it's a fatal *faux pas*. But don't be surprised at constant interruptions during meetings in India, Africa and the Middle East, especially with ministry officials. People rarely instruct the secretary to hold calls or tell unscheduled visitors to wait. This would be inexcusably rude to legions of friends and relatives who are likely to drop by unannounced at any time.

Meetings themselves can drive Anglo-Saxons to distraction. The French style of working is often incomprehensible to us. For example, in America or northern Europe, the point of having a meeting is to get decisions made or to allocate projects. The French meeting (which can go on for three or four hours, even longer than the business lunch) may not have a particular agenda. People simply talk and talk, with the idea of putting themselves in context – as the sociologists say — with other people. It's a form of jockeying for position and networking. Consequently, the French work long hours. You often find French managers in the office at seven in the evening. They manage to get things done, although not always to deadlines, which don't have the same awesome imperative as they do *chez nous*. People set great store by details of etiquette. Gestures need not be extravagant or deliberate to be considered offensive. For example, in the Middle East, never give or receive anything with the left hand (which was traditionally used for cleaning up after bodily functions) or sit showing the sole of your shoes. And it's often considered impolite to refuse refreshments.

Even a classic Anglo-Saxon OK sign — a thumb-finger circle – can get you into trouble. In Brazil, Russia and Greece it is considered vulgar, even obscene. In Japan it signifies money and in France zero or worthless. In Finland, folded arms are a sign of arrogance, while in Fiji, the gesture shows disrespect. In Java, placing your hands on hips means you are looking for a fight. So place your hands on the table out of trouble.

Except at an English dinner party, of course, when they should be placed on your knees, when you're not actually eating. (In France, place them by the side of your plate.) And in Japan remember not to speak when you're eating (not to be confused with speaking with your mouth full). And, of course, Americans have this curious habit of cutting a piece of something, putting the knife down then switching the fork to their right hand. No wonder they invented fast food.

People do business with those whom they feel comfortable. It comes down to sincerity and spontaneous good manners.

If you're not sure how to behave in someone else's culture, then at least be polite in your own. Unless, of course, you are into power behaviour.

But that's another story.

Making your presents felt

As we all know, the most serious challenge as the year draws to a close is not how to survive the budget review but how to choose the right gifts for customers and contacts around the world, especially across cultural boundaries. The art of giving is a crucial management skill.

An ill-considered gift can easily turn out to be an exploding cigar. Remember that gift-giving is a form of communication; it says as much about the giver as the receiver.

Take the case of the hapless executive who destroyed a carefully nurtured relationship in China by giving a clock, a symbol of death, as a New Year present. On the other hand, get it right, and you may come home with a contract: that happened to the smart lad who offered his Saudi contact a sounding device for calling back falcons.

When is a business gift a bribe? This is often the kind of 'now you see it, now you don't' distinction that has proved an ethical minefield for executives on both the giving and receiving end – not to mention those in the middle. You might say that a bribe is open persuasion done covertly ('Give us the Fingelstein contract and we'll open a holiday fund for you in Zurich') and a gift is hidden persuasion done openly ('Please accept this Picasso lithograph for your boardroom as a small token...').

One Africa hand stocks up with gifts for any hierarchical contingency, from plastic ballpoints ('for anyone you meet') and imitation marble desk-sets to solid gold fountain pens. Closer to home, we like to think we do things with a bit more style. But, let's face it, gift-giving, however gracefully done, is rarely an act of disinterested generosity.

A genuine gift – as distinct from a bribe – is a gesture of friendship. The personal touch is more important than monetary value. It can help avoid one of the pitfalls of gift-giving called 'escalation', a kind of arms race in which the recipient feels obliged to reciprocate with a more lavish gift. This is what the economists call 'gift-push' inflation. Try to make sure you get something that the other person wouldn't think of buying for him or herself.

You may find original ideas stalking the pages of the glossy mags. You know the sort of thing – 'Model 1800 British 12-pounder campaign cannons in valuable brass – a lifelong talking point', or 'Tom Byrd Gift Apples are so expensive because they're so good. From the Shenandoah Valley, hand-polished by little old ladies'.

One way to make a gift memorable but not embarrassing is to offer something from your own country (say a Feinschmecker ham from the Black Forest or an Ansel Adams print of Yosemite) or one of your company's products. Candied fruits are likely to go down better than fan belts, but you never know.

Perception of equality is important for a relationship to survive. Anglo-Saxons are much more comfortable giving than receiving; but not to allow the recipient to repay can cause him or her to lose face.

Balance of power is related to what one might call the 'expectation threshold'. This needs to be measured carefully, and depends on who is doing the giving. A peon may make just the right impression with, say, a first-day cover of the Sydney Olympics, but a chairman-to-chairman gift requires a more lavish approach, such as the use of one's yacht for a fortnight. Nothing offends people more than the impression that they are being bought cheaply.

Another thing to consider is how to reach the right recipient in an organization. This is often a matter of knowing your way around the invisible hierarchy. For example, the chairman's PA may be much more useful to you than the boss. A warehouse dispatcher may be able to do more for you than the production director, and so on. What's more, such people are less likely to be highly gifted (this has nothing to do with talent) than the chairman, who is so flooded with gifts that he may not notice yet another desk diary.

Buying a gift for a foreign business contact requires special care; you have to familiarize yourself with local customs as well as individual tastes. The Japanese, a ceremonious people who set great store by long-term relationships and human values, have developed gift-giving into an art form. Don't try to out-gift them, and never surprise them with a gift: they may be embarrassed by not having one for you.

The French, as everyone knows, can be tricky. To offer a gift at the first encounter is likely to be considered gauche (although this may change at the next elections). Avoid home decoration gifts (your taste will be on the line) or anything too personal; when invited for a meal, send flowers beforehand (never chrysanthemums, which are associated with funerals) rather than afterwards or the gift may be interpreted as a reward rather than a thoughtful gesture.

In Germany, avoid red roses (they are for lovers) and the number 13, and get local advice on wrapping a gift. Germans do not like anything ostentatious or garish. Entertainment is welcome, but it should be well planned and somewhat formal.

Arabs are magnanimous and appreciate generous people. If you're well off, it's best to be generous or they'll have no respect for you. Never offer a gift to a wife (or wives) and do not admire an object openly; you may find it's yours!

In Latin America, never give a knife (it implies cutting off a relationship) or a handkerchief (it's associated with tears). Never go empty-handed to a home but otherwise do not give a gift until you have developed a personal relationship with a business contact.

Like politics, gift-giving is the art of the possible. It's knowing how to bridge the gaffes.

Useful travel sites

www.A2BTravel.com
Claims to be the biggest online travel information site in the United Kingdom, run by EMAP Online. Home page is very crowded. Has ferry information and handy online mapping for the United Kingdom. Flight arrival details for UK airports.

www.airease.net
Allows you to organize your portfolio of mileage programmes and lets you know when you've reached award levels.

www.arab.net
A copious resource comprising thousands of pages on the geography, culture, history and cuisine of North Africa and the Middle East.

www.biztravel.com/
Track your frequent-flier miles, get an update on the status of your flight, gate number and weather at your departure point. You can book flights, hotels and car rental, and send in an upgrade request.

www.cdc.gov/travel/bluesheet.htm
United States Centers for Disease Control (CDC) provides comprehensive briefings and advice on all aspects of travel.

www.cheapflights.com
A UK database for flights run by the exemplary John Hatt, former travel editor, publisher of Eland books and author of *The Tropical traveler*. It is easy to use and offers business and economy fares, plus a 'fare of the day'. Each destination has its own page of e-mail and Web links to travel agents for easy booking.

www.cityguide.lycos.com
Select a destination city from regional maps for local information and the cheapest way of getting there.

www.cnn.com/WEATHER/
Global weather forecasts.

www.cnntraveler.com
A leading-edge site for the international traveler with the latest travel news and features, hotel reservation service and 'hot hotel deals'.

www.crg.com
Control Risks Group. Worldwide security and safety advice for business travelers includes country risk forecasts.

www.ebookers.com
Savings on flights, hotels and car rentals.

www.excite.com
One of the best search engines. It can be used for any search. Click on to a travel channel before you start a search.

www.expedia.co.uk
A UK version of Microsoft US site. Links to a vast database of flights (including some consolidated fares from the United Kingdom), hotels and car rental with booking capability.

www.fco.gov.uk
Travel advice from the UK Foreign Office. Ask for detailed advice on specific regions of the world to be sent direct by e-mail to your PC.

www.hardens.com
London Restaurants 2000, Good Cheap Eats in London, Top UK Restaurants 2000, plus regular updates.

www.HotelsCentral.com
A composite site for booking hotels at discounts of up to 50 per cent in 27 countries, especially in Western and Eastern Europe, the Middle East and Asia.

www.iht.com
International Herald Tribune has Roger Collis's latest columns, as well

as weather and currency information for hundreds of countries, holidays available and travel agents.

www.lastminute.com
A one-stop shop for last-minute flight and hotel offers.

www.login.net/imperial
Specializes in 'creative ticketing' for first- and business-class travelers. Fill out a 'travel analysis' form and Imperial Travel Consultants will tell you how they can get you there cheaper.

www.lonelyplanet.com.au
Summaries of every country in the Lonely Planet series. Includes health precautions.

www.mapquest.com
One of the first online maps sites. You can search for a map by postcode in the United States and the United Kingdom, then either print out or e-mail to a colleague. It also tells you the best way to get from one place to another. Linked to Pegasus' http://travelweb.com, which provides online booking at more than 30,000 hotels worldwide.

www.mapsonus.com
Key into any US address and generate a map. Gives directions on how to get from one place to another. Linked to Yellow Pages.

www.masta.org/home.html
Medical Advisory Services for travelers Abroad (MASTA), based at the London School of Tropical Medicine.

www.maxmiles.com
MaxMiles Mileage Miner consolidates all your mileage accounts into one document. It calculates flight miles, flight segments and year-to-date miles for all major airlines and monitors expiration dates, reconciles your FFP statements, generates missing mileage credit requests and assists with mileage redemption planning. Costs $2.95 a month.

www.netcafeguide.com
Information on 2,000 cafes around the world where you can log on and pick up your e-mail.

www.1travel.com
'Farebeater' offers easy access to 8 million discount fares from 400 airlines.

A booking engine that retrieves the best prices on flights that have seats available by searching published fares, discounted consolidated fares and 1travel.com negotiated deals.

www.PASSENGERRIGHTS.com
An easy and free way for airline passengers to file complaints without making dozens of phone calls, spending countless hours searching their rights or finding the proper channels for complaining. An invaluable resource for people to research their rights.

www.rosenbluth.com
A comprehensive site for corporate and individual business travelers from Rosenbluth International, 'third-largest travel management company' in the world.

www.seaforths.com
Flight and hotel reservations through Galileo.

www.skymalltravel.com
Your gateway to almost everything travel-related on the Web. A link is provided to www.intellitrip.com, which will search the Internet for the best fare, plus a link to www.MileageManager.com, which will track your miles with various programmes. Another link allows you to create your own itinerary to include appointments, with reminders e-mailed to you.

www.teleadapt.com
Plugs and connections for getting connected anywhere in the world. Plus hot-line advice.

www.teletext.co.uk
Extensive destination and weather information for hundreds of places worldwide along with travel news and features. Latest flight offers but no booking capability.

www.thetrip.com/
Aimed at frequent business travelers. Flight reservations and how to get the best fares. Travel news includes airport and city information with maps. Will e-mail you last-minute deals.

www.timeout.com
Restaurant and entertainment listing and guides to 30 cities worldwide.

Plus essential information for travelers, from visas and hotels to sight-seeing and clubbing.

www.travelhealthline.com/cicc_report.html
Travel Health Line covers all aspects of personal well-being, including security and safety. Customized reports based on your personal itinerary.

www.travelocity.com
Airline, hotel and car rental information, scheduling and booking service from the Sabre global distribution system for more than 700 airlines, 34,000 hotels and 80 car rental firms. You must sign up as a member before your first visit.

www.travelselect.com
Discount tickets from Globepost, one of the biggest consolidators in the United Kingdom.

www.travelweb.com
An easy way to book hotel rooms for major chains across the world.

www.travsoft.com
'Laplink, Remote Control and File Transfer.' How to get connected. 'For telecommuters and road warriors.'

www.webflyer.com
Comprehensive up-to-date information on all frequent-flier programmes from FFP guru Randy Petersen. More than 2,000 screens of news and resources in an easy-to-use format. Includes the US domestic and international editions of *InsideFlyer* magazine. Links take you to Deal Watch, which searches the best flight deals, and MileMarker, which acts as a mileage calculator.

www.webreservations.com
Sabre reservations system. Mainly for travel agents and corporate travel managers.

www.which.net
Independent advice from the British Consumers' Association. Allows you to sample *Holiday Which*? and other publications such as food and hotel guides.

www.xe.net/currency/full/
Convert 180 currencies.